Study Guide

Physics
for CSEC®

Lancelot Caesar
Darren Forbes
Yvette Mayers
Earl Skerritt

OXFORD
UNIVERSITY PRESS

Great Clarendon Street, Oxford, OX2 6DP, United Kingdom

Oxford University Press is a department of the University of Oxford.
It furthers the University's objective of excellence in research, scholarship,
and education by publishing worldwide. Oxford is a registered trade mark of
Oxford University Press in the UK and in certain other countries

First published by Nelson Thornes Ltd in 2013
This edition published by Oxford University Press in 2014

British Library Cataloguing in Publication Data
Data available

978-1-4085-2245-5

11

Printed in Great Britain by CPI Group (UK) Ltd., Croydon CR0 4YY

Acknowledgements
Cover photograph: Mark Lyndersay, Lyndersay Digital, Trinidad
www.lyndersaydigital.com
Illustrations include artwork drawn by GreenGate Publishing
Page make-up: GreenGate Publishing

Thanks are due to Lancelot Caesar, Yvette Mayers and Earl Skerritt for their
contributions in the development of this book.

Although we have made every effort to trace and contact all
copyright holders before publication this has not been possible in all
cases. If notified, the publisher will rectify any errors or omissions at
the earliest opportunity.

Links to third party websites are provided by Oxford in good faith
and for information only. Oxford disclaims any responsibility for
the materials contained in any third party website referenced in
this work.

The manufacturer's authorised representative in the EU for product
safety is Oxford University Press España S.A. of El Parque Empresarial
San Fernando de Henares, Avenida de Castilla, 2 – 28830 Madrid
(www.oup.es/en or product.safety@oup.com).
OUP España S.A. also acts as importer into Spain of products
made by the manufacturer.

Contents

Contents

This Study Guide has been developed exclusively with the Caribbean Examinations Council (CXC®) to be used as an additional resource by candidates, both in and out of school, following the Caribbean Secondary Education Certificate (CSEC®) programme.

It has been prepared by a team with expertise in the CSEC® syllabus, teaching and examination. The contents are designed to support learning by providing tools to help you achieve your best in Physics and the features included make it easier for you to master the key concepts and requirements of the syllabus. *Do remember to refer to your syllabus for full guidance on the course requirements and examination format!*

Inside this Study Guide is an interactive CD which includes electronic activities to assist you in developing good examination techniques:

- **On Your Marks** activities provide sample examination-style short answer and essay type questions, with example candidate answers and feedback from an examiner to show where answers could be improved. These activities will build your understanding, skill level and confidence in answering examination questions.

- **Test Yourself** activities are specifically designed to provide experience of multiple-choice examination questions and helpful feedback will refer you to sections inside the study guide so that you can revise problem areas.

- **Answers** are included on the CD for summary questions and practice exam questions, so that you can check your own work as you proceed.

This unique combination of focused syllabus content and interactive examination practice will provide you with invaluable support to help you reach your full potential in CSEC® Physics.

1 Mechanics

1.1

Base units, derived units and measuring density

LEARNING OUTCOMES

At the end of this topic you should be able to:

- state and use a range of SI units and prefixes
- derive units for quantities
- measure the density of regularly and irregularly shaped objects.

When we measure a quantity we need to include the **units** of the measurement. The length of a desk should be given as, for example, 1.2 metres or 1.2 m, not just 1.2.

Base units

A set of seven units, based on the metre, kilogram and second, has been agreed internationally. They are known as the SI base units and are shown in Table 1.1.1.

Derived units

There are many more units in addition to the seven base units. These units can all be derived directly from the seven, based on mathematical relationships and definitions.

For example, the speed of an object is defined from the equation:

$$\text{speed} = \frac{\text{distance moved (m)}}{\text{time (s)}}$$

This means that the unit for speed is a distance divided by a time: metres per second (m s^{-1}).

Every other derived quantity can be worked out this way.

For convenience (and to honour important scientists) some of the derived units have been given special names. For example, the unit for a potential difference derived from the base units would be $\text{m}^2\,\text{kg}\,\text{s}^{-3}\,\text{A}^{-1}$. This unit is given the special name volt (V).

Table 1.1.1

Quantity	Base unit	Symbol
mass	kilogram	kg
length	metre	m
time	second	s
current	ampere	A
temperature	kelvin	K
amount of substance	mole	mol
luminous intensity	candela	cd

Standard form

To avoid using very large or very small numbers, scientists use **standard form**. In standard form the number is always written in the format $A \times 10^x$, where A is a number between 0 and 10 and x is the number of places to move the decimal point. A positive value of x indicates movement to the right while a negative value indicates movement to the left.

- 4500 is written as 4.5×10^3
- 0.0006 is written as 6×10^{-4}

Prefixes

Scientists often need to use very large or very small numbers and so use a set of prefixes which may be attached to any unit. These are shown in Table 1.1.2. This set of prefixes allows a quantity like 8.4×10^6 watts to be written as 8.4 megawatts or 8.4 MW.

ACTIVITY

The SI base units have very precise definitions or derivations. Find out what these are.

Figure 1.1.1 SI units were used in all the calculations needed in designing the Half-Way Tree Transport Centre in Kingston, Jamaica.

Using units: density

The **density** of a material is the mass per unit volume. In non-scientific language this is how much mass there is in a cubic metre or cubic centimetre of the material. The equation defining density is:

$$\text{density} = \frac{\text{mass}}{\text{volume}} \text{ or } \rho = \frac{m}{V}$$

WORKED EXAMPLE 1

Find the derived SI unit of density.

Mass is measured in kilograms (kg). Volume is measured in cubic metres (m^3).

The equation defining density shows that density is a mass divided by a volume and therefore the SI unit of density is $kg\,m^{-3}$.

Measuring density

To measure the density of a regularly shaped object you must measure the mass using a balance and then calculate the volume by taking appropriate measurements for the dimensions and using a formula.

To measure the volume of an irregular object, place the object inside a measuring cylinder partly full of water. The level of the water will rise by the volume of the object.

WORKED EXAMPLE 2

A rough stone has a mass of 30 g. It is placed in a measuring cylinder containing $20\,cm^3$ of water and the level of the water rises to the $24\,cm^3$ mark (Figure 1.1.2).

The density of the stone is found using:

$$\text{density} = \frac{\text{mass (g)}}{\text{volume (cm}^3)} = \frac{30\,g}{(24 - 20)\,cm^3} = 7.5\,g\,cm^{-3}$$

Table 1.1.2   Prefixes for SI units

Prefix	Symbol	Represents
tera	T	10^{12}
giga	G	10^{9}
mega	M	10^{6}
kilo	k	10^{3}
centi	c	10^{-2}
milli	m	10^{-3}
micro	μ	10^{-6}
nano	n	10^{-9}
pico	p	10^{-12}

ACTIVITY

Use the technique described on these pages to find the density of a range of irregularly shaped objects.

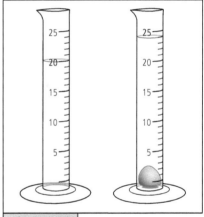

Figure 1.1.2

KEY POINTS

1 Scientists use a standard set of base units (SI) for quantities.

2 Units for most quantities are derived from these base units.

3 The density of an object is given by $\text{density} = \dfrac{\text{mass}}{\text{volume}}$ and the unit is $kg\,m^{-3}$ or $g\,cm^{-3}$.

SUMMARY QUESTIONS

1 Use the following equations to work out the appropriate derived units for velocity, acceleration and force.

$$\text{velocity} = \frac{\text{distance}}{\text{time}}$$

$$\text{acceleration} = \frac{\text{change in velocity}}{\text{time}}$$

$$\text{force} = \text{mass} \times \text{acceleration}$$

2 Write these quantities using the base unit and standard form: 83 milliamperes, 4.9 micromoles, 2400 picoseconds, 0.2 gigavolt.

Making measurements

At the end of this topic you should be able to:

- select an appropriate instrument to measure length in a range of experiments
- identify systematic error and random error in measurements
- use the appropriate number of significant figures in calculations and answers.

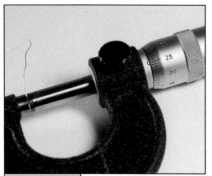

Figure 1.2.1 This micrometer is being used to measure the gauge of a wire.

Figure 1.2.2 Human reaction time is a factor when using a stopwatch.

Common measurements

Length

Many lengths can be measured with a ruler or tape measure. These instruments typically have a **resolution** of 1 mm. The resolution of an instrument is the smallest difference in a reading the instrument can measure.

If a smaller length needs to be measured, callipers or a micrometer can be used. Callipers have a resolution of 0.1 mm and a high quality screw gauge micrometer will have a resolution of 0.01 mm.

Time

Time intervals are generally measured with a digital stopwatch. Many stopwatches have a resolution of 0.01 second but, as human reaction times are more than 0.1 second, it may be unnecessary to measure to the full resolution.

To measure times more precisely, we can use automatic stopwatches triggered by events such as the breaking of a light-beam. These have much better response times.

Mass

Mass is measured by a balance which compares an unknown mass to a known one or, more often, by a top-pan balance. A variety of top-pan balances is available, some with a resolution of 0.01 g.

Uncertainty and error

When we make a measurement it may not be exactly the same as the 'true value'. Readings from instruments introduce error in measurements leading to some uncertainty in our calculations.

Systematic error

A systematic error is usually the result of some flaw in the measuring device or the measurement technique. For example, a metre rule could have a damaged end so that it shows all lengths as 1 mm too short.

Systematic errors will make the readings recorded shift away from the true measurement.

Random error

Random error is an unpredictable error introduced into a measurement when you take a reading. Sometimes this is because of the technique you use such as poor positioning of your line of sight while measuring length (Figure 1.2.3).

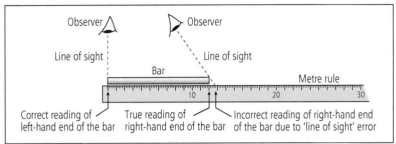

Correct reading of left-hand end of the bar · True reading of right-hand end of the bar · Incorrect reading of right-hand end of the bar due to 'line of sight' error

Figure 1.2.3 A line of sight error

Random errors will cause readings to be scattered around the true value. The effects of random error can be reduced by performing repeat readings and finding a mean value. Readings which were slightly too high will tend to cancel readings which were slightly too low.

Accuracy and precision

If a measurement is close to the true value of a quantity it is said to be **accurate**. It is not possible to know if a reading is accurate without repeating the measurement several times and calculating a mean value. All possible systematic errors must be avoided. If all of the measurements taken are close to the mean then you can be confident that the results are accurate.

A **precise** measurement is a measurement where all of the repeated readings show very little difference. They are all very close to the mean value of the readings.

It is possible to obtain results which are precise but not accurate due to a systematic error (Figure 1.2.4a). Results can also be accurate but not precise (Figure 1.2.4b). The very best experiments produce results which are both accurate and precise.

Quoting answers

The number of significant figures you quote in any answers is a reflection of how certain you are of the precision of your answer. You should never use more significant figures than are justified by the resolution of your instruments. In general, answers should be given to two or three significant figures unless more significant figures are given in questions or by measuring instruments.

ACTIVITY

Use a range of instruments to take measurements of the properties of objects. Find out how to measure the thickness of a sheet of paper.

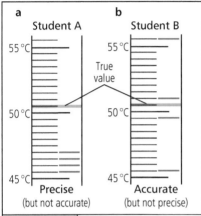

Figure 1.2.4 Demonstrating **a** precision and **b** accuracy

WORKED EXAMPLE

The diameter of a small ball bearing is measured with callipers giving a value of 6.4 mm. Using the formula for volume gives an answer of 137.258 mm³. Record the volume to a sensible number of significant figures.

The volume is recorded as 1.4×10^2 mm³.

KEY POINTS

1 Systematic errors produce a constant amount of uncertainty in measurements.

2 Random errors produce a varying amount of uncertainty in measurements.

3 The number of significant figures shown in the result of a calculation is an indication of the uncertainty in the answer.

SUMMARY QUESTIONS

1 How can you increase the accuracy of a measurement?

2 Table 1.2.1 shows three sets of results for the measurement of the diameter of a metal rod of true diameter 5.0 mm. Which sets of results are accurate, which are precise and which are both?

Table 1.2.1

Set a/mm	4.3	5.6	5.5	4.2	4.9	5.1
Set b/mm	5.1	4.9	5.0	4.9	4.9	5.1
Set c/mm	4.7	4.8	4.6	4.8	4.6	4.7

Variables and graph plotting

Scientific investigations are highly controlled in order to reveal connections between quantities and behaviour. In an ideal experiment a physicist would be able to alter one variable in an experiment and see the effect of this change in isolation.

Key variables

The **independent variable** is the variable which is manipulated by the experimenter to see what effect changing it has on the experiment.

The **dependent variable** is the variable which is expected to change in response to altering the independent variable.

Scientists explore the connection between these two variables in an experiment by finding a relationship between them and then explaining the cause of that relationship.

For example, if you were investigating the hypothesis 'The colder a sample of water is the denser it will be' then the independent variable would be the temperature of the water as this is what you would be manipulating. The dependent variable would be the density of the water, as this is the quantity you expect to change in response to changing the temperature.

Control variables

There are usually a wide range of other factors that need to be taken into account during an experiment so that they do not have an effect on the results. These are known as **control variables**. Good experimental designs ensure that these factors do not alter during the experiment.

Graphs

One of the best ways to show the relationship between two variables is to plot a graph (Figure 1.3.1). If there is a clear pattern shown in the graph then a clear relationship has been demonstrated. Scientists would then try to explain how this relationship occurs. If an explanation can be given then the relationship is causal.

Perfect graph plotting takes time and practice. Use these tips to help produce yours.

- Use a sharp pencil and ruler.
- When you draw the axes make sure you leave enough space to label them clearly.
- Plot the independent variable on the *x*-axis.
- Plot the dependent variable on the *y*-axis.
- Plot the graph so that the data points occupy as much of the graph paper as possible horizontally and vertically.
- Use increments of 2, 5 or 10 (or their multiples) for your scales if possible.

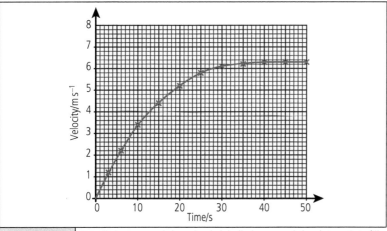

Figure 1.3.1 A well-drawn graph has clearly labelled axes and the data points fill up the available space.

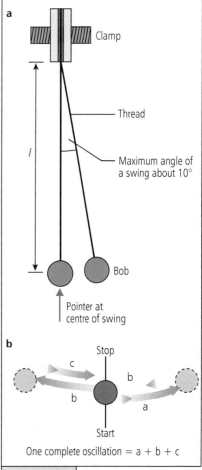

Figure 1.3.2 Timing a pendulum

ACTIVITY

A pendulum is a simple device that can be used to measure time. A mass on the end of a thread or wire is allowed to swing freely from side to side (Figure 1.3.2). One complete oscillation is a swing back and forth to the same position.

The following three factors **may** affect the period (time it takes for one complete oscillation).

Investigate each of the three factors independently while controlling the other two. Collect data and plot separate graphs comparing each of the independent variables to the period.

- Length of the thread
- Mass of the pendulum bob
- Initial angle of displacement

You will need to use the data to produce a graph in the next topic.

SUMMARY QUESTIONS

1 Think about the following hypotheses and outline a basic experiment to investigate them. For each one identify clearly the independent variable, dependent variable and any other variables you will have to control.

   a The greater the current in a light bulb the brighter it will be.

   b The further away from a sound you are the quieter it will seem.

   c The larger the force you put onto a spring the more it will stretch.

2 Table 1.3.1 shows the data from an investigation into resistance. Plot a graph using this data.

Table 1.3.1

Potential difference/V	0.0	0.1	0.2	0.3	0.4	0.5	0.6
Current/A	0.00	0.60	1.02	1.57	2.07	2.52	3.01

KEY POINTS

1 An independent variable is a variable that is changed during an investigation to see if this change has any effect.

2 A dependent variable is a variable which is measured to determine the effect of changing the independent variable.

3 To make sure that only the effect of altering the independent variable affects the outcome of the experiment, other factors have to be carefully controlled. These are control variables.

A graph can be analysed to find the relationship between the two variables.

Graphs showing linear relationships

Lines of best fit are drawn onto graphs to identify the relationship between the independent and dependent variables. These lines follow simple shapes (straight lines or curves) that pass through or close to the points.

Straight lines

If the points on a graph appear to be in a straight line, you can use a ruler to draw a line of best fit (Figure 1.4.1). Draw the line so that it passes through the points with an equal number above and below the line.

Some data points may not fit the pattern of results. These may be due to unexpectedly large random errors or uncertainties produced during the experiment. You may also have made mistakes in recording the data. Do not use these anomalous results when drawing the line of best fit.

ACTIVITY

Use the data you collected when investigating the relationship between the period of a pendulum's swing and the length of the pendulum or use the data provided in Table 1.4.1.

Table 1.4.1

Length/m	Period²/s²
l	T^2
0.05	0.20
0.10	0.40
0.15	0.60
0.20	0.80
0.25	1.01
0.30	1.21
0.35	1.41
0.40	1.61

• Plot a graph comparing the length of the pendulum with the square of the period (T^2).

• Describe the relationship shown in the graph.

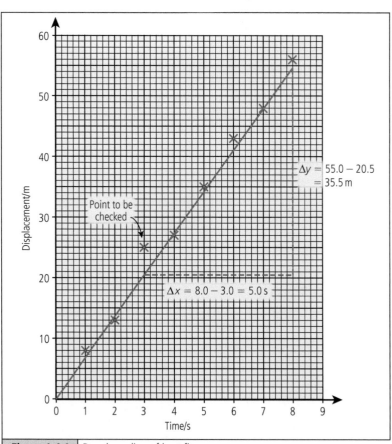

$\Delta y = 55.0 - 20.5$
$= 35.5\,\text{m}$

Point to be checked

$\Delta x = 8.0 - 3.0 = 5.0\,\text{s}$

Figure 1.4.1 Drawing a line of best fit

Gradients

The gradient of a line can be used to find a mathematical relationship between the two variables.

To find the gradient:

- Draw a large, right-angled triangle on the graph so that the triangle meets two points on the line of best fit. If possible, select points that are widely spaced and those whose values are easily read (for example, points that lie on the gridlines).
- Use the triangle to find the change in the y-value (Δy) and the change in the x-value (Δx).
- The gradient (m) is given by $m = \dfrac{\Delta y}{\Delta x}$

Intercepts

Sometimes the line of best fit will pass directly through the origin. In this case the two variables are in **direct proportion** to each other:

independent variable $\propto$ dependent variable

If the line does not pass through the origin the relationship is described as linear. The line will cut the y-axis at a point known as the intercept (c) and the relationship between the variables will be of the form:

$$y = mx + c$$

where y is the dependent variable, x is the independent variable, m is the gradient and c is the intercept on the y-axis.

Graphs showing other relationships

The points on a graph may also follow a curve. This may also represent a simple mathematical relationship between the variables.

Instead of plotting a graph comparing the x and y variables directly, functions such as plotting y^2 or $\dfrac{1}{y}$ may show the relationship more clearly.

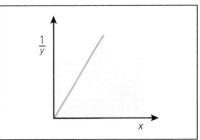

| Figure 1.4.2 | You can sometimes find a pattern by plotting x against $\dfrac{1}{y}$ |

Table 1.4.2 Examples of relationships which occur between variables in physics

Relationship	Produces a straight-line graph when
$x \propto y$	x plotted against y
$x \propto y^2$	x plotted against y^2
$x \propto \dfrac{1}{y}$	x plotted against $\dfrac{1}{y}$

Figure 1.5.1 Vector calculations are used in predicting the paths of hurricanes.

WORKED EXAMPLE 1

Find the resultant of the three forces acting on the ball in Figure 1.5.2.

6.1 N   5.2 N

4.8 N

Figure 1.5.2

Resultant = 5.2 N + 4.8 N − 6.1 N = 3.9 N to the right

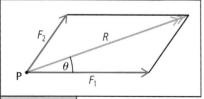

Figure 1.5.3 The parallelogram rule

There are two classes of quantity in physics: scalars and vectors.

• A **scalar** quantity has magnitude (size) but no direction.
• A **vector** quantity has magnitude and direction.

Comparing a scalar and a vector

Distance and displacement are both lengths which can be measured in metres:

• Distance is a scalar quantity. It is how far an object moves without reference to the direction.
• Displacement is a vector quantity. It is a measure of how far an object is from its origin (original position).

For example, if you walk 10 metres northwards, turn around and walk 5 metres back towards your starting point you have covered a distance of 15 metres. However, your displacement is 5 metres north of your starting point.

Combining quantities

Scalars, such as mass and volume, simply add together or are subtracted from each other:

• Adding a mass of 40 kg to a mass of 30 kg gives a mass of 70 kg.
• Removing 40 cm³ of water from 100 cm³ of water will always leave 60 cm³ of water.

Vectors, such as velocity and force, cannot be simply added together. To find the resultant of vectors you must also take their direction into account.

Parallel vectors

If the vectors are parallel to each other, then you can add or subtract to find a resultant. Always give the direction of the resultant in your answer.

Non-parallel vectors: the parallelogram rule

The parallelogram rule allows us to find the resultant of two non-parallel vectors by drawing a scale diagram (Figure 1.5.3). Two adjacent sides of the parallelogram (in red) represent the two vectors to be added (F_1 and F_2). The lengths of F_1 and F_2 are in proportion to their magnitude. The resultant (R) of the two vectors is represented by the diagonal of the parallelogram, shown in green.

WORKED EXAMPLE 2

What is the resultant of the two vectors shown in Figure 1.5.4?

50 N

75 N

Figure 1.5.4

Check that the vectors are drawn to the same scale. Then draw the other two sides of the parallelogram and the diagonal (Figure 1.5.5). Measure the length and angle of the diagonal, and use the scale factor to find its value in newtons.

120 N

50 N   15°

75 N

Figure 1.5.5

Vectors at right angles

Where the vectors are at right angles to each other, you can use Pythagoras's theorem and trigonometry. The two vectors form two sides of a right-angled triangle with the resultant forming the hypotenuse of the triangle (Figure 1.5.6). The size of the hypotenuse can be found using:

$$\text{hypotenuse}^2 = \text{adjacent}^2 + \text{opposite}^2$$

$$R^2 = x^2 + y^2$$

The angle of the resultant vector can be found using:

$$\tan\theta = \frac{\text{opposite}}{\text{adjacent}} = \frac{y}{x}$$

which leads to the relationship: $\theta = \tan^{-1}\left(\frac{y}{x}\right)$.

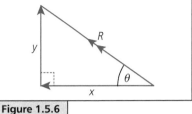

Figure 1.5.6

SUMMARY QUESTIONS

1 You follow the instructions below in a treasure hunt. Calculate the total distance travelled and the final displacement: Walk 50 m north, then 40 m east, then 70 m south and finally 10 m east.

2 Draw a scale diagram to find the resultant of two velocity vectors acting on a boat crossing a river, as shown in Figure 1.5.7.

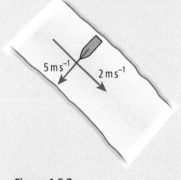

5 m s⁻¹   2 m s⁻¹

Figure 1.5.7

WORKED EXAMPLE 3

A remote-controlled toy is instructed to move 80 m south followed by a movement of 60 m west. What is the displacement of the toy after this movement?

Magnitude of displacement:

$$R^2 = 80^2 + 60^2 = 10\,000\,\text{m}^2$$

$$R = \sqrt{10\,000} = 100\,\text{m}$$

Direction of displacement:

$$\theta = \tan^{-1}\left(\frac{60}{80}\right) = 37°$$

KEY POINTS

1 Scalars have magnitude (size) but not direction. They can be added or subtracted simply.

2 Vectors have both magnitude and direction. Addition of vectors has to take into account the direction of the vectors.

Forces

EXAM TIP

Most questions involving weight are set on the Earth where $g = 10\,N\,kg^{-1}$. However, the gravitational field strength at other places is different (e.g. $g_{Moon} = 1.6\,N\,kg^{-1}$), so make sure you check where the question is set.

Forces acting on an object can change its shape or the way it is moving.

Describing forces

As forces are vector quantities (they have size **and** direction) they are represented in diagrams as arrows. The direction of the arrow gives the direction of the force and the length represents the size of the force.

The unit of force is the **newton** (N).

Example forces

Contact forces

When objects need to be touching for the force to exist, these forces are described as **contact forces**.

- When two surfaces move past each other, forces attempt to prevent this movement. These types of forces are known as **friction**, drag, or air resistance depending on where they originate from. This gives objects grip against each other.
- Floating objects experience **upthrust** from the fluid in which they float.

Non-contact forces

In some situations the objects are not in direct contact but forces still exist between them.

- Planets are held in orbit around the Sun by the forces of **gravity**.
- Electrons are bound to atoms by **electromagnetic** forces. The same forces cause attraction and repulsion in magnets.
- The nucleus of an atom is held together by strong **nuclear** forces.

Combining forces

The combination of all of the forces acting on an object is called the **resultant force**. In many situations you will find that the resultant force is zero.

Weight

Weight is a force which acts on an object because of the gravitational attraction between the object and the Earth.

The weight of the object depends on two factors: the mass of the object and the gravitational field strength ($g = 10\,N\,kg^{-1}$ on Earth).

$$W\,(N) = m\,(kg) \times g\,(N\,kg^{-1})$$

Figure 1.6.1 shows a tug-of-war. Which team is winning?

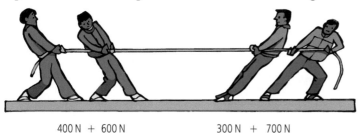

400 N + 600 N   300 N + 700 N

Figure 1.6.1

Forces to the left = 400 N + 600 N = 1000 N

Forces to the right = 300 N + 700 N = 1000 N

The forces are balanced so the resultant is zero.

WORKED EXAMPLE 2

A student of mass 45 kg jumps off a diving board into a deep pool. After the dive the student then floats on the surface of the pool.

a Calculate the weight of the student.

$$W = mg$$
$$= 45 \, kg \times 10 \, N \, kg^{-1} = 450 \, N$$

b Draw a diagram showing the forces acting on the student as he falls and as he floats on the surface of the water. Give the size of these forces where possible.

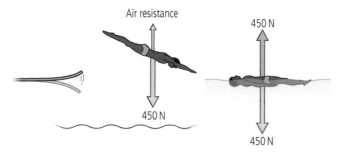

Air resistance

450 N

450 N

450 N

Figure 1.6.2

KEY POINTS

1. Forces are vector quantities.

2. The resultant of a force is a single force which would have the same overall effect of the other forces combined.

3. The weight of an object is the product of the mass and the gravitational field strength. ($W = mg$)

ACTIVITY

Use some plasticine to explore the effects of forces.

- Stretch it until it snaps.
- Squash it.
- Roll it into a ball shape and then roll the ball along the desk.
- Throw a ball against the wall.
- Rub it along the desk to feel the frictional force and see what it does to the plasticine.

Draw force diagrams to explain what happens.

Now explore the effects that bar magnets have on each other.

- Arrange them so they repel or attract.
- Try to balance one magnet so that the N-pole floats above the N-pole of the other.

Draw force diagrams for these situations.

SUMMARY QUESTIONS

1. The lunar landing module which visited the Moon had a mass of 15 000 kg. What would this weigh on the Earth and on the Moon? ($g_{Moon} = 1.6 \, N \, kg^{-1}$)

2. If the largest mass you could lift on the Earth is 150 kg. What is the largest mass you could lift when standing on the Moon?

Moments

At the end of this topic you should be able to:

- determine the moment of a force acting about a fulcrum (pivot)
- combine moments to find a resultant moment
- analyse systems in equilibrium to find forces and distances.

The turning effect of a force

When a force acts on an object it may cause a turning effect, known as the **moment** of the force. This turning effect depends on the size of the force applied and the distance from the pivot or point of rotation.

Calculating moments

The moment of a force is the product of the force and the perpendicular distance to the pivot:

$$M \text{ (N m)} = F \text{ (N)} \times d \text{ (m)}$$

Combining moments

When there are several forces acting a resultant moment can be found.

WORKED EXAMPLE 1

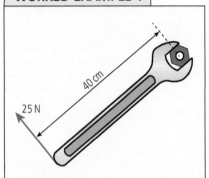

Figure 1.7.1

A long spanner is used to turn a nut using a force of 25 N. What is the moment of the force when the spanner is held 40 cm from the nut?

$$M \text{ (N m)} = F \text{ (N)} \times d \text{ (m)}$$
$$M = 25 \text{ N} \times 0.4 \text{ m}$$
$$M = 10 \text{ N m}$$

WORKED EXAMPLE 2

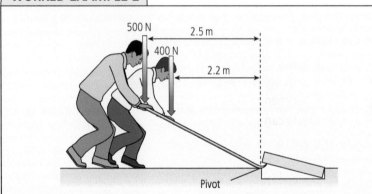

Figure 1.7.2

Two workers are using a large lever to lift up a concrete slab (Figure 1.7.2). Worker A applies a force of 400 N at a distance 2.2 m from the pivot. Worker B applies a force of 500 N at a distance 2.5 m from the pivot. What is the total turning effect produced?

Total moment = moment (worker A) + moment (worker B)

$$= (400 \times 2.2) + (500 \times 2.5) = 880 + 1250$$
$$= 2130 \text{ N m}$$

Moments acting against each other can be subtracted in a similar way.

Clockwise and anticlockwise

When describing the action of moments, the terms *clockwise* and *anticlockwise* are used to describe the direction of action (Figure 1.7.3).

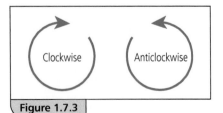

Figure 1.7.3

Moments and equilibrium

When an object is in equilibrium it is not accelerating or rotating. The two equilibrium conditions are:

• There is no resultant force acting on the object.
• The clockwise moment is equal to the anticlockwise moment.

The second of these points is called the **principle of moments**.

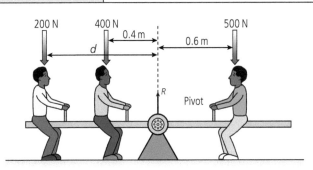

Figure 1.7.4

Find the distance d of the third child from the pivot if the seesaw is in equilibrium (Figure 1.7.4).

For a seesaw in equilibrium:

• there is no overall resultant force
• clockwise moments = anticlockwise moments.

These two facts can be used to find the values of the force R and distance d.

The upwards force R must equal the sum of the downward forces:

$$R = 400\,N + 200\,N + 500\,N = 1100\,N$$

The moments are also balanced.

Clockwise moments = anticlockwise moments

$$(0.6\,m \times 500\,N) = (0.4\,m \times 400\,N) + (d \times 200\,N)$$
$$300\,Nm = 160\,Nm + 200d\,Nm$$
$$200d = 300 - 160$$
$$d = \frac{140}{200} = 0.7\,m$$

Test the principle of moments by suspending a ruler from its centre (a hole through the centre works best) and then suspending masses on either side. Try various combinations of masses until the ruler is balanced (Figure 1.7.5).

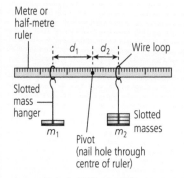

Figure 1.7.5   Testing the principle of moments

Calculate the moments acting on each side using the weights of the masses and the distance from the pivot point.

You should find that the ruler is only balanced when the clockwise moments are equal to the anticlockwise moments.

1 A force can cause a turning effect (moment).

2 The moment of a force is the product of the force and the perpendicular distance to the pivot. ($M = Fd$)

3 An object is in equilibrium when the clockwise moments are equal to the anticlockwise moments and there is no overall resultant force.

1 What are the two conditions required for an object to be in equilibrium?

2 Three people of equal weight sit on a seesaw of total length 4.0 m. Sketch a diagram showing the possible positions where the three people could sit so that the seesaw would be balanced.

Stability

Objects are composed of billions of particles each of which is attracted by the gravitational pull of the Earth. Instead of considering each of these forces separately we use a single equivalent resultant force and call this the weight of the object as a whole. This single force seems to come from a single point in the object. This is called the **centre of gravity**.

The centre of gravity is the point from which the weight appears to act.

Finding the centre of gravity

As the weight of an object acts from the centre of gravity an object will always be in equilibrium when it is suspended from a point directly above the centre of gravity.

This idea can be used to find the centre of gravity for a lamina (Figure 1.8.1). A lamina is a thin sheet of material in any shape.

WORKED EXAMPLE

Why do some tightrope walkers carry a very long flexible pole?

The pole can be held so that it lowers their centre of gravity and increases stability. The ends of the pole bend downwards and lower the centre of gravity even further (Figue 1.8.2).

Figure 1.8.2   A tightrope walker

ACTIVITY

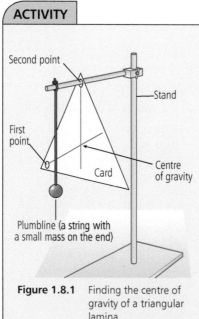

Figure 1.8.1   Finding the centre of gravity of a triangular lamina

- Make several small holes near the edges of the lamina. Suspend the lamina so that it can rotate freely. When it comes to rest the centre of gravity is directly below the point of suspension.
- Attach a plumbline at the point of suspension. Use a pencil to draw a line from the point of suspension and following the plumbline. (This line must pass through the centre of gravity.)
- Repeat the process using at least two more points of suspension.
- The point where the lines meet is the centre of gravity.

Three-dimensional objects

Three-dimensional objects are a little more difficult to investigate. They can also be suspended from a number of points but it's hard to draw lines and see where they meet. The centre of gravity is usually where you would expect for regularly shaped objects (e.g. where the diagonal lines joining the corners of a cube meet, the centre of a sphere, the middle of a uniform ruler).

Stability

An object standing on a table will be in equilibrium when its centre of gravity is directly above the point where the reaction force acts, i.e. above the base. If the object is tilted and the centre of gravity moves beyond the base it will topple (Figure 1.8.3c).

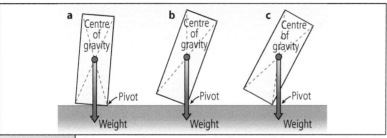

Figure 1.8.3 | If the centre of gravity is outside the base of the object it will topple.

An object that can be tilted and will return to its original position when released is said to be in **stable equilibrium**. This occurs if tilting the object results in the centre of gravity being moved upwards.

If the object falls over with a slight push then the object was in **unstable equilibrium**. This happens when the centre of gravity lowers and so the object falls into a position where it is more stable.

Designing for stability

A stable object has a low centre of gravity and a wide base. A racing car has a wide wheelbase and low centre of gravity to make it more stable when it travels around corners. A car with a higher centre of gravity might topple over.

Figure 1.8.4 | During a judo match the competitors spread their feet and bend down. Both of these actions make them more stable.

SUMMARY QUESTIONS

1 Why does a chest of drawers become more unstable if you only fill the top drawers?

2 Describe how you could find the centre of gravity for a laboratory stool.

3 Which of the objects in Figure 1.8.5 is in stable equilibrium and which is in unstable equilibrium?

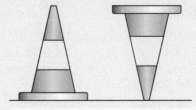

Figure 1.8.5

KEY POINTS

1 The centre of gravity of an object is the point at which the weight of the object appears to act.

2 The centre of gravity can be found by suspending the object from different points.

3 Stability of an object depends on the position of its centre of gravity.

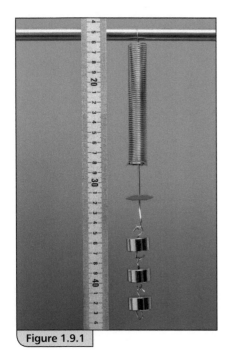

Figure 1.9.1

Extension

The increase in length of a spring caused by a stretching force is called the **extension**. When the force is removed the spring may return to its original shape and size.

In the 17th century, Robert Hooke found that there was a simple relationship between the extension of the spring and the force acting on it.

The extension of a spring is proportional to the force acting on it.

Expressed mathematically Hooke's law is:

$$F = kx$$

where F is the force, x is the extension and k is a constant known as the **spring constant**. The spring constant represents the size of the force required to stretch the spring by one metre. The spring constant is effectively a measure of the stiffness of a spring. A high spring constant indicates a stiff spring.

WORKED EXAMPLE

A spring is loaded with a 5.0 kg mass and its length increases from 20 cm to 45 cm.

a What is the spring constant of this spring?

$$F = kx$$

$$k = \frac{F}{x} = \frac{5.0\,\text{kg} \times 10\,\text{N kg}^{-1}}{0.45\,\text{m} - 0.20\,\text{m}} = \frac{50\,\text{N}}{0.25\,\text{m}} = 200\,\text{N m}^{-1}$$

b How long is the spring if a load of 7.0 kg is applied?

$$x = \frac{F}{k} = \frac{7.0\,\text{kg} \times 10\,\text{N kg}^{-1}}{200\,\text{N m}^{-1}} = 0.35\,\text{m}$$

The spring has extended by 0.35 m from its original length of 0.2 m, so the new length is 0.55 m.

Limit of proportionality

Hooke's law only applies up until a point called the **limit of proportionality**. If the load is increased after this point the spring will continue to extend but this additional extension will not be in proportion to the force applied.

Elastic limit

If the spring is stretched even further then it will become permanently deformed. This means it will not return to its original length. This deformation happens when the spring is stretched beyond a point called the **elastic limit**.

The graph in Figure 1.9.2 shows the extension of a spring when a force is applied. The spring follows Hooke's law up to point P (the limit of proportionality). It continues to stretch up to point E (the elastic limit). Up to this point the spring is able to return to its original length if the force is removed. Beyond the elastic limit the spring will be permanently deformed.

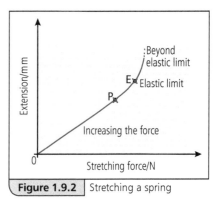

Figure 1.9.2 | Stretching a spring

ACTIVITY: FINDING THE SPRING CONSTANT

Investigate a spring using the technique described here.

- Suspend a spring from a stand as shown in Figure 1.9.3.
- Measure and record its length.
- Add a small mass and record the new length.
- Add more masses one at a time, recording the length each time.
- Calculate the extension for each length.
- Remove the masses one by one to check that the same pattern is followed during unloading. If not, then the spring was loaded beyond the elastic limit and the last few data points may be invalid.
- Plot a graph of the load (x-axis) against total extension (y-axis) and find the gradient using a line of best fit.
- The gradient of this graph is:

$$\frac{\Delta y}{\Delta x} = \frac{\text{extension}}{\text{load}}$$

and so the spring constant is given by $k = \dfrac{1}{\text{gradient}}$.

- Investigate the extension of a rubber band using the same process.
- To what extent do the spring and the rubber band obey Hooke's law?

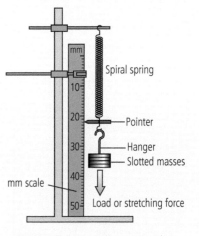

Figure 1.9.3 | Investigating Hooke's law

SUMMARY QUESTIONS

1 Calculate the length of a spring of original length 50 cm and spring constant 40 N m⁻¹ when a mass of 2.0 kg is suspended from it.

2 Use the data in Table 1.9.1 to determine the spring constant.

Table 1.9.1

Force applied/N	0	1	2	3	4	5	6
Length/cm	0	3.2	6.4	9.6	12.8	16.0	19.2

KEY POINTS

1 Hooke's law states that the extension of a spring is proportional to the load acting on it. ($F = kx$)

2 The spring constant for a spring is the force required to produce unit extension.

3 Stiffer springs have a larger spring constant.

SECTION 1: Practice exam questions 1

1 What SI units are used for the following quantities?

  a Mass

  b Time

  c Length

  d Speed

  e Density

  f The moment of a force

  g Pressure

2 Complete this table of descriptions of measurements with the appropriate prefixes and standard forms.

Description	Using prefixes	SI unit and standard form
a force of 5000 newton	.......kN	5×10^3 N
a length of seven hundred and twenty nanometres	.......nm	7.2×10^{-7} m
a current of 30 milliampere	.......mA	
	990 µg	

3 Use a scale diagram to find the resultant of these combinations of forces.

  a

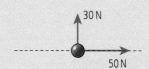

  b

  c

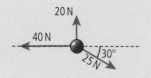

4 Find the resultants of these displacements using Pythagoras' theorem.

  a 16 km east and 20 km south

  b 27 km west and 50 km north

5 The mass and volume of a small sample of meteorite are measured as shown in the diagrams. Calculate the density of the sample.

6 An expedition to the planet Mars is being planned. The landing module has a mass of 50 000 kg.

  a Draw a labelled force diagram showing this module resting on the surface of Mars. Include the size of the forces. ($g_{Mars} = 3.7$ N kg^{-1})

  b The closest approach between Mars and Earth is 56 million kilometres. If the spacecraft can only carry supplies for 600 days how fast must it travel in order to get to Mars and back before these supplies run out?

7 On a building site a crane is used to lift heavy iron girders. To counteract the turning effect a concrete block, of mass 2.0×10^3 kg, is mounted on the other side of the crane. The position of this block can be adjusted between 2.0 m and 10.0 m from the pivot in order to balance loads of different sizes.

The mass of the girder is 4.2×10^3 kg and the lifting cable is connected 3.0 m from the pivot.

a Where should the concrete block be placed for the crane to be in equilibrium?

b What is the largest load the crane can lift while staying in equilibrium if the load always has to be connected 3.0 m from the pivot?

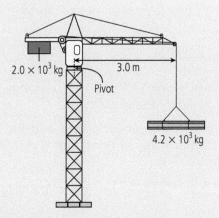

8 Describe how to find the centre of gravity of an irregularly shaped metal sheet of uniform thickness.

9 A group of students were asked to investigate the stretching of a spring and elastic band. They measured the extension of the spring and then the elastic by loading masses and recording the extension, producing the results shown in the table.

Load/N	Spring length/cm	Elastic length/cm
0	5.5	8.0
1	6.2	8.9
2	6.9	10.4
3	7.6	12.2
4	8.3	14
5	9.0	15.8
6	9.7	17.6
7	10.4	19.4
8	11.1	20.9
9	11.8	22.2

a Plot a suitable graph allowing the comparison of the extensions of the spring and the elastic.

b During which part of the extension was the elastic band stretching proportionally to the load?

c Determine the spring constant for the spring.

10 A single spring was used to suspend a block of mass 40 kg. The spring extended by 0.5 m.

a What is the spring constant for this spring?

b How can two identical springs be arranged so that the spring constant for the combination is:

i twice that of a single spring

ii half that of a single spring?

Moving objects and displacement–time graphs

Key definitions

Displacements and distances

The **displacement** of an object is the distance it is from the **origin** (starting point) in a stated direction.

The total **distance** an object travels is not always the same as the displacement, as the object may move backwards or forwards during the motion. A pendulum swinging will travel a considerable distance during one minute but its displacement will never be very large.

Speed and velocity

The speed of an object is the distance it covers in a particular time.

The **average speed** for a whole journey (or part of that journey) is given by:

$$\text{average speed} = \frac{\text{distance}}{\text{time}} \text{ or } v = \frac{x}{t}$$

The SI unit of speed is the metre per second (m s^{-1}) but kilometres per hour (km h^{-1}) and miles per hour are also used.

At different points an object may be travelling faster or more slowly than average. The speed at any particular time is called the **instantaneous speed**.

The velocity of an object is the speed in a particular direction.

Table 1.10.1 Units and symbols used in motion equations

Quantity	Unit	Symbol
distance	m	x
displacement	m	s
time	s	t
speed	m s^{-1}	v or c
velocity	m s^{-1}	v or u
acceleration	m s^{-2}	a

Displacement–time graphs

Displacement–time graphs represent the distance of an object from the origin over a period of time. The time is plotted on the horizontal axis while the displacement is plotted on the vertical axis.

The graph in Figure 1.10.1 can be used to determine how far away the sprinters are from the starting line at any time. It also shows that the blue sprinter took longer than the red sprinter to reach the 100 m finishing line.

The velocity can be found from the gradient of a displacement–time graph:

$$\text{velocity} = \frac{\Delta s}{\Delta t} = \frac{\text{change in displacement}}{\text{change in time}}$$

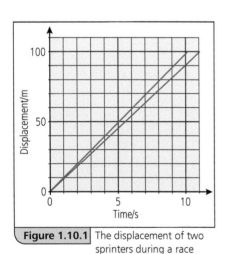

Figure 1.10.1 The displacement of two sprinters during a race

WORKED EXAMPLE

What is the velocity of the red sprinter as shown in Figure 1.10.1?

$$\text{Velocity } (\text{m s}^{-1}) = \frac{\Delta s}{\Delta t} = \frac{100\,\text{m}}{10\,\text{s}} = 10\,\text{m s}^{-1}$$

More complex journeys, involving changes in velocity, can be represented by a graph (Figure 1.10.2). These changes will be shown as changes in the gradient:

- The steeper the gradient the greater the velocity.
- A zero gradient (flat line) indicates zero velocity.
- A negative gradient (downward slope) will indicate movement back towards the starting point.

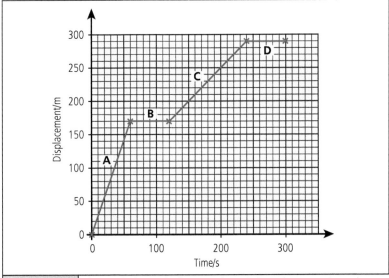

SUMMARY QUESTIONS

1 Calculate the velocity of the blue sprinter in Figure 1.10.1 and the taxi during parts A and C of Figure 1.10.2.

2 Sketch a more realistic displacement graph for a sprinter showing him speeding up at the start of the race and then slowing down after he has passed the 100 m finish line.

Figure 1.10.2 The graph shows the journey of a taxi through a town. It can be analysed to give the information shown in Table 1.10.2.

Table 1.10.2 Describing the motion of a taxi

Journey part	Description of the movement of the taxi	How the graph shows this movement
A 0–60 s	During the first sixty seconds the taxi is moving at a steady speed.	The line on the graph slopes upwards showing that the displacement is increasing.
B 60–120 s	The taxi stops for 60 seconds.	From 60 s to 120 s the line on the graph is horizontal. The displacement is not changing and so the taxi is not moving.
C 120–240 s	The taxi moves at a steady speed again. This speed is slower than for part A of the journey.	The slope of the line on the graph is upwards but has a shallower slope than for part A. This means the taxi is travelling more slowly.
D 240–300 s	Finally, the taxi stops again.	The line on the graph is horizontal again and so the taxi has stopped.

Acceleration

When an object changes velocity it **accelerates**. The graph above is unrealistic as it shows instant changes in velocity. In reality the taxi would accelerate for several seconds and, instead of a sharp change, the displacement–time graph would show a curve as the speed changed gradually. Similarly the sprinters would accelerate from the starting blocks until they reached a top speed and then slow after the finishing line.

KEY POINTS

1 A displacement–time graph shows the movement of an object over a period of time.

2 The velocity of an object can be found from the gradient of a displacement–time graph.

Acceleration and velocity–time graphs

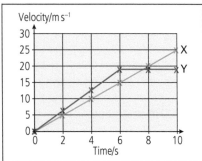

Figure 1.11.1 A simple velocity–time graph

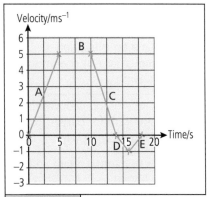

Figure 1.11.2 Motion of a toy. During phase A the toy is accelerating. In phase B the toy is at a constant velocity. During phase C the toy decelerates. Phase D shows that the toy is now moving with a negative velocity; it is moving backwards and accelerating. Finally, during phase E the toy slows and comes to rest.

Acceleration

The acceleration of an object is the rate of change of velocity:

$$\text{acceleration (m s}^{-2}) = \frac{\text{change in velocity (m s}^{-1})}{\text{time (s)}} \text{ or } a = \frac{v - u}{t}$$

where u is the initial velocity, v is the final velocity and t is the time during which the object changed velocity.

WORKED EXAMPLE 1

A rally car accelerates to $25\,\text{m s}^{-1}$ from a standing start in $15\,\text{s}$. What is the acceleration of the car?

Noting that the initial velocity is 0 gives:

$$a = \frac{v - u}{t} = \frac{(25 - 0)\,\text{m s}^{-1}}{15\,\text{s}} = 1.7\,\text{m s}^{-2}$$

Velocity–time graphs

A second way to represent the motion of an object is through a **velocity–time graph**. On these graphs:

- the time is represented on the x-axis
- the velocity is represented on the y-axis.

Figure 1.11.1 compares the movements of two cars. Car X accelerates uniformly from 0 to 10 seconds. Car Y accelerates for the first six seconds but then reaches a steady speed. It is important to notice that car Y does not stop. It keeps travelling at $18\,\text{m s}^{-1}$ until the end of the test.

Using velocity–time graphs to find acceleration

The acceleration can be found from the gradient of a velocity–time graph:

$$\text{acceleration} = \frac{\Delta v}{\Delta t} = \frac{\text{change in velocity}}{\text{change in time}}$$

WORKED EXAMPLE 2

What is the acceleration of car X throughout the test, shown in Figure 1.11.1?

$$a = \frac{v - u}{t} = \frac{(25 - 0)\,\text{m s}^{-1}}{10\,\text{s}} = 2.5\,\text{m s}^{-2}$$

As with displacement–time graphs, velocity–time graphs can show several phases of motion (Figure 1.11.2).

Using velocity–time graphs to find the distance travelled by an object

You can find the distance travelled by an object by measuring the area beneath the line on a velocity–time graph. This area can be broken down into simple shapes and the area calculated. Where simple shapes cannot be used the area may be estimated.

WORKED EXAMPLE 3

The simple velocity–time graph in Figure 1.11.3 represents the motion of a robot. What distance does it travel?

The graph is broken down into three simple shapes: triangle A, rectangle B and triangle C.

The areas are calculated:

Area A = $\frac{1}{2}$ × base × height = $\frac{1}{2}$ × 5 × 4 = 10

Area B = base × height = 10 × 4 = 40

Area C = $\frac{1}{2}$ × 6 × 4 = 12

The total area is 10 + 40 + 12 which represents a distance travelled of 62 m.

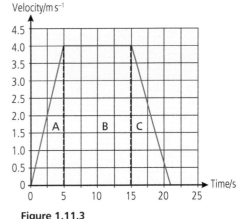

Figure 1.11.3

ACTIVITY

- Attach ticker tape to an object. Thread the tape through a vibrating pin or pen which produces a dot on the paper at regular intervals (usually 50 dots per second).
- Let the object fall, allowing a pattern of dots to be made on the strip.
- This pattern reveals the distance the object has travelled in each $\frac{1}{50}$th of a second and so the velocity and acceleration can be calculated.

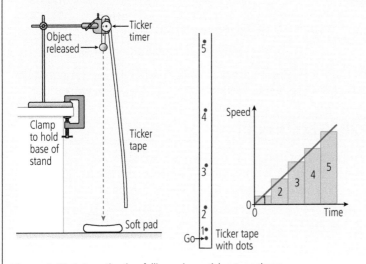

Figure 1.11.4 Investigating falling using a ticker tape timer

---

SUMMARY QUESTIONS

1 Calculate the acceleration of the toy in each part of the graph in Figure 1.11.2.

2 a Calculate the total distance travelled by the toy in Figure 1.11.2.

  b What is the final displacement of the toy?

KEY POINTS

1 The acceleration of an object can be found from the gradient of a velocity–time graph.

2 The distance travelled by an object can be found using the area under the line of a velocity–time graph.

1.12 | Newton's laws of motion

EXAM TIP

Be careful not to get confused about the first law and the third law. Just because there are equal and opposite forces does not mean that there is no resultant force. The paired forces always act on different objects, such as the girl and the chair (Figure 1.12.2a).

The Greek scientist Aristotle thought that a force was required to keep an object moving at a constant velocity. The greater the force the faster the object would be moving ($v \propto F$). He based this idea on his observation that an object tends to come to rest unless there is an obvious force acting on it. However, Aristotle performed no experiments to verify his idea and when, hundreds of years later, tests were carried out by Galileo, the idea was found to be wrong. Isaac Newton fully developed our ideas about forces and movement. Some of his key discoveries are called the laws of motion.

First law of motion

If there is no resultant force acting on an object it will remain at constant velocity.

The object will continue to move in a straight line at constant speed (or remain unmoving) unless acted on by a resultant force. This reluctance to change behaviour is called **inertia**.

Roll a marble along a smooth desk and you will see that it continues in a straight line unless it encounters something that produces a force on it. Note that frictional forces are acting and these will slow the marble down.

This first law leads to the idea that it is always resultant forces which cause an object to accelerate.

Second law of motion

The acceleration of an object is proportional to the resultant force acting on the object and inversely proportional to the mass of the object.

This statement leads to the mathematical relationship:

$$\text{force} = \text{mass} \times \text{acceleration or } F = ma$$

When mass is expressed in kg and acceleration in m s^{-2} the unit of force is called the newton (N) in honour of Newton's work.

Figure 1.12.1 The acceleration of a ship depends on its mass and the resultant force.

WORKED EXAMPLE 1

A cruise ship of mass 1.5×10^7 kg is pushed by an engine force of 2.3×10^4 N. The water resistance acting on the ship is 1.2×10^4 N. What is the acceleration of the ship?

The resultant force acting on the ship is $(2.3 - 1.2) \times 10^4$ N $= 1.1 \times 10^4$ N.

$$a = \frac{F}{m} = \frac{1.1 \times 10^4 \, \text{N}}{1.5 \times 10^7 \, \text{kg}} = 7.3 \times 10^{-4} \, \text{m s}^{-2}$$

Third law of motion

When an object A exerts a force on object B then object B exerts an equally sized force in the opposite direction on A.

- When you sit on your chair your weight acts downwards on the chair. The chair produces a reaction force equal to your weight but in an upwards direction (Figure 1.12.2a).
- The Sun exerts a force on the Earth which keeps it in orbit, but the Earth also exerts an equally sized force on the Sun causing it to wobble (Figure 1.12.2b). These stellar wobbles have been used to detect some large planets orbiting other stars.

Rockets

Gases from burning fuel are expelled from the base of a rocket as they expand. These hot gases gain momentum as they are pushed downwards and the rocket gains an equal and opposite momentum upwards.

As the fuel is used and leaves the rocket, its mass decreases and the acceleration of the rocket will increase $\left(\text{as } a = \dfrac{F}{m}\right)$.

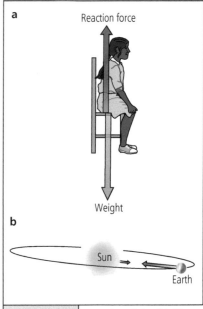

Figure 1.12.2 Examples of the third law in action

WORKED EXAMPLE 2

At launch, the initial mass of a rocket and fuel is 7.80×10^5 kg. The rocket produces a maximum force of 13.5 MN.

a What is the acceleration of the rocket at launch?

Remember that the resultant force acting on the rocket will be the thrust minus the weight.

The weight of the rocket is given by:

$$W = mg = 7.80 \times 10^5 \text{ kg} \times 10 \text{ N kg}^{-1} = 7.80 \times 10^6 \text{ N}$$

$$a = \frac{F}{m} = \frac{13.5 \times 10^6 \text{ N} - 7.80 \times 10^6 \text{ N}}{7.80 \times 10^5 \text{ kg}} = 7.3 \text{ m s}^{-2}$$

b One minute into the flight the rocket has used 1.0×10^5 kg of fuel but still produces the same thrust. What is the acceleration of the rocket at this stage?

Now use the reduced mass of the rocket to find the acceleration:

$$a = \frac{F}{m} = \frac{13.5 \times 10^6 \text{ N} - 6.80 \times 10^6 \text{ N}}{6.80 \times 10^5 \text{ kg}} = 9.9 \text{ m s}^{-2}$$

Figure 1.12.3 An Ariane rocket system is used to launch satellites from French Guiana.

SUMMARY QUESTIONS

1 Draw a diagram showing a ladder leaning against a wall, so that someone can climb up it. Draw all of the forces acting on the ladder, wall and floor.

2 A skydiver of mass 60 kg experiences an air resistance of 400 N just before opening her parachute and an air resistance of 1000 N just after. Calculate the acceleration of the skydiver at these two instants. ($g = 10$ N kg^{-1})

KEY POINTS

1 The first law of motion shows that resultant forces are needed to cause acceleration.

2 The second law of motion shows that $F = ma$

3 The third law of motion shows that forces always act in equal and opposite pairs.

Momentum and impulse

Momentum

Momentum is a vector quantity related to the mass and velocity of an object.

$$p = mv$$

An analysis of the units shows that the units of momentum are $kg\,m\,s^{-1}$.

WORKED EXAMPLE 1

What is the momentum of a minibus of mass 2000 kg when moving at $5.0\,m\,s^{-1}$?

$$p = mv = 2000\,kg \times 5.0\,m\,s^{-1} = 1.0 \times 10^4\,kg\,m\,s^{-1}$$

Impulse

As you saw in the previous topic, resultant forces are required to change the velocity and therefore the momentum of an object. The change in momentum caused by a force is called the **impulse** of the force and this impulse is the product of the force and the time for which it acts:

$$\text{impulse} = Ft = \text{change in momentum}$$

The units for impulse are $N\,s$. As this is a change of momentum this means that the units of impulse and momentum are identical:

$$kg\,m\,s^{-1} \equiv N\,s$$

The symbol $\equiv$ means 'is identical to'.

Conservation of momentum

As the momentum of an object can only be changed when a force acts on it then, from Newton's third law, you can see that when the momentum of an object changes then the momentum of another object must change by an equal and opposite amount.

In an interaction between two objects A and B the forces acting on the two objects must be of the same size and last for the same amount of time. This means that the impulse on object A is given by Ft and the impulse on B is given by $-Ft$. The two objects gain equal quantities of momentum but in opposite directions (Figure 1.13.1).

This gives the law of conservation of linear momentum:

In any interaction the total amount of momentum is conserved.

This law means that the amount of momentum after any collision is exactly the same as the momentum before the collision. This law can be used to analyse situations where two objects collide with each other.

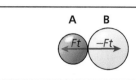

Figure 1.13.1 Momentum is conserved as the impulse is the same size on both objects.

Investigating momentum and movement

To investigate the law of conservation of momentum, trolleys can be used (Figure 1.13.2). Their movement is monitored using a ticker tape timer or by ultrasonic measurements of their position.

To carry out the experiment successfully the effect of frictional forces needs to be reduced. To do this a trolley is placed on a ramp and the ramp is tilted so that a ticker tape attached to the trolley has equally spaced dots. This shows that the trolley is moving at constant velocity and the friction forces have been compensated. The masses of the trolleys can be varied by placing additional blocks of metal onto them.

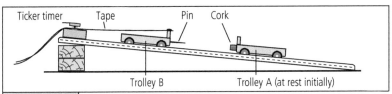

Figure 1.13.2 A ramp can be used to compensate for frictional forces.

The first trolley is pushed and allowed to collide with a second trolley partway down the ramp. The trolleys may have Velcro strips, magnets or a pin and cork to make them stick to each other after the collision. The movement data can then be analysed to confirm the law of conservation of momentum.

WORKED EXAMPLE 2

In a ramp experiment a trolley of mass 0.5 kg is pushed at a velocity of 0.3 m s^{-1}. It collides with a second stationary trolley of mass 1.0 kg and sticks to it. The resulting trolley pair moves off with a velocity of 0.1 m s^{-1}. Has momentum been conserved?

Find the momentum before the collision:

$$p = mv = 0.5\,\text{kg} \times 0.3\,\text{m s}^{-1} = 0.15\,\text{kg m s}^{-1}$$

Find the momentum after the collision remembering that the trolleys have a combined mass of 1.5 kg.

$$p = mv = 1.5\,\text{kg} \times 0.1\,\text{m s}^{-1} = 0.15\,\text{kg m s}^{-1}$$

This shows that momentum was conserved in the collision (as it always is).

WORKED EXAMPLE 3

Why does running into a wall hurt more than walking into it?

The change of momentum will be greater when you are moving faster and the impact time will also be shorter. This means that the force

$$\left(F = \frac{\text{change in momentum}}{\text{time}}\right)$$

will be much larger.

SUMMARY QUESTIONS

1 Copy and complete Table 1.13.1 by finding the missing values.

Table 1.13.1

Object	Mass/kg	Velocity/m s^{-1}	Momentum/kg m s^{-1}
cricket ball	0.16	20	
meteorite	5000		6.5×10^6

2 A car is pushed using a constant force of 500 N for 5 seconds. How much momentum does the car gain?

KEY POINTS

1 Momentum is the product of the mass and the velocity of an object. ($p = mv$)

2 Momentum is a vector quantity.

3 Momentum is conserved in **all** interactions.

The concept of momentum can be applied to situations where objects collide and bounce off each other and also to explosions and rocket propulsion.

More collisions

During collision both objects could be moving. This is often the case in a traffic collision. The objects may not stick together in a collision, instead they can rebound and separate after the impact.

WORKED EXAMPLE 1

In a game of billiards/pool, balls of mass 0.20 kg are used. During a match the white cue ball collides head on with the object ball. Initially the balls are moving in opposite directions. The cue ball has velocity of 0.30 m s^{-1} and the object ball has velocity −0.10 m s^{-1}. After the collision the cue ball continues to move in its original direction but at a reduced velocity of 0.05 m s^{-1}. What is the velocity of the object ball after the collision?

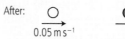

Before: 0.30 m s^{-1} −0.10 m s^{-1}

After: 0.05 m s^{-1} ?

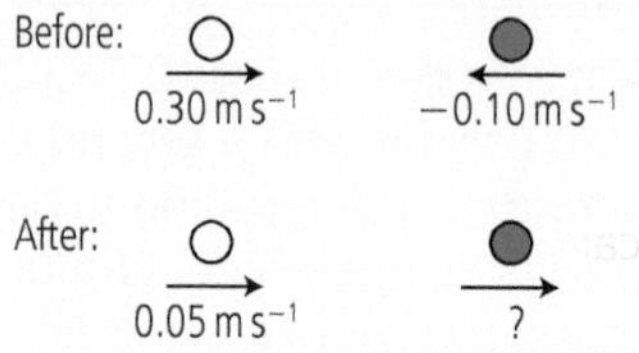

Figure 1.14.1

Choose the cue ball direction as positive, and the opposite direction as negative. Subscripts t, c and o identify the total, cue ball and object ball.

Find the initial total momentum of the balls:

$$p_t = p_c + p_o = (0.20\,\text{kg} \times 0.3\,\text{m s}^{-1}) + (0.20\,\text{kg} \times -0.1\,\text{m s}^{-1})$$
$$= 0.04\,\text{kg m s}^{-1}$$

Find the momentum of the cue ball after the collision:

$$p_c = 0.20\,\text{kg} \times 0.05\,\text{m s}^{-1} = 0.01\,\text{kg m s}^{-1}$$

The total momentum after the collision is the same as the momentum before and so the momentum of the object ball must be $0.04 - 0.01 = 0.03$ kg m s^{-1}.

Finally find the velocity of the object ball:

$$v_o = \frac{p_o}{m_o} = \frac{0.03\,\text{kg m s}^{-1}}{0.20\,\text{kg}} = 0.15\,\text{m s}^{-1}$$

As the answer is positive, this means that the object ball is now moving in the same direction as the cue ball.

Figure 1.14.2 When billiard balls collide they don't stick together. They often move off with different velocities.

Explosions

The law of conservation of momentum applies even when the initial momentum of a system is zero. This can be demonstrated in the following way (Figure 1.14.3).

- Two identical gliders are placed in the centre of a linear air track. The track floats the gliders on a cushion of air and so eliminates most of the friction.
- The gliders are held together with a small spring between them so that when they are released they will be forced apart by the spring.
- The initial momentum of the system is zero as their velocity is zero.
- When the gliders are released they will move apart and reach the end of the track at the same time showing that they have equal and opposite velocities and therefore equal and opposite amounts of momentum. This means that the total momentum after the release (explosion) is still zero.
- Further experiments can be carried out using gliders of different masses and measuring the velocities after the explosion.

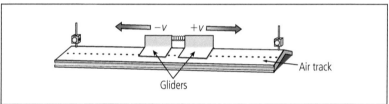

Figure 1.14.3 Using a linear air track to investigate explosions

Similar experiments can be carried out using two trolleys on a track.

Recoil

When a gun is fired the bullet is propelled forwards at high velocity by rapidly expanding gases. The bullet has gained momentum. At the same time the gun must gain an equal and opposite amount of momentum. It therefore moves backwards (recoils).

WORKED EXAMPLE 2

A rifle of mass 4.5 kg fires a bullet of mass 10 g forwards with a velocity of $300\,\text{m s}^{-1}$. What is the recoil velocity of the rifle?

Use a subscript b to identify the bullet and r for the rifle.

Find the momentum of the bullet:

$p_b = m_b v_b = 0.01\,\text{kg} \times 300\,\text{m s}^{-1} = 3.0\,\text{kg m s}^{-1}$

The rifle must also gain the same momentum but in the opposite direction.

$v_r = \dfrac{p_r}{m_r} = \dfrac{-3.0\,\text{kg m s}^{-1}}{4.5\,\text{kg}} = -0.67\,\text{m s}^{-1}$

SUMMARY QUESTIONS

1 A satellite has a mass of 500 kg. To adjust its speed it ejects 50 kg of fuel at $40\,\text{m s}^{-1.}$ What is the change in momentum and change in speed of the satellite?

2 If the fuel ejected in Question 1 is ejected over a period of 1 minute what is the average force acting on the satellite?

1 The displacement–time graph shows the height of a skydiver during a dive.

    a Find the velocity of the skydiver between 20 s and 50 s.

    b Find the velocity of the skydiver between 50 s and 100 s.

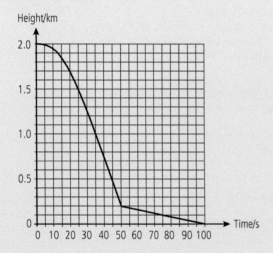

2 A car takes 8 s to slow down from a speed of 15 m s^{-1} to 5 m s^{-1} as it approaches a junction.

    a What is the acceleration of the car?

    b If the car has a mass of 800 kg, what is the braking force required to slow the car?

3 During take-off a jet aeroplane of mass 10 000 kg can produce a maximum thrust of 40 kN. At the point of take-off the plane experiences a drag force of 20 kN.

    a Calculate the initial acceleration of the plane.

    b Calculate the acceleration of the plane at the point of take-off.

4 During an experiment a trolley of mass 4.0 kg moves with a velocity of 0.5 m s^{-1}. It collides with a stationary trolley of mass 3.0 kg and the two trolleys stick together moving off at a new velocity. What is the velocity of the trolley combination?

5 During a docking manoeuvre a supply pod of mass 4000 kg accidently collides with the International Space Station (mass 100 000 kg) with a relative velocity of 2.0 m s^{-1}. Assuming the pod attaches to the station what is the change in velocity of the space station?

6 During a game of snooker a player attempts to pot the final black. The white ball strikes the stationary black with a velocity of 1.2 m s^{-1} and the black ball is propelled forwards with a velocity of 1.0 m s^{-1} after the impact. Assuming that both balls have equal mass, calculate the velocity of the white ball after the impact.

7 A billiard ball of mass 0.3 kg hits a cushion with a velocity of 2.5 m s^{-1}. It rebounds off the cushion in the opposite direction with a velocity of -2.4 m s^{-1}.

    a What is the initial momentum of the billiard ball?

    b What is the final momentum of the billiard ball?

8 An artillery gun of mass 1500 kg fires a shell of mass 10 kg at a velocity of 400 m s^{-1}. What is the recoil velocity of the gun?

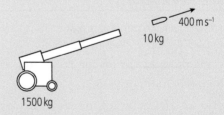

9 A group of students investigated the law of conservation of momentum using two trolleys, X and Y. Trolley X was allowed to roll along a ramp and accelerated before moving along a ramp adjusted to counteract frictional forces. The trolley then collided with trolley Y causing both trolleys to continue to move forwards separately.

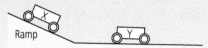

The graph shows the motion of the two trolleys during an investigation.

a What is the acceleration of trolley X as it travels down the ramp?

b What distance did trolley X travel before the impact with trolley Y?

The mass of trolley X was 0.5 kg.

c Calculate the momentum of trolley X just before and just after the impact.

d Calculate the mass of trolley Y.

The impact between the two trolleys lasts for 0.25 s.

e What is the average force acting on trolley Y during the impact?

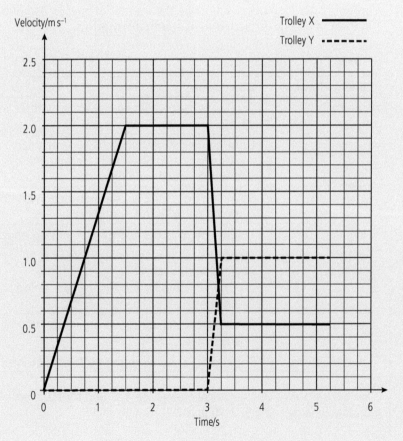

1.15 Energy and energy transformations

At the end of this topic you should be able to:

- define energy
- describe energy transfers and energy transformations
- calculate the work done (energy transferred) by a force acting through a distance.

The concept of **energy** is fundamental to physics. All events occur due to a transfer or transformation of energy.

Energy is defined as the capacity to do **work,** for example when a force moves an object through a distance. This is sometimes referred to as mechanical work.

All energy (and work done) is measured in a unit called the joule (J). One joule of energy is quite a small quantity and so kilojoule (kJ) is often used.

The forms of energy

Energy is sometimes referred to as being in different forms, as shown in Table 1.15.1, to help us describe the transfer of energy. A change in form of energy is referred to as a **transformation**.

Table 1.15.1   Forms of energy

Energy form	Description
thermal	This refers to the heat energy stored within an object.
light	Light is an electromagnetic wave and it can carry energy from place to place very quickly without the need for a medium.
sound	Sound energy is the energy associated with the vibrating particles in a sound wave.
kinetic	Kinetic energy is the energy of a moving object.
potential energy	Potential energy is the energy stored in an object due to its position (being off the ground), its physical state (such as a spring being stretched) or chemical state.
electrical energy	Electrical circuits transfer energy through wires in an electric current.
nuclear energy	This energy is stored in the nucleus of atoms.

For transfers involving electrical energy see 4.5, and for transfers of thermal energy see 2.9, 2.10 and 2.11.

Energy transfer and transformation

The ideas of energy transfer and transformation can be used to explain how devices operate.

ACTIVITY

Think about a range of electrical devices and why they are so useful to us. Describe the energy transformations that take place in as many as you can, including radios, televisions, telephones, microphones, electric motors and light bulbs.

Make sure that you identify any wasted energy.

Examples:

- When you walk up stairs the potential energy stored in the chemicals in your body is transferred into gravitational potential energy and heat energy (Figure 1.15.1).
- When you stretch a catapult to fire a stone, potential energy is stored in the elastic. When you release it the energy is transformed into kinetic energy as the stone flies outwards (Figure 1.15.2).
- Fireworks transform the potential energy stored in their chemicals into heat, light, sound, kinetic energy and even gravitational potential energy as they shoot up into the air (Figure 1.15.3).

Wasted energy

In any energy transfer or transformation some of the energy is transformed into thermal energy which cannot be used to do any more useful work. This energy has not disappeared. It has just become spread out to the surroundings or **dissipated**.

Mechanical work

When a force acts and moves an object through a distance we say that work has been done by the force. The amount of work done is given by the relationship:

work done = force × distance moved in the direction of the force

or $W = Fd$

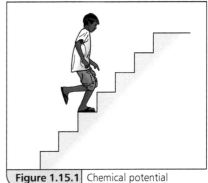

Figure 1.15.1 Chemical potential energy in your cells $\longrightarrow$ gravitational potential energy + heat energy

Figure 1.15.2 Elastic potential energy in the elastic $\longrightarrow$ kinetic energy of the stone

---

WORKED EXAMPLE

A broken-down motorcycle has to be pushed to a garage 2.5 km away along a flat road using a force of 80 N. How much work will be done?

$W = Fd = 80\,\text{N} \times 2.5 \times 10^3\,\text{m} = 2.0 \times 10^5\,\text{J}$

SUMMARY QUESTIONS

1 Describe the energy transformations involved in:

  a using a battery-operated torch

  b charging a mobile phone

  c boiling a kettle.

2 Copy and complete Table 1.15.2 comparing work done, force and distances for mechanical work.

Table 1.15.2

	a	b	c
Work done		5.0 kJ	4.3 J
Force	40 N	2000 N	
Distance	60 m		20 cm

Figure 1.15.3 Chemical potential energy $\longrightarrow$ heat + light + sound + kinetic energy + gravitational potential energy

KEY POINTS

1 Scientists describe events in terms of energy transformation and energy transfer.

2 A mechanical transfer of energy is called work done and this is found using the equation $W = Fd$

Energy sources for electricity

ACTIVITY

Research the use of fossil fuels and renewable energy in the Caribbean and write a short report about what should be done to reduce the dependency on fossil fuels.

SUMMARY QUESTION

1 Which energy sources:
  a require a large amount of land?
  b damage the atmosphere?
  c are unreliable?
  d can be used on a small scale near to where the electricity is required?

KEY POINTS

1 Large-scale electricity production takes place in fossil fuel burning or nuclear power plants.

2 There are a range of other renewable energy sources which can produce electricity on a smaller scale.

Electricity is an important form of energy as it is simple to transfer over very large distances and to transform it into other forms such as light, kinetic energy or heat. There is a constantly increasing demand for electricity which is met by using a wide range of energy sources.

Non-renewable energy sources

Non-renewable energy sources are fuels that cannot be replaced and so are in limited supply or have limited lifespans.

Fossil fuels

Fossil fuels include coal, oil and natural gas, formed from the remains of plants and animals that died millions of years ago.

These fuels are burnt in a furnace producing waste gases and large amounts of thermal energy. The heat is used to produce high pressure steam to spin turbines which drive electricity generators.

Burning fossil fuels can produce very large amounts of energy but vast quantities of carbon dioxide are released leading to global warming. Sulfur dioxide is also released, especially from burning coal, and this causes acid rain.

Oil is the most significant energy source used in the Caribbean, accounting for more than 90% of the total electricity production.

Nuclear power

A nuclear power station produces heat using nuclear fuels such as uranium. These fuels are not burnt but release thermal energy inside a reactor core when the nuclei split through a process called nuclear fission.

Nuclear power plants are very expensive to build and dismantle but are fairly cheap to operate. They can produce very large quantities of electricity. However, they also produce radioactive waste which is very dangerous and requires safe storage for thousands of years. Accidents are very rare but the escaping radioactive material can contaminate large areas of land.

No nuclear power stations operate in the Caribbean and none are currently planned. Cuba started construction of a nuclear power station in the 1980s but abandoned the project before the reactor had been built. You can find additional detail about nuclear reactions in 5.4.

Renewable energy sources

Renewable energy sources produce electricity without being used up. The sources are either quickly replaceable or have effectively unlimited lifespans. Several examples are shown in Table 1.16.1.

Table 1.16.1 A summary of some renewable energy sources in the Caribbean

Energy source	Example	How it operates	Key advantages	Key disadvantages
Solar power (photovoltaic cells)	There are no large-scale solar power plants in the Caribbean but many new buildings have panels installed. Most homes in Barbados have solar water heaters on their roofs.	The energy from sunlight is converted directly to electricity using semiconductor cells.	No fuel required. Plenty of sunlight in the Caribbean. Electricity can be produced on the building in which it is to be used.	Can't produce electricity at night so battery storage required. Quite expensive to build.
Hydroelectricity	The Dominican Republic has twenty dams providing 10% of the electricity needs.	Water is trapped behind a dam and used to drive turbines as it is allowed to escape.	No fuel required. Can produce large amounts of electricity very quickly.	Floods large amounts of land which is a precious resource on islands. Only small- and medium-scale systems can be used on Caribbean islands as there are few large valleys or rivers.
Tidal power	Tidal flows around the Caribbean could provide energy but are not used currently.	Water is trapped in estuaries and drives turbines.	No fuel required. Predictable energy output.	There are very few suitable estuaries in the Caribbean islands. Alters habitats and wildlife.
Wind turbines	The Wigton wind farm on Jamaica produces 20 MW of electricity.	The wind spins turbine blades mounted on towers.	No fuel required. Plenty of wind around island systems. Large-scale wind farms or small-scale local generation possible.	Offshore turbines could affect tourism by spoiling views. Some noise pollution is produced especially from large wind farms.
Geothermal energy	Beneath the volcanic islands of St Kitts and Nevis there are vast reserves of geothermal energy. Research projects are underway to develop a power station.	Thermal energy released by radioactive decay within the Earth is used to heat water into steam and the steam drives turbines.	No pollution is caused and sources are very reliable.	Only a very few locations are suitable.
Biofuels	Sugar cane is grown on many islands and some could be used to produce oils or ethanol to replace crude oil.	Biological material, such as wood, sugar cane, or ethanol, is burnt.	New supplies can be grown fairly quickly. Does not add extra carbon dioxide to the atmosphere.	The land used to grow fuel crops may be better used to grow food for increasing populations.

Potential energy and kinetic energy

EXAM TIP

The transposition of the kinetic energy equation is probably the most difficult one you will need to do. If you struggle then memorise the alternate versions shown on these pages.

WORKED EXAMPLE 2

a A fast bowler can bowl a cricket ball of mass 160 g at 40 m s⁻¹. How much kinetic energy does this ball have?

$E_k = \frac{1}{2}mv^2$

$= \frac{1}{2} \times 0.16\,\text{kg} \times (40\,\text{m s}^{-1})^2$

$= 128\,\text{J}$

b What is the speed of a powerboat of mass 600 kg if it has 40 kJ of kinetic energy?

The rearrangement of the kinetic energy equation gives:

$v = \sqrt{\dfrac{2 \times E_k}{m}} = \sqrt{\dfrac{2 \times 40 \times 10^3\,\text{J}}{600\,\text{kg}}}$

$= 11.5\,\text{m s}^{-1}$

Potential energy can arise because an object is stretched or compressed. When you investigated Hooke's law in 1.9 you added masses to the spring and the force caused the spring to stretch. This force acted through a distance and therefore did work in stretching the spring.

Gravitational potential energy

An object that can fall due to the pull of gravity has **gravitational potential energy**. When it changes its height then there is a change in its gravitational potential energy:

$$\text{change in gravitational potential energy} = \text{mass} \times \text{gravitational field strength} \times \text{change in height}$$

or

$$\Delta E_p = mg\Delta h$$

This equation matches the equation for mechanical work done.

WORKED EXAMPLE 1

How much energy is required to lift 500 kg of sand to a height of 20 m (Figure 1.17.1)?

The work done lifting the sand will be equal to the gravitational potential energy gained:

$\Delta E_p = mg\Delta h$

$= 500\,\text{kg} \times 10\,\text{N kg}^{-1} \times 20\,\text{m}$

$= 1.0 \times 10^5\,\text{J}$

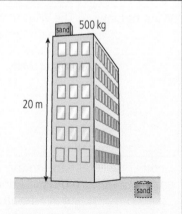

Figure 1.17.1 Gaining gravitational potential energy

Kinetic energy

The **kinetic energy** of an object is the energy associated with its movement. The relationship is:

$$\text{kinetic energy} = \frac{1}{2} \times \text{mass} \times \text{speed}^2 \text{ or } E_k = \frac{1}{2}mv^2$$

As you can see an object with a large mass and high speed will have more kinetic energy than a small, slow moving object.

Transposition of the equation

To find v if given the mass and the kinetic energy, you need to rearrange the equation. Here is the process.

- Original equation: $E_k = \frac{1}{2}mv^2$
- Multiply both sides by 2: $2E_k = mv^2$
- Divide both sides by m: $\dfrac{2E_k}{m} = v^2$
- Take the square root of both sides: $\sqrt{\dfrac{2E_k}{m}} = v$

Transfer between E_p and E_k

Transformation of gravitational potential energy to kinetic energy is common. It happens every time something falls. The equations for kinetic energy and potential energy can be used to calculate the speed of the falling object, assuming there is negligible air resistance.

Oscillations of a pendulum

A pendulum serves as an example of the transfer between kinetic and gravitational potential energy. As the pendulum swings from side to side there is a transfer of gravitational potential energy to kinetic energy and back again. The quantities of energy involved can be calculated using the equations in the worked example for the falling coconut.

WORKED EXAMPLE 4

A pendulum bob of mass 60 g is displaced sideways so that it is 3 cm above its equilibrium position and then allowed to swing freely. What is the maximum speed of the bob?

Find the gravitational potential energy the bob loses as it swings to the equilibrium position:

$\Delta E_p = mg\Delta h = 0.06\,\text{kg} \times 10\,\text{N kg}^{-1} \times 0.03\,\text{m} = 1.8 \times 10^{-2}\,\text{J}$

When the pendulum reaches the central position all of this potential energy will be lost, matched by a gain in kinetic energy and the speed can be calculated (Figure 1.17.2).

$v = \sqrt{\dfrac{2 \times E_k}{m}}$

$= \sqrt{\dfrac{2 \times 1.8 \times 10^{-2}\,\text{J}}{0.06\,\text{kg}}}$

$= 0.77\,\text{m s}^{-1}$

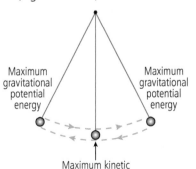

Maximum gravitational potential energy

Maximum gravitational potential energy

Maximum kinetic energy

Figure 1.17.2 Energy changes in a pendulum swing

Conservation of energy

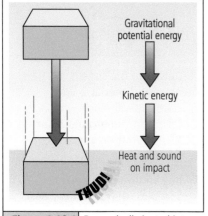

Figure 1.18.1 Energy is dissipated into the surroundings.

The most important rule about energy is the law of conservation of energy which states:

Energy cannot be created or destroyed. It can only be transferred or transformed.

This rule allows us to analyse and explain a wide variety of systems.

Spotting energy loss to the surroundings

There is always a loss of energy to the surroundings in energy transformations, usually as heat. This means that it often looks as though energy is disappearing when in fact the energy is still present but no longer useful for doing work.

Dropping objects

If you pick up a wooden block and drop it onto the ground the gravitational potential energy will transform to kinetic energy as the block falls but then the block will stop. The original energy has been transformed into thermal energy warming up the block and some sound energy (Figure 1.18.1). Even the sound energy dissipates into the surroundings and becomes heat.

A similar process happens when you kick a football. With repeated kicks the ball gains and loses kinetic energy. Over time the ball will warm up as some of the energy turns into heat within the ball. The rest is lost to the surroundings.

Pendulums

When a pendulum oscillates over a period of time, the height of the swing will decrease. Some of the energy is leaving the system. There are two transformations happening leading to this loss. As the pendulum moves through the air it experiences frictional forces. This frictional force will reduce the kinetic energy of the pendulum bob. The kinetic energy is transformed into random motion of the air particles (heat energy). At the point where the pendulum wire is attached to the stand there will be a small frictional force as the wire rubs against the stand. This also reduces the kinetic energy of the system and transfers it into heat energy.

Eventually the pendulum will stop swinging due to these energy losses. Because of this gradual energy loss the pendulums in clocks need to be provided with energy to keep swinging for long periods of time. Masses are attached to a system which drives the pendulum. As these masses move downwards very slowly their gravitational potential energy is provided to the pendulum.

Swinging

When you are on a swing you can keep it moving for a long time even though there is energy loss to the surroundings. By adjusting your centre of gravity you can drive the swing and so you seem to gain kinetic or gravitational potential energy. However, you are using chemical potential energy to drive the swing when you produce forces with your muscles.

ACTIVITY

Investigate the energy losses due to friction by rolling a trolley or ball down a ramp of different gradients (Figure 1.18.3).

- Measure the height difference to calculate the loss of gravitational potential energy.
- Measure the speed of the trolley or ball at the end of the ramp to find the kinetic energy.

Explain the losses: does a steeper ramp waste more or less energy?

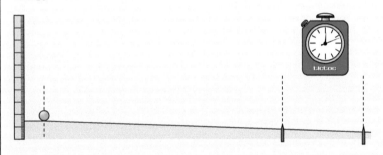

Figure 1.18.3 Investigating energy losses

EXAM TIP

If you do not know where the missing energy has gone in a transformation it has probably transformed into heat.

KEY POINTS

1 Energy is always conserved.

2 During energy transfers some energy is transformed into heat in the surroundings and this energy can no longer be used.

WORKED EXAMPLE

Describe the changes when a heavy ball is dropped onto a trampoline.

The ball starts with gravitational potential energy and this is transformed into kinetic energy as it falls. When the ball hits the trampoline the trampoline stretches, this is because the kinetic energy is being transformed into elastic potential energy. When the ball has no kinetic energy left the elastic strain energy will be transferred back into kinetic energy and the ball will move upwards gaining kinetic energy and gravitational potential energy. The ball will continue upwards until all of its kinetic energy has been transferred to gravitational potential energy.

The cycle will continue but during each stretching of the trampoline some energy will be converted to heat until eventuallly all of the initial energy will have been tranferred to heat and the ball will stop moving.

SUMMARY QUESTIONS

1 How is energy lost when you push a book across your desk?

2 When you place a mass onto a spring it stretches. If the mass is then pulled downwards and released the system oscillates up and down. Describe the energy transfers in this process and explain why the mass eventually stops.

Some devices transfer energy at a greater rate than others. For example, a large car engine will be able to transfer more energy in one second than a small moped engine, as it is more powerful.

Power

The rate of energy transfer is called **power** and is defined by the equation:

$$\text{power} = \frac{\text{work done (energy transferred)}}{\text{time taken}}$$

or

$$P = \frac{E}{t}$$

The unit of power is the $J\,s^{-1}$ which has the special name watt (W). The power equation applies to any transfer of energy or any work done and so can be used for mechanical work, electrical energy transfer or heating.

WORKED EXAMPLE 1

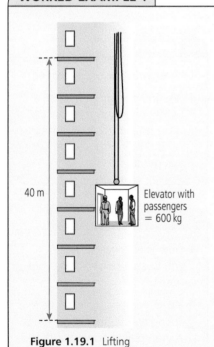

Figure 1.19.1 Lifting

An electric motor is used to lift an elevator and passengers with total mass of 600 kg through a height of 40 m (Figure 1.19.1). This process takes 30 seconds.

a What is the work done by the elevator motor?

Remember to use the weight of the elevator and not the mass:

Weight = mass × gravitational field strength

$$= 600\,kg \times 10\,N\,kg^{-1}$$

$$= 6000\,N$$

Now calculate the weight:

$$W = Fd = 6000\,N \times 40\,m = 2.4 \times 10^5\,J$$

b What is the effective power rating of the elevator motor?

$$P = \frac{E}{t} = \frac{2.4 \times 10^5\,J}{30\,s} = 8.0\,kW$$

Efficiency

During any energy transfer some energy is wasted and lost to the environment. This wasted energy depends on the specific device but there is always some heat produced.

The **efficiency** of a transfer is a measure of how much energy is transferred usefully:

$$\text{efficiency} = \frac{\text{output value}}{\text{input value}} \times 100\%$$

Here the output value represents the *useful* energy or power output of a transfer and the input value represents the *total* energy or power input. As there is always some energy wasted the output is always smaller than the input and so no transfer can have an efficiency of greater than 100%.

EXAM TIP

If you ever find an efficiency of greater than 100% then go back and try the question again. Your answer is definitely not correct.

WORKED EXAMPLE 2

If the lift motor mentioned in Worked example 1 is 70% efficient, how much energy is wasted when lifting the elevator and passengers?

First find out how much energy was supplied to the motor:

$$\text{efficiency} = \frac{\text{output value}}{\text{input value}} \times 100\%$$

$$\text{input value} = \frac{\text{output value}}{\text{efficiency}} \times 100\% = \frac{2.4 \times 10^5\,\text{J}}{70\%} \times 100\%$$

$$= 3.4 \times 10^5\,\text{J}$$

The energy wasted by the motor can now be found using the law of conservation of energy:

Energy wasted = energy supplied – useful energy output

$$= (3.4 - 2.4) \times 10^5\,\text{J} = 1.0 \times 10^5\,\text{J}$$

ACTIVITY

Use a small electric motor attached to a joulemeter to lift objects (Figure 1.19.2). Calculate the gain in potential energy and the electrical energy supplied to the motor to find its efficiency.

• Does the efficiency of the motor change when the load is changed?

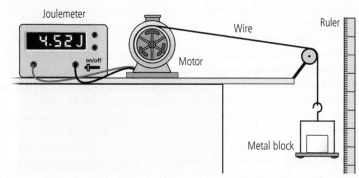

Figure 1.19.2 Measuring the efficiency of an electric motor

SUMMARY QUESTIONS

1 What is the power rating of an engine which transfers 40 kJ per minute?

2 How much useful energy is provided by an electrical motor with an efficiency of 75% in one hour if it has a power rating of 150 W?

KEY POINTS

1 The power of a device is the rate at which it does work (transfers energy) as given by $P = \dfrac{E}{t}$

2 Efficiency is a measure of how effective an energy transfer is at producing useful energy.

At the end of this topic you should be able to:

- calculate the pressure acting on a surface
- describe how pressure increases with the depth in a fluid.

Figure 1.20.1

WORKED EXAMPLE 1

I have a mass of 60 kg and the total area of my feet is 0.04 m². What is the pressure on the sand?

$$p = \frac{F}{A} = \frac{600\,N}{0.04\,m^2} = 15\,kPa$$

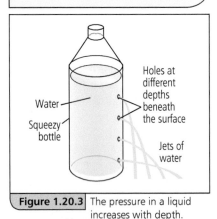

Figure 1.20.3 The pressure in a liquid increases with depth.

Water — Squeezy bottle

Holes at different depths beneath the surface

Jets of water

Pressure on surfaces

When you walk on a sandy beach you leave a trail of footprints behind. Your weight is pushing down on the sand and it acts over the area of your feet causing a pressure.

$$\text{Pressure} = \frac{\text{force}}{\text{area}} \text{ or } p = \frac{F}{A}$$

The unit of pressure is $N\,m^{-2}$ which is also known as the **pascal** (Pa).

Pressure can also be measured in $N\,cm^{-2}$. As $1\,m^2 = 10\,000\,cm^2$, $1\,N\,cm^2 = 10\,000\,Pa$.

ACTIVITY

Draw around your feet onto some squared paper. Use the squares to estimate the area of your feet and then measure your weight. Calculate the pressure you exert on the floor (Figure 1.20.2).

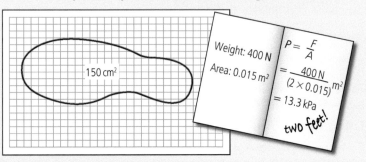

150 cm²

Weight: 400 N
Area: 0.015 m²

$$P = \frac{F}{A}$$
$$= \frac{400\,N}{(2 \times 0.015)}\,m^2$$
$$= 13.3\,kPa$$

two feet!

Figure 1.20.2 How much pressure do you produce on the floor?

Pressure in liquids

Pressure acts throughout a liquid and increases with depth. This can be demonstrated simply by allowing water to flow out of holes in a container. The further down the hole is from the surface of the liquid the further the water squirts out. This shows that it is experiencing a greater force or pressure.

ACTIVITY

Drill some small holes into a tall, plastic, measuring cylinder and fill it with water. Compare the distance the water is ejected to the depth of the water in the container. What happens as the water level decreases (Figure 1.20.3)?

Another pressure experiment uses Pascal's vases.

Explaining the increase in pressure

When a submarine is under water the weight of the water acts downwards onto the skin of the submarine. This produces pressure acting on the surface of the submarine.

- Imagine the water above the submarine to be a rectangle with width w and length l giving an area of $l \times w$ (Figure 1.20.4).
- The volume of the water directly above the submarine would be given by:

  volume = length × width × height or $V = l \times w \times h$
- The mass of the water above the submarine would be given by:

  mass = volume × density or $m = l \times w \times h \times \rho$
- The force acting downwards on the submarine would be the weight of the water which would be given by:

  weight = mass × gravitational field strength

  or $W = l \times w \times h \times \rho \times g$
- The weight of the water acts over the surface of the submarine, $l \times w$.
- The pressure acting on the submarine is:

$$\text{pressure} = \frac{\text{force}}{\text{area}} = \frac{l \times w \times h \times \rho \times g}{l \times w} = h \times \rho \times g$$

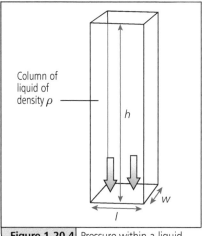

Figure 1.20.4 Pressure within a liquid

Column of liquid of density ρ

h

w

l

Figure 1.20.4 Pressure within a liquid

This shows that the pressure in a liquid is constant at a particular depth (h) as long as the density of the liquid is the same throughout. At very great depths the pressure is so high that the liquid is compressed and the density increases slightly.

WORKED EXAMPLE 2

Mercury has a density of $13.5 \times 10^3 \, \text{kg m}^{-3}$. What is the increase in pressure at a depth of 30 mm beneath the surface of a pool of mercury?

$p = h \times \rho \times g = 0.030 \, \text{m} \times 13.5 \times 10^3 \, \text{kg m}^{-3} \times 10 \, \text{N kg}^{-1}$

$= 4.05 \times 10^3 \, \text{N m}^{-2}$

Pressure in gases

The atmosphere

The Earth's atmosphere is a deep layer of gases reaching beyond 100 km above the Earth's surface. Pressure in the atmosphere increases in depth in a similar way to the pressure in a liquid but the difference in density as you travel deeper into the atmosphere is far greater than that in liquids and so the relationship is not as simple.

At sea level the pressure is approximately 100 kPa which is often referred to as 'one atmosphere' pressure. If you climbed to the top of the Blue Mountain Peak in Jamaica you would reach a height of 2.2 km above sea level. At this height the air pressure is only 80 kPa (0.8 atmosphere).

As water is much denser than air, travelling to a depth of 10 metres in water will increase the pressure acting on you to two atmospheres. Deep-sea divers can reach a depth of nearly 500 m causing them to experience a pressure of 50 atmospheres.

SUMMARY QUESTIONS

1 A nail is knocked into a plank of wood using a force of 60 N. The point on the nail has an area of 1.0 mm² ($1.0 \times 10^{-6} \, \text{m}^2$). What is the pressure acting on the wood when the nail is hit?

2 Water has a density of 1000 kg m⁻³. What is the pressure 40 m beneath the surface? Don't forget to include the pressure of the atmosphere above the water.

KEY POINTS

1 The pressure acting on a surface is given by $p = \dfrac{F}{A}$

2 The pressure in a liquid is given by $p = h\rho g$

Floating, sinking and density

At the end of this topic you should be able to:

* explain why some objects float and why some sink
* calculate the resultant force acting on an object as a result of its weight and buoyancy.

Archimedes was a Greek scientist who lived in the 3rd century BCE. Legend has it that, when asked to investigate if a crown was made from pure gold, he discovered a key principle which explains why objects float or sink.

Archimedes' principle

Any object, wholly or partially immersed in a fluid, is buoyed up by a force equal to the weight of the fluid displaced by the object.

It is important to note that this principle applies to objects which are floating and to objects which are submerged in the fluid.

In addition submerged objects will displace a volume of water equal to their own volume. This fact is often used to calculate the **density** of materials.

When you get into a bath of water you will notice the water level rise. The weight of that displaced water will be the same as the upthrust you feel.

ACTIVITY

Investigate Archimedes' principle using a displacement can (also called a Eureka can) (Figure 1.21.1).

Measure the weight of water displaced when an object is submerged in the water. Compare this to the apparent reduction in the weight.

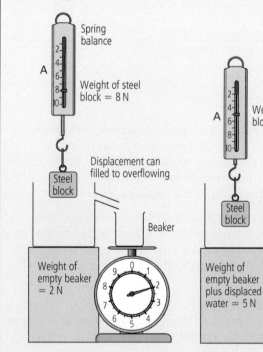

Figure 1.21.1 Investigating Archimedes' principle

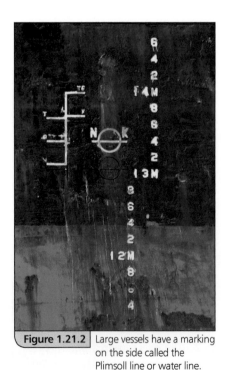

Figure 1.21.2 Large vessels have a marking on the side called the Plimsoll line or water line.

Floating objects

An object will float as long as the upthrust (or buoyancy) is equal to the weight of the object. Solid objects with a density greater than that of water will always weigh more than the water they displace and so will sink.

Ships are built from steel which has a much higher density than water. They float because they contain large volumes of air and this reduces their average density to much lower than the density of water.

For the ship to float it must displace the same weight of water as it weighs. Loading up the ship with cargo will increase the weight of the ship and therefore the weight of water displaced. This means that the ship will sink lower into the water.

If too much cargo is added to the ship then it will sink too low in the sea. The Plimsoll line indicates how heavily loaded the ship is and ensures that enough extra buoyancy is kept in reserve in case waves cause water to start entering the ship (Figure 1.21.2).

If the ship is damaged and water enters into the hull then the weight of the ship increases and it sinks lower into the water until, eventually, it sinks. The average density of the ship as a whole becomes greater than the density of the water.

Submerged objects

When an object is beneath the surface of a fluid Archimedes' principle tells us there will be an upthrust force acting on the object equal to the weight of the fluid displaced. This upthrust force will seem to reduce the weight of the object by decreasing the resultant force.

Submarines

Submarines can alter their average density by allowing ballast tanks to fill with water. This increases the weight of the submarine which makes it sink in the water. To gain additional buoyancy the water can be pushed out of the tanks using compressed air and this decreases the weight of the submarine.

Balloons

A balloon or airship is also submerged in a fluid, the air. This means that there will be a force acting upwards on the balloon equal to the weight of air which has been displaced. This buoyancy allows balloons and airships to float as long as the upthrust is greater than their weight.

1 A student has been asked to investigate the motion of a ball bearing fired from a spring mounted at the edge of a table. The ball bearing is pushed into the spring so that the spring is compressed a distance x. The spring is then released and the ball bearing follows a curved trajectory as it falls to the floor. The student measures the distance travelled by the ball bearing for a range of compressions of the spring and investigates the relationship between the length of the compression of the spring and distance the ball bearing travels before reaching the floor. The ball bearing is fired three times for each compression of the spring.

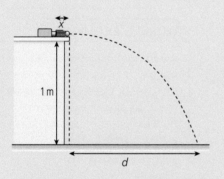

Compression distance, x/cm	2.0	3.0	4.0	5.0	6.0
Travel distance, d/cm	26.2	38.8	51.0	63.4	76.2
Travel distance, d/cm	26.6	38.8	51.0	63.4	75.8
Travel distance, d/cm	26.6	39.0	51.2	63.4	76.0

a Calculate the average travel distance for the ball bearing for each compression distance.

b Plot a graph comparing the compression distance (x-axis) to the travel distance (y-axis).

c Draw a straight line of best fit.

d Calculate the gradient of this line.

e To what extent does the data support the hypothesis that the travel distance is proportional to the compression of the spring?

2 Describe the energy transfers and transformations that take place when:

a a helicopter takes off

b a bungee jumper dives off a bridge

c a tree falls over in a forest.

3 A car of mass 600 kg is pushed up a hill using a force of 500 N. The slope is 50 m long and the car rises by 4 m.

a How much work is done in pushing the car?

b How much gravitational potential energy does the car gain?

c Assuming that gain in potential energy is counted as useful work, calculate the efficiency of the energy transfer.

4 During a competition to determine the world's strongest human a competitor pulls a tractor along a flat road. A force of 4000 N is required and the tractor is moved through a distance of 20 m in 70 s.

a What is the work done in moving the tractor?

b What is the effective power of the competitor?

5 State the law of conservation of energy. Describe how this law is applied when finding the efficiency of an electric motor.

6 A new business wished to generate its own electricity. They are considering the use of a wind turbine or photovoltaic cells. Write a paragraph for each system describing the advantages and disadvantages.

7 A pulley system consisting of three pulleys is used to lift a pallet of bricks weighing 600 N through a height of 40 m. The force required to lift the pallet at a steady speed is 210 N and the rope is pulled through a distance of 120 m.

  a Neglecting the mass of the pulleys and rope, calculate the useful work done in lifting the pallet.

  b What is the efficiency of the pulley system?

  c In what form is energy wasted in the lifting process?

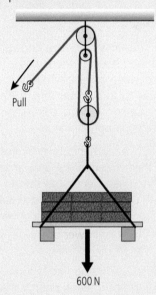

Pull

600 N

8 A tourist submarine has a glass dome to allow clear views of aquatic life. The dome can withstand a maximum absolute external pressure of 12 000 kPa. The density of seawater is 1.02×10^3 kg m^{-3} ($g = 10$ N kg^{-1}). What is the maximum safe diving depth of the submarine?

9 The density of water is 1000 kg m^{-3} (1 g cm^{-3}). Which of the following cubes of material will float in water?

Material	Length of side	Mass
a	4.0 cm	60 g
b	10 cm	1.2 kg
c	3.1 m	2.3×10^4 kg

10 A ship is made of 4000 m^3 steel of density 7900 kg m^{-3}.

  a What volume of fresh water ($\rho_{water} = 1000$ kg m^{-3}) would the ship need to displace in order for it to float?

  b Explain how the design of the ship enables it to displace this much water.

11 A rectangular block of polystyrene foam with dimensions 2.0 m × 1.0 m × 0.3 m is used to make a raft. The density of the polystyrene foam is 50 kg m^{-3} and that of water is 1000 kg m^{-3}.

  a What is the mass of the polystyrene block?

  b What volume of water will be displaced when the block floats?

  c How much additional weight could the raft support before beginning to sink?

12 Explain why a helium-filled balloon rises in the atmosphere.

13 The following table shows the power output from hydroelectric plants on Jamaica.

Location	Installed	Power output/MW
Upper White River	1945	3.8
Lower White River	1952	4.9
Roaring River	1949	3.8
Rio Bueno A	1949	2.5
Maggotty Falls	1966	6.3
Constant Spring	1989	0.8
Rams Horn	1989	0.6
Rio Bueno River	1989	1.1

  a Find the total power output of the hydroelectric system.

  b Assuming that the turbines operate all year around (365 days), estimate the total energy production of the system over a year.

  c The total electrical energy production in Jamaica was 2.0×10^{16} J. What percentage of Jamaica's electricity is produced by hydroelectricity?

  d Suggest why no new hydroelectric power stations have been built since 1989.

2 Thermal physics and kinetic theory

2.1 Heat, energy and temperature

A good understanding of **thermal energy** is required to explain the behaviours of different materials and the energy transfers between them. It took many years for scientists to explain why some objects were hot and why objects cooled.

The end of the caloric theory

During the 18th century the most commonly held idea about heat was caloric theory. This theory used the idea that there was a fluid called *caloric* that was transferred between objects when heat moves. The caloric would flow from a hot object to a colder one, meaning that the hot object would lose some caloric and the cold object gain some. Objects could only have a limited supply of caloric.

Count Rumford noted the heating effect of mechanical work involved in boring holes into cannons. Although there was clearly a large amount of heat released, the filings from the cannon had identical properties to the original cannon material. This meant that there was no physical substance (the caloric) being transferred. If the cannons were placed under water the mechanical work would always heat the water to boiling point. There seemed to be an unlimited supply of heat being released.

Over the next few years other scientists, including James Joule, developed the idea that heat was a form of internal energy that could be generated by mechanical energy. Joule measured the mechanical energy provided to water and measured the temperature increase (Figure 2.1.2). He found that the increase in temperature was proportional to the energy supplied. This research eventually led to the ideas behind the principle of conservation of energy.

Figure 2.1.1 The mechanical work done in boring out this cannon was converted to heat.

EXAM TIP

Thermal energy always moves from an object at a higher temperature to an object at a lower temperature.

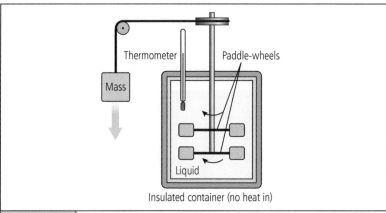

Figure 2.1.2 Joule's apparatus for transferring mechanical energy into heat

The kinetic theory and thermal energy

The thermal energy (heat energy) of an object is mainly the result of the motion of the particles within the object. As the theory describes motion it is called the **kinetic theory**. Some potential energy is associated with the bonding between, and the arrangement of, the atoms in materials.

Thermal energy transfers from a hotter object to a cooler one. This means that thermal energy flows from an object at high temperature to an object at a lower temperature. This process **always** occurs in this direction.

Temperature scales

A temperature scale is simply a way of expressing the relative hotness and coldness of objects. Hotter objects have a higher temperature. There are several temperature scales including:

The **Celsius scale**: This is a scale based on the properties of water. The freezing point of pure water is set at $0\,^\circ C$ and the boiling point at $100\,^\circ C$ producing a centigrade (100 step) scale. Celsius is the most commonly used temperature scale in school science and in industry.

The **Kelvin scale**: The Kelvin scale is based on the properties of ideal gases and the energy of particles. The low point of the scale is **absolute zero**. At this temperature the particles have zero thermal energy and so they cannot become any colder. An increase of one kelvin is defined to be the same as an increase of one degree Celsius. This makes conversion between the scales fairly easy:

- Temperate in kelvin = temperature in degrees Celsius + 273
- Temperature in degrees Celsius = temperature in kelvin − 273

ACTIVITY

- Use three bowls, one of iced water, one of lukewarm water and one containing hot water (Figure 2.1.3).
- Place one hand in the hot water and one in the iced water.
- After thirty seconds place both hands into the lukewarm water.

The hand which has been in the hot water will feel cold and the hand which has been in the cold water will feel hot. However, both hands are experiencing the same temperature.

Ice-cold water   Hot water
Room temperature

Figure 2.1.3   Hot or cold?

SUMMARY QUESTIONS

1 What would have happened in Count Rumford's experiments if the caloric theory had been correct?

2 Copy and complete Table 2.1.1 which shows some important temperatures.

Table 2.1.1

	Temperature in degrees Celsius	Temperature in kelvin
Absolute zero		0
Boiling point of liquid nitrogen		77
Freezing point of ethanol	−117	
Freezing point of water	0	
Body temperature		310
Boiling point of ethanol	79	
Boiling point of water	100	

KEY POINTS

1 The thermal energy of an object is a measure of the kinetic energy and potential energy of all of the particles that make up the object.

2 Temperature is a measure of the 'hotness' of an object.

3 Thermal energy is transferred from an object at higher temperature to an object at lower temperature.

Thermometers and temperature scales

At the end of this topic you should be able to:

- describe the characteristics and operation of different types of thermometer
- select an appropriate thermometer for use in a range of situations.

A thermometer is a device to measure the temperature of an object or substance. Thermometers rely on properties that vary with temperature.

Liquid-in-glass thermometers

Liquid-in-glass thermometers are based on the principle that the liquid will expand as its temperature increases and that this expansion is proportional to the increase in temperature (Figure 2.2.1).

A reservoir of liquid, mercury or coloured alcohol, is contained at the bottom of the thermometer in a 'bulb'. This is required so that there will be enough liquid to give a measurable expansion. The reservoir is connected to a narrow capillary tube through which the liquid will expand and rise upwards. The higher the temperature of the liquid the further up the capillary tube the liquid will rise.

The thermometer can be calibrated by placing the bulb of liquid in melting ice and then marking the level of the liquid in the capillary tube. This point represents 0 °C. The bulb of liquid is then placed in boiling water and the level of liquid in the capillary tube is marked to give the 100 °C point. The distance between these two points is then divided into 100 equal divisions giving a centigrade scale.

Figure 2.2.1 Most thermometers used in schools are liquid-in-glass.

Clinical thermometers

As human body temperature is approximately 37 °C and will generally vary between 35 °C and 42 °C, a clinical thermometer is designed to cover only this narrow range (Figure 2.2.2). The small range allows the thermometer to be designed to be very precise, with temperature divisions of 0.1 °C. The shape of the thermometer is designed to magnify the capillary tube and make it easier to read the temperature.

Clinical thermometers need to be removed from the patient before they can be read. To prevent an inaccurate reading as the liquid contracts, a small constriction is built into the thermometer that breaks the liquid thread. The liquid can be returned to the bulb after the reading by flicking the thermometer.

Clinical thermometers take a few minutes to reach thermal equilibrium and display an accurate temperature. Because of this, most are now being replaced by electronic thermometers.

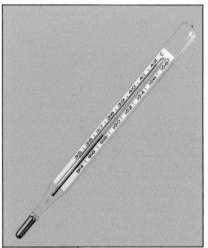

Figure 2.2.2 A clinical thermometer follows the same basic principles as a liquid-in-glass thermometer.

Thermocouples

A thermocouple is an electrical thermometer which relies on the potential difference (p.d.) produced when two different metals are connected. The p.d. produced varies with temperature.

Thermocouples can measure very high temperatures (beyond the melting point of glass) and they respond very quickly to changes. The p.d. they produce can also be recorded quite simply by data loggers or computers. This can then be converted and a temperature shown on a digital display making them very easy to read. These properties mean that thermocouples are used extensively in industry.

More thermometers

There are several other types of thermometers:

- **Gas thermometers** use the fact that a gas expands when its temperature increases. This expansion is proportional to the temperature change.
- **Infra-red thermometers** measure the rate of emission of infrared radiation from objects. The intensity of this radiation depends on the temperature of the object: hotter objects emit more radiation. This measurement can be used to find the temperature of something without needing to touch it.

ACTIVITY

Make your own thermometer using a conical flask containing dyed water and capillary tube. Place the flask in iced water and mark the level of the dyed water for 0 °C point. Then place it in boiling water to find the level for 100 °C. Divide the range into suitable divisions.

SUMMARY QUESTIONS

1 What are the ranges, precisions and temperature readings on the three liquid-in-glass thermometers shown in Figure 2.2.3?

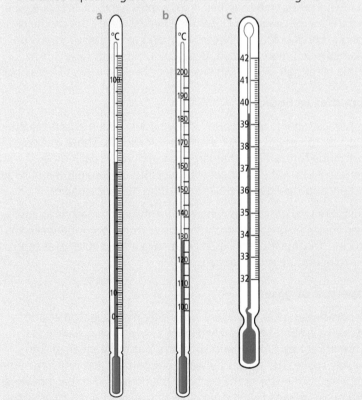

Figure 2.2.3

2 What are the advantages of using a thermocouple compared to a liquid-in-glass thermometer?

KEY POINTS

1 All thermometers rely on physical changes in substances caused by changes in temperature.

2 Thermometers have a range of scales, precisions and response times.

The states of matter

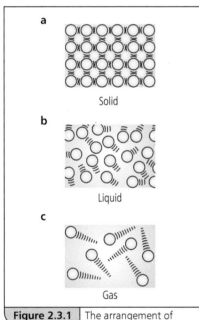

Figure 2.3.1 The arrangement of particles in **a** a solid, **b** a liquid and **c** a gas.

Most materials can be placed into three categories based on their properties and behaviour: solids, liquids and gases.

The particle model of matter

All materials are composed of tiny particles in different arrangements. These particles are atoms or molecules. The behaviour and physical properties of materials can be explained by describing the behaviour of these particles and the forces between them.

Properties of solids

In solid materials the particles are closely packed together and are held in place with relatively strong inter-molecular forces (Figure 2.3.1a). The particles are not free to move around but instead vibrate about their fixed positions. This means that solid materials maintain their own shape.

It is not easy to compress solids. This is because the particles are already tightly packed together. If a compressive force is applied then the particles move slightly closer together. However, this produces a strongly repulsive force between them and so further compression becomes much more difficult. Because of this solids have a fixed volume (although this can change when the solid is heated or cooled).

Properties of liquids

The particles in liquids are also closely packed together but the inter-molecular forces are weaker than those for solids. These weaker, short-range forces allow the particles to flow past each other (Figure 2.3.1b). When a liquid is placed into a container the particles will flow and the liquid will fill the bottom of the container.

Liquids are very difficult to compress for the same reasons as solids. When they are squashed strong repulsive forces occur between the particles. This means that liquids also have a fixed volume as long as their temperature is unchanged.

Properties of gases

The particles in gases have very weak inter-molecular forces and they move around very quickly (Figure 2.3.1c). The gas particles do not attract each other and so spread out to fill up all of the available space. The spaces between gas particles are very large when compared to the size of the particles themselves. The space between the particles means that it is possible to compress a gas by applying a pressure to it.

Thermal expansion

When a material is heated the particles gain thermal energy. In a solid this increase in energy causes the particles to vibrate more while staying in the same position. This increase in vibration will force the particles slightly further apart and as a result the material expands (Figures 2.3.2 and 2.3.3).

The forces which produce the expansion are very large and can cause even very strong objects to distort. Long metal bridges may expand by several centimetres on a hot day. To allow for this expansion the bridges have expansion gaps at each end. As the bridge warms up it lengthens and the gaps close. Similar gaps are used in railway lines to prevent them buckling in hot weather.

As you have already seen, both liquids and gases will expand when heated. The volume of a liquid will increase with temperature. Gases in containers will not be able to expand and so their pressure increases instead.

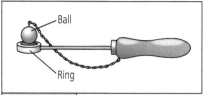

Figure 2.3.2 | A metal ball can pass through a ring. Heating the ball will cause it to expand and it will no longer fit through the ring.

Figure 2.3.3 | Overhead power cables or telephone lines expand on hot days, causing them to sag.

SUMMARY QUESTIONS

1 Summarise the properties of solids, liquids and gases using a table like Table 2.3.1. Add additional categories if you can.

Table 2.3.1

	Shape	Does it flow?	Volume	Density	Separation of particles	Forces between particles
Solid						
Liquid						
Gas						

2 Draw a diagram showing what happens to the particles in a gas as it is compressed inside a syringe.

3 Use ideas about expansion to explain why:

a running the lid of a jar under hot water makes it easier to open

b a house roof sometimes creaks during the night.

KEY POINTS

1 In solids the particles vibrate about fixed positions.

2 Liquids and gases are both fluids. Their particles are free to move.

3 Gases can be compressed as there is a large amount of space between the particles.

ACTIVITY

You can test the compressibility of solids, liquids and gases.

- Seal the end of a plastic syringe. Place a solid such as modelling clay inside the syringe and push on the plunger.
- Repeat with a liquid, such as water, and a gas (air).

The solid and liquid will be incompressible but it should be possible to compress the gas to about half of its original volume.

55

2.4 Gas laws

LEARNING OUTCOMES

At the end of this topic you should be able to:

- state the gas laws and describe how they can be demonstrated
- use the gas laws to describe changes in the properties of gases.

The gas laws describe the behaviour of gases when their temperature, pressure or volume is altered. A change in one of these quantities will result in a change in one, or both, of the others. For example, increasing the temperature of a gas will cause an increase in the pressure or volume of the gas.

The gas laws apply to a fixed mass of gas. This means that the number of particles in the gas sample does not change.

Charles' law

Charles' law describes the relationship between the volume V and temperature T of a gas and is usually stated as:

The volume of a fixed mass of gas is directly proportional to its temperature (in kelvin) if the pressure is kept constant.

$$V \propto T \text{ or } = \frac{V}{T} = \text{constant}$$

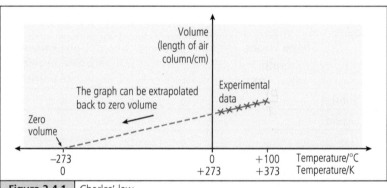

Figure 2.4.1 Charles' law

One key consequence of this law is the idea of absolute zero. As a gas is cooled, the kinetic energy of the particles decreases until they stop moving altogether. At this point the gas will have zero volume and cannot be cooled any further (Figure 2.4.1). This is the lowest possible temperature: absolute zero, 0 K.

WORKED EXAMPLE 1

A sample of gas occupies 600 cm³ while its temperature is 300 K. The gas is heated to 400 K and allowed to expand so that the pressure remains the same. What volume would the gas occupy?

Before expansion:

$$\frac{V}{T} = \frac{600 \text{ cm}^3}{300 \text{ K}} = 2 \text{ cm}^3\text{K}^{-1}$$

After expansion:

$$\frac{V}{T} = 2 \text{ cm}^3\text{K}^{-1}$$

So $V = T \times 2 \text{ cm}^3\text{K}^{-1}$

$= 400 \text{ K} \times 2 \text{ cm}^3\text{K}^{-1}$

$= 800 \text{ cm}^3$

Boyle's law

Boyle's law deals with the relationship between the volume V of a gas and its pressure p while the temperature is kept constant.

The volume of a fixed mass of gas is inversely proportional to its pressure if the temperature is kept constant.

$$V \propto \frac{1}{p} \text{ or } = pV = \text{constant}$$

An increase in pressure will cause the volume to decrease in proportion so applying pressure squashes the gas into a smaller space.

The pressure law

The **pressure law** connects temperature T and pressure p.

The pressure of a fixed mass of gas is directly proportional to the temperature (in kelvin) when the volume is kept constant.

$$p \propto T \text{ or } = \frac{p}{T} = \text{constant}$$

This means that heating a gas in a closed container will cause the pressure to increase. As the temperature decreases to absolute zero the pressure decreases to zero (Figure 2.4.2).

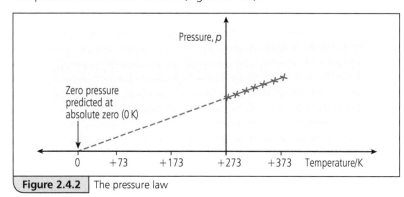

| **Figure 2.4.2** | The pressure law |

The gas equation

All three of the gas laws can be combined together to form a single **gas equation** that describes the relationship between the pressure, volume and temperature of a gas. As before, the mass of the gas must be constant.

$$\frac{pV}{T} = \text{constant}$$

WORKED EXAMPLE 2

A weather balloon containing hydrogen gas is released from the ground into the atmosphere. The volume of the gas in the balloon at launch is $40\,m^3$ while the pressure of the gas is $1.0 \times 10^5\,Pa$ ($N\,m^{-2}$) and the temperature is $35\,°C$ ($308\,K$).

The balloon rises into the upper atmosphere where the temperature is $-50\,°C$ ($223\,K$) and the pressure is only $1.0 \times 10^4\,Pa$. What is the new volume of the balloon?

Let the conditions on the ground be represented by V_1, p_1 and T_1 and the conditions in the upper atmosphere by V_2, p_2 and T_2.

Find the value of the constant at ground level:

$$\frac{p_1V_1}{T_1} = \text{constant} = \frac{1.0 \times 10^5\,N\,m^{-2} \times 40\,m^3}{308\,K} = 1.3 \times 10^4\,N\,m\,K^{-1}$$

Use the value of the constant to find the new volume:

$$\frac{p_2V_2}{T_2} = \text{constant}$$

$$\text{So } V_2 = \frac{T_2 \times \text{constant}}{p_2} = \frac{223\,K \times 1.3 \times 10^4\,N\,m\,K^{-1}}{1.0 \times 10^4\,N\,m^{-2}} = 290\,m^3$$

SUMMARY QUESTIONS

1 What happens when:

   a the volume of a gas is decreased while the temperature remains constant?

   b the temperature of a gas is increased while the volume remains constant?

   c the pressure of a gas is increased while the temperature is kept constant?

2 A $500\,cm^3$ sample of gas is compressed until it occupies only $100\,cm^3$ while the temperature is kept constant. The final pressure of the gas is found to be $600\,Pa$. What was the initial pressure of the gas?

KEY POINTS

1 The behaviour of gases can be described by the gas laws which link the pressure, temperature and volume of a gas.

2 The gas laws lead to the idea of a minimum temperature called absolute zero ($0\,K$, $-273\,°C$).

WORKED EXAMPLE 1

A bath full of water has been provided with 5.0×10^6 J of energy and the temperature of the water has risen by $8.0\,°C$ ($8.0\,K$). What is the heat capacity of the water?

$$C = \frac{E_H}{\Delta\theta}$$

$$C = \frac{5.0 \times 10^6\,J}{8.0\,K}$$

$$C = 6.3 \times 10^5\,J\,K^{-1}$$

Table 2.5.1 Some examples of specific heat capacity

Material	Specific heat capacity /J kg^{-1}K^{-1}
air	1003
aluminium	897
copper	385
gold	129
water	4181
diamond	509
glass	840

Heat capacity

The **heat capacity**, C, of an object is the amount of energy required to increase the temperature of the object by $1\,°C$ ($1\,K$).

$$\text{Heat capacity} = \frac{\text{heat energy}}{\text{temperature rise}} \text{ or } C\,(J\,K^{-1}) = \frac{E_H\,(J)}{\Delta\theta\,(K)}$$

Specific heat capacity

The heat capacity of an object is directly proportional to the mass. For example, a 2 kg block of aluminium takes twice as much energy to increase its temperature by 1 K as a 1 kg block. This leads to the concept of **specific heat capacity**, c. This is a measure of the amount of energy required to increase the temperature of 1 kg of a material by 1 K. Specific heat capacity allows us to directly compare materials and the amount of energy required to increase their temperatures. Some typical specific heat capacities are shown in Table 2.5.1.

Specific heat capacity is defined by the relationship:

$$\text{specific heat capacity} = \frac{\text{heat energy}}{\text{mass} \times \text{change in temperature}}$$

$$\text{or} \qquad c\,(J\,kg^{-1}\,K^{-1}) = \frac{E_H\,(J)}{m\,(kg) \times \Delta\theta\,(K)}$$

Investigating heat capacity and specific heat capacity

The heat capacity of a metal block can be found using an electrical heating element (Figure 2.5.1). The energy provided is measured with a joulemeter or calculated from the electrical power equation:

energy provided = heater current × heater p.d. × heating time

The temperature rise in the block is measured with a thermometer. It is important to insulate the block to reduce heat loss to the surroundings.

A similar method can be used to find the heat capacity of water. The heating element is placed in a sample of water inside an insulated container such as a plastic beaker or a polystyrene cup.

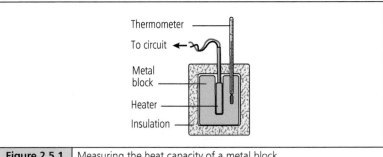

Figure 2.5.1 Measuring the heat capacity of a metal block

To find the specific heat capacity the mass of the metal block or water must also be measured.

Method of mixtures

We can use the known value of specific heat capacity of water to measure the heat capacity (or specific heat capacity) of a solid object (Figure 2.5.2).

- The mass of the object is measured and recorded.
- The object is heated and its temperature is recorded.
- The object is placed in water and the water is stirred thoroughly.
- Energy is transferred from the object into the water until they both reach the same temperature.
- Energy gained by water is calculated using the rise in temperature, the mass of water and the specific heat capacity of water.
- The energy gained by the water equals the energy lost by the object. The heat capacity of the object can be calculated using its temperature change. The specific heat capacity can be calculated using the temperature change and the mass.

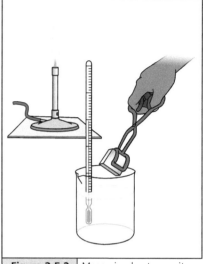

Figure 2.5.2 | Measuring heat capacity

WORKED EXAMPLE 2

A metal block of mass 3 kg is heated until its temperature rises to 140 °C. The metal is then placed into a container of water and stirred until the temperature of the water stops rising. The mass of water is 10 kg and its temperature increases from 15 °C to 20 °C. If the specific heat capacity of water is 4200 J kg^{-1} K^{-1} what is the specific heat capacity of the metal?

Energy gain by water: $E_H = mc\Delta\theta$

$$= 10\,kg \times 4200\,J\,kg^{-1}\,K^{-1} \times 5\,K = 210\,kJ$$

Energy loss from metal = 210 kJ

Specific heat capacity of metal: $c_{metal} = \dfrac{E_H}{m\Delta\theta} = \dfrac{210\,kJ}{3\,kg \times 120\,K}$

$$= 583\,J\,kg^{-1}\,K^{-1}$$

KEY POINTS

1. The heat capacity, C, of an object is the amount of heat energy required to raise its temperature by 1 °C.

2. The specific heat capacity, c, of a material is the amount of energy required to raise the temperature of 1 kg of that material by 1 °C.

SUMMARY QUESTIONS

1 Describe the difference between heat capacity and specific heat capacity.

2 Copy and complete Table 2.5.2.

Table 2.5.2

Object	Mass /kg	Temperature change /K	Energy provided /J	Heat capacity /J K^{-1}	Specific heat capacity /J kg^{-1} K^{-1}
water in a beaker	2.0	15			4200
gold block	0.3		500		129
copper pan	1.5	120		585	

When a solid gains thermal energy it may change into a liquid. With further heating the liquid may also change into a gas. When energy is lost by a gas it can change into a liquid and, if further cooling occurs, into a solid. These processes are called changes of state (or changes of phase). The names of the changes are shown in Figure 2.6.1. All of the changes involve a change in the thermal energy of the substance, although during the change there is no change in temperature. Sublimation is the process in which a solid changes directly to a gas.

During changes of state the particles form or break inter-molecular bonds and this causes changes in the properties of the materials.

Evaporation

Evaporation is a process which occurs at the surface of a liquid. The particles in the liquid have a range of kinetic energies and the temperature of the liquid is related to the average kinetic energy of the particles. The higher the temperature is, the greater the average kinetic energy.

The particles near the surface are held in place by forces within the liquid. However, the more energetic particles may escape from the liquid and form a gas. This process is called **evaporation**. During evaporation the particles with the greatest amount of energy are more likely to escape from the surface. When these fast-moving particles escape, the average energy of particles in the liquid decreases. This decrease in the average energy of the liquid means that the temperature of the liquid decreases (Figure 2.6.2).

Examples

• When you perspire, the moisture on your skin spreads over its surface and evaporates quickly. The evaporation takes energy from the surface of your skin and cools you down.

• In a similar way, coating earthenware jars in water will help keep the contents cold. The water will evaporate and remove some of the thermal energy from the containers.

• Refrigerators and air-conditioning units are also cooled by evaporation processes.

Factors affecting the rate of evaporation

There are several factors that affect the rate of evaporation:

• The **temperature** of the liquid. The higher the temperature is, the higher the average kinetic energy of the particles and so the more chance they have of escaping the surface.

• The **surface area** of the liquid. A large surface area will allow particles to escape at a greater rate and so evaporation will be faster.

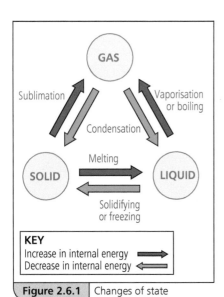

Figure 2.6.1 Changes of state

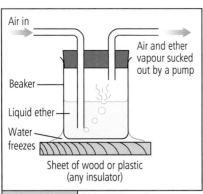

Figure 2.6.2 The cooling effect produced by the evaporation of ether is large enough to freeze the water.

- The **humidity** and **air flow**. If the air above the liquid is already saturated with vapour from the liquid some of the vapour will condense and reduce the overall rate of evaporation.
- The type of liquid. Some liquids evaporate much more rapidly than others as the forces holding the particles together in the liquid state are weaker. Ether evaporates more readily than water.

Comparing evaporation and boiling

Evaporation and **boiling** are often confused but they are different processes:

- Evaporation is a process which can only happen at the surface of a liquid and it happens whatever the temperature of the liquid. A puddle of water will evaporate away even though the temperature of the water never reaches anywhere near 100 °C.
- When a liquid is heated it will eventually reach a maximum temperature. This is the boiling point. Boiling occurs throughout the liquid and happens at a specific temperature for that liquid. During boiling the liquid turns into a gas throughout the whole volume and bubbles of gas can be seen forming within the liquid.

Figure 2.6.3 The flow of air will help speed up evaporation.

ACTIVITY

Pour a little ethanol on the back of your hand and blow over it. You should feel the cooling effect of evaporation on your skin.

SUMMARY QUESTIONS

1 A flask of ethanol will take many hours to evaporate if the lid is left off but it will evaporate in a few minutes if it is spilt on the floor. Explain how this happens.

2 Explain why, after getting out of the sea on a sunny but breezy day, you feel cooler.

3 Draw a table stating the differences between boiling and evaporation.

KEY POINTS

1 During a change of state a solid can change into a liquid, a liquid to a gas, a gas to a liquid or a liquid to a solid.

2 It is possible for a solid to change to a gas directly in a change called sublimation.

3 Changes of state involve the gain or loss of thermal energy in a substance.

Figure 2.6.4 The water has evaporated but did not boil.

Heating, cooling and latent heat

EXAM TIP

Remember, the temperature remains constant during a change of state.

Figure 2.7.1 The temperature will stay at 100°C until all of the water has turned to gas.

When water is heated and its temperature rises the particles are gaining energy. However, when the temperature reaches 100°C and water begins to boil, the temperature stops increasing even though more energy is being provided. This additional energy is being used to change the state of the water. This is because the bonds between the molecules are being altered. A similar thing happens when ice is heated to convert it to water. The temperature stops increasing when the ice reaches 0°C and the energy taken in breaks the inter-molecular forces and causes the ice to melt.

Latent heat

The energy used to change the state of a substance is referred to as **latent heat**. As there are two changes of state, there are two separate latent heats:

- for the change between solid and liquid, **latent heat of fusion**
- for the change between liquid and gas, **latent heat of vaporisation**.

During cooling, the latent heat is released when a gas changes into a liquid or a liquid changes into a solid. During the change of state, the temperature will stay constant. Also, exactly the same amount of energy will be released as the amount of energy taken for changes of state that take place during heating.

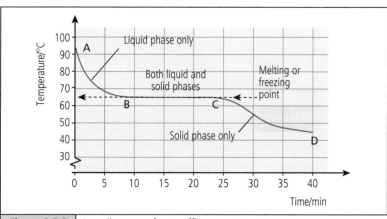

Figure 2.7.2 A cooling curve for paraffin wax

Between A and B the cooling curve graph shows that the temperature of the liquid wax decreases until it reaches the freezing point (Figure 2.7.2). Once it reaches its freezing point (B to C) the wax continues to lose energy to the surroundings. Note that the temperature does not change until all of the wax has solidified. During this phase, latent heat is being lost by the wax. In the final phase (C to D) the temperature of the solid wax decreases as the wax continues to lose energy.

ACTIVITY: EXPLORING HEATING AND COOLING

- Place some granulated wax (or stearic acid) into a boiling tube and suspend the tube in a beaker of water (Figure 2.7.3a).
- Place a thermometer into the wax and heat the water while stirring it to make sure the temperature is even throughout.
- Watch the thermometer to see how the temperature changes as the wax is heated past its melting point.

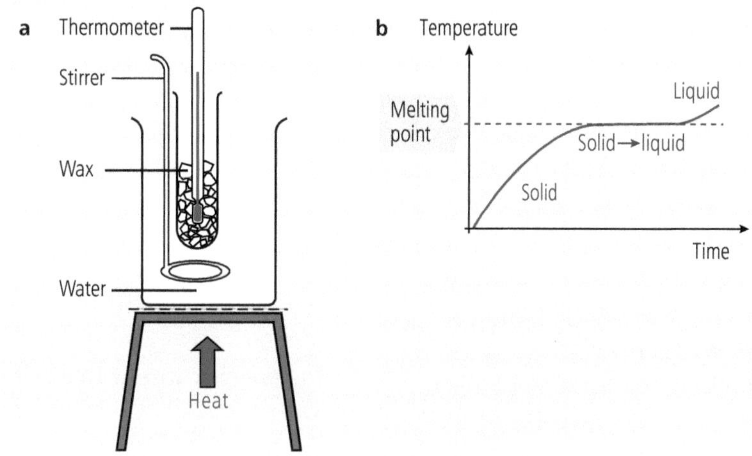

At first the temperature of the wax will increase as it approaches its melting point (Figure 2.7.3b). As the wax reaches its melting point the temperature stops increasing and the wax begins to melt instead. This allows the melting point to be measured accurately. After all of the wax has melted, the temperature of the liquid wax will begin to increase again.

- Remove the boiling tube from the water and monitor the cooling of the wax as it solidifies (Figure 2.7.4).
- Record the temperature of the wax every minute.

If you plot a graph showing the temperature of the wax against time it will show a **cooling curve** (Figure 2.7.2).

Figure 2.7.3 Heating wax and finding the melting point

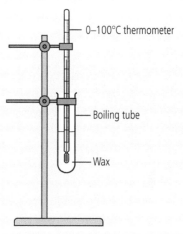

Figure 2.7.4 Monitoring the cooling of the wax

SUMMARY QUESTIONS

1 Use the graph in Figure 2.7.2 to find the freezing point for the sample of wax.

2 A small sample of beeswax is heated until it melts and then allowed to cool, providing the data in the table.

Table 2.7.1

Time/min	1	2	3	4	5	6	7	8	9	10	11
Temp./°C	85	80	74	69	65	62	62	58	55	52	50

a Plot a cooling curve for the beeswax.

b Find the melting point for the beeswax.

c Would using a larger sample of beeswax give a more accurate result?

KEY POINTS

1 During a change of state the temperature of a material does not change.

2 Additional energy (latent heat) is required when a substance changes state during heating.

3 Latent heat is released when a substance changes state during cooling.

At the end of this topic you should be able to:

- describe the energy transfers that take place during changes of state
- calculate the energy required or produced during a change of state.

To compare latent heats of different materials, we need to find the amount of energy required to change the state of a unit mass of the materials. This gives a quantity known as the **specific latent heat**. As there are two changes of state, each material has two specific latent heats:

- The **specific latent heat of fusion** (l_f) is the energy required to change 1 kg of a solid into liquid without a change in temperature.
- The **specific latent heat of vaporisation** (l_v) is the energy required to change 1 kg of a liquid into gas without a change in temperature.

Both of these terms can be represented by the same equation:

$$\text{specific latent heat (J kg}^{-1}) = \frac{\text{energy provided (J)}}{\text{mass (kg)}} \text{ or } l = \frac{E_H}{m}$$

Measuring the specific latent heat of water

Specific latent heat of vaporisation

To measure the specific latent heat of vaporisation of water, an electrical heating element can be used to heat a sample of boiling water so that some of it is converted into steam (Figure 2.8.1). A well-insulated container needs to be used to prevent energy loss through the container.

WORKED EXAMPLE

A small block of lead of mass 300 g is heated until it reaches its melting point of 327 °C. How much additional energy is required to melt the lead?

($l_f = 2.3 \times 10^4$ J kg^{-1})

$l_f = \dfrac{E_H}{m}$

$E_H = l_f \times m$

$= 2.3 \times 10^4$ J kg^{-1} $\times$ 0.3 kg

$= 6.9 \times 10^3$ J

ACTIVITY

- Record the mass of the boiling water and its container.
- Allow the water to boil for several minutes while being heated by the heating element.
- Find the energy supplied using a joulemeter or the electrical power equation:

  energy supplied = current × p.d. × time

- After heating, record the new mass of the water and container.
- Calculate the change in mass of the water and container to find the mass of water that has boiled off.
- Calculate the specific latent heat of vaporisation using the equation:

  specific latent heat of vaporisation

  $= \dfrac{\text{energy supplied}}{\text{change in mass}}$ or $l_v = \dfrac{E_H}{\Delta m}$

Specific latent heat of fusion

As a sample of ice melts naturally at room temperature, it is more difficult to find out how much melts as a result of heating by an electrical element. The following technique takes the natural melting into account (Figure 2.8.2).

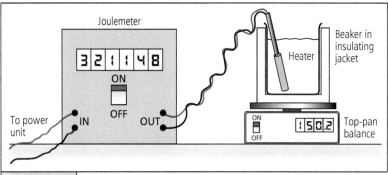

Figure 2.8.1 | Measuring the specific latent heat of steam

ACTIVITY

- Allow the ice to melt for a fixed period of time (such as five minutes) without any heating. Record the mass of water collected, m_1.
- Use an electrical heater to melt a similar sample of ice for the same period of time and record the mass of water collected, m_2.
- Find the difference in these two mass measurements ($m_2 - m_1$). This gives the mass of ice that has melted as a result of the energy provided by the heater.

The energy provided and the mass of melted ice as a result are used in the calculation for the latent heat.

- Calculate the specific latent heat of fusion using the equation:

$$\text{specific latent heat of fusion} = \frac{\text{energy supplied}}{\text{change in mass } (m_2 - m_1)}$$

$$\text{or } l_f = \frac{E_H}{m_2 - m_1}$$

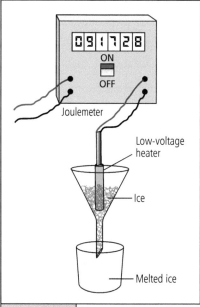

Figure 2.8.2 | Measuring the specific latent heat of ice

SUMMARY QUESTIONS

1 a Calculate the energy required to change 250 g of liquid oxygen into oxygen gas at the same temperature. ($l_v = 2.1 \times 10^5\,\text{J kg}^{-1}$)

b Calculate the energy released when 4.5 kg of lead solidifies, without change in temperature. ($l_f = 2.3 \times 10^4\,\text{J kg}^{-1}$)

2 In an experiment to find the latent heat of ice as described in the activity above, the following measurements were recorded when the ice was allowed to melt for five minutes.

- Mass of ice melted without heater = 5.3 g
- Mass of ice melted when heater is on = 15.7 g
- Energy provided to heater = 3500 J

a Calculate the specific latent heat of fusion for ice (l_{ice}) using this data.

b The agreed value for l_{ice} is 334 kJ kg^{-1}. Explain why the value obtained by the experiment is higher than this value.

KEY POINT

1 The amount of energy released or absorbed during a change of state for 1 kg of a material is the specific latent heat.

Thermal conduction

At the end of this topic you should be able to:

• describe conduction processes in metals and non-metals

• perform an experiment to measure the rates of thermal conduction in different materials.

Table 2.9.1 Some examples of thermal conductivity

Material	Thermal conductivity /$W\,m^{-1}\,K^{-1}$
air	0.024
wood	~0.06
brick	0.2
glass	0.8
cast iron	55
aluminium	204
copper	385
diamond	2200

ACTIVITY

Diamond has a surprisingly high thermal conductivity, especially as it is a non-metal. Find out why this is and how this property is used to detect fake diamonds.

The particles in a solid are in fixed positions. When they gain heat energy they vibrate more rapidly about these positions. When one part of a solid object is heated, the energy passes through the object by a process called **conduction**.

When a sample rod is heated using a Bunsen burner, the part of the rod in the flame will become hot. The particles will start to vibrate rapidly. The vibrations of the particles will cause nearby particles to gain energy and begin to vibrate more. This process will continue along the rod until, eventually, all of the particles are vibrating more rapidly and the whole rod has increased in temperature. The process of passing energy along is called **lattice vibration**.

The rate of thermal conduction varies from material to material. The better a material is at transferring thermal energy, the higher its **thermal conductivity** (Table 2.9.1).

The rate of thermal energy transfer by conduction also depends on the temperature difference between the parts of the object. A large temperature difference will increase the rate of thermal conduction.

Conduction in metals

Metals have significantly higher thermal conductivities than non-metals. This is because there is a second process transferring the energy in metals (Figure 2.9.1). This is energy transfer by **free electrons**. Metals contain a lattice of metal ions surrounded by a 'sea' of free electrons. The same electrons allow electrical conduction. When a metal is heated, the electrons rapidly gain energy and can pass along the metal carrying the thermal energy. This process is far quicker than the lattice vibration method described above and so metals are good thermal conductors.

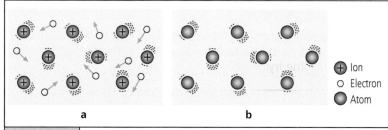

	Ion
+	
○	Electron
●	Atom

Figure 2.9.1 Conduction in **a** a metal and **b** a non-metal

Insulators

Poor thermal conductors are called **insulators**. Air is a very poor thermal conductor. It is very difficult for energy to be passed from particle to particle. For this reason materials, such as sponges or foams, containing lots of trapped air are used to insulate objects.

Measuring rates of thermal conduction

To demonstrate different rates of thermal conduction, samples of the materials can be heated with a Bunsen burner. There are several ways to monitor or compare the rates of conduction:

- The rod can be completely coated in a thin wax layer that melts as the rods heats up. Observing the rate at which the wax melts gives an indication of how quickly the thermal energy is being transferred.
- The far end of each rod can be coated in petroleum jelly and a drawing pin attached (Figure 2.9.2). When the far end of the rod heats up the pin will fall off. Measuring the time it takes from starting heating until each pin falls off can be used to compare the thermal conductivity of the material of each rod.

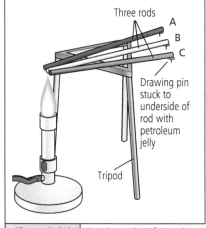

Figure 2.9.2 The time taken for a pin to fall off indicates how quickly heat energy is transferred along the rod.

Comparing insulators

The insulating properties of materials can be investigated by placing hot liquids inside identical containers lagged with these materials and monitoring the temperature fall for each (Figure 2.9.3). Alternatively the materials can be used to lag identical containers of cold water and the temperature rise can be monitored over a period of time.

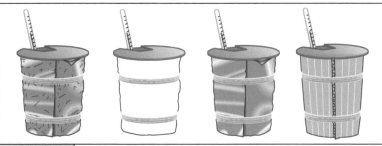

Figure 2.9.3 Comparing insulators

ACTIVITY

Carry out an experiment to test the properties of insulating materials using cups or beakers lined with the material. You will need to make sure there are lids to prevent evaporation.

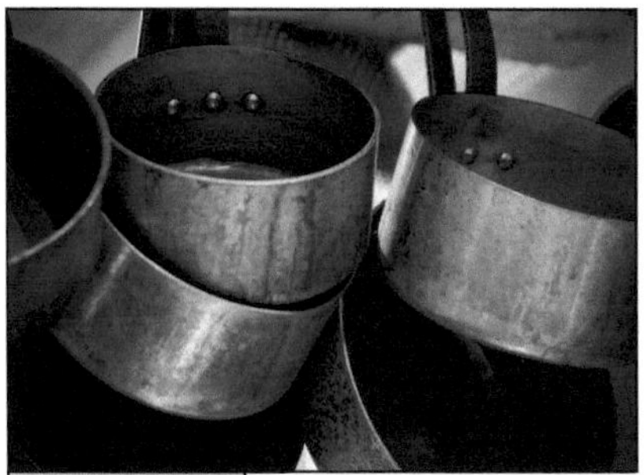

Figure 2.9.4

SUMMARY QUESTIONS

1 Explain why hot drinks are sometimes sold in polystyrene cups.

2 Why do some frying pans have a copper base?

KEY POINTS

1 Thermal conduction involves the transfer of energy from particle to particle.

2 Metals have free electrons which transfer energy by conduction much more quickly than is possible in non-metals.

3 Materials which conduct poorly are classed as insulators.

2.10 Convection currents

LEARNING OUTCOMES

At the end of this topic you should be able to:

- describe convection processes in fluids and explain how thermal energy can be transferred by them
- explain how convection currents produce breezes in coastal areas.

Liquids and gases are both **fluids**. The particles they are composed of are able to move around within them. Because the particles can move they can carry thermal energy from place to place as they travel.

Convection currents

When a substance increases in temperature it expands. When it cools it contracts. During expansion the particles in the substance move further apart and so the density of the substance decreases. During contraction the particles move closer together so the density of the substance increases. This behaviour can transfer heat energy by producing **convection currents**. These are flows of particles within the substance. For example, a convection current in air is produced by these processes:

- When air is heated the particles move further apart from each other and the air expands.
- The air becomes less dense.
- Because the warm air is less dense that the cooler, surrounding air, it floats upwards carrying heat energy with it.
- The hot air spreads out as it rises, loses energy and cools.
- As the air cools the particles become closer together and so the air becomes denser.
- The dense air sinks back downwards and the cycle continues.

This process produces a continual flow of air.

Demonstrating convection currents

Observing convection currents in air and water can be quite difficult as they are both transparent. These two simple demonstrations can be used to show convection currents.

ACTIVITY: USING A LIQUID

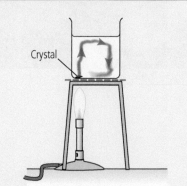

Crystal

Figure 2.10.1 Demonstrating a convection current in water

- Place a small crystal of potassium manganate(VII) (also known as potassium permanganate) at the bottom and towards one side of a large beaker of water (Figure 2.10.1).
- Heat the water directly beneath the crystal and a convection current will form.

The water near the crystal expands as it is heated and as the water rises upwards the purple colouration from the dissolving crystal will rise with it. As the water reaches the surface it will spread out, cool, and at the other side of the beaker begin to sink.

- Start with a glass-fronted chamber with two chimneys (Figure 2.10.2).
- Light a candle positioned under one chimney.
- Close the front glass panel.
- Hold a smoking piece of cardboard above the other chimney.

The smoke from the cardboard moves downwards. This is because cool air is being drawn down through the chimney to replace the hot air rising out of the chimney above the candle.

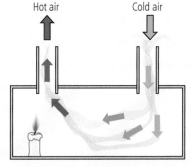

Figure 2.10.2 Demonstrating a convection current in air

Air conditioning

Air-conditioning units cool air using a system of expanding gases. The cool air will be denser than the surrounding air and so sink downwards. Air-conditioning units are positioned towards the top of the room to produce a cold flow of air downwards.

Thermal convection in the atmosphere

Convection currents produce breezes near the coast (Figure 2.10.3). During the day the land heats up more rapidly than the sea and this causes air above the land to warm up. The warm air rises and is replaced by cooler air flowing in from above the sea. At night the sea remains warm and the land cools. This causes air above the sea to rise and cooler air flows from the land to the sea.

Convection currents within the oceans have a significant effect on the temperatures across the globe.

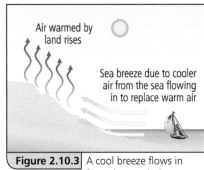

Figure 2.10.3 A cool breeze flows in from the sea during the day.

1 Explain why, during a fire in a room, you should crawl across the floor to make your escape.

2 How can a hot-air balloon control its height?

Convection currents are responsible for the movement of the continents across the surface of the Earth. Find out how this process works.

1 Convection can only occur in fluids as it involves the movement of particles from place to place.

2 Changes in density caused by expansion result in convection currents.

Infra-red radiation

EXAM TIP

See 3.3 to find out more about the electromagnetic spectrum and the ideas of absorption and emission.

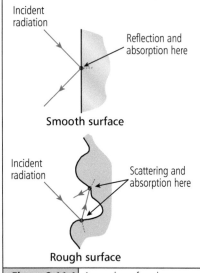

Incident radiation

Reflection and absorption here

Smooth surface

Incident radiation

Scattering and absorption here

Rough surface

Figure 2.11.1 A rough surface has a larger overall surface area so is able to absorb more infra-red radiation.

Thermal energy can be transferred by infra-red radiation (IR radiation). This is a part of the electromagnetic spectrum with a wavelength longer than visible light. IR radiation shares many of the properties of visible light including the ability to travel through empty space (a vacuum).

All objects are constantly emitting and absorbing IR radiation from their surfaces. This gives three possible conditions for an object:

• *Warming up* – an object will warm up if it is absorbing IR radiation at a greater rate than it is emitting it. A cold drink placed in direct sunlight will warm up rapidly.

• *Cooling down* – an object cools down when it is emitting more IR radiation than it is absorbing from its surroundings. Freshly cooked food will gradually cool to room temperature.

• *Constant temperature* – if the rate of absorption and the rate of emission are the same then the object will not gain or lose energy and so will stay at a steady temperature. Most objects in a room will be at 'room temperature'. They are at the same temperature as each other.

Factors affecting the rate of heating or cooling

Temperature

A hot object will emit far more IR radiation then a cool one. This means that very hot objects lose energy at a greater rate than cooler objects. If you monitor the temperature of a cooling drink then you will see that the temperature drops more rapidly at the start of the experiment than later on. Eventually the drink will reach room temperature and stop cooling.

Properties of the surface

The absorption or emission of IR radiation happens at the surface of an object and so the properties of the surface are very important:

• The *surface area* of the object. A larger surface area will allow energy to escape or be absorbed more rapidly.

• The *colour* of the surface. Dark surfaces are much better absorbers and emitters of IR radiation than white surfaces. If you step out into bright sunlight wearing dark clothes you will notice this effect immediately. Your clothes start to feel hot.

• The *roughness* of the surface. A rougher surface will effectively have a larger surface area when compared to a smooth surface (Figure 2.11.1).

ACTIVITY

A Leslie's cube is a metal container with the surfaces painted different colours or with different textures. Boiling water is poured into the container and all of the sides rapidly reach the same temperature.

- Place a temperature sensor (or the back of your hand) close to the different surfaces to measure (or feel) the thermal energy being radiated.

You should find that the dark or rough surfaces emit more thermal radiation than the white and shiny surfaces.

Similar experiments can be carried out with metal plates with one side painted matt black and the other left shiny.

Investigating cooling and heating

To investigate the factors affecting the cooling of materials you can place hot water into beakers that have been painted with different colours, for example silver and black (Figure 2.11.2). The temperature of each beaker is recorded every minute over a period of twenty minutes and a graph is plotted to compare the patterns in cooling.

A similar experiment, using very cold water, can be used to investigate how different surfaces absorb IR radiation. The different coloured beakers are placed in direct sunlight or near to a radiant heater and the temperature rises are monitored.

Both experiments confirm that the beakers with the black surfaces cool down or heat up more rapidly than the silvered surface. The rate of cooling also slows as the difference in temperature between the water and the room decreases.

Figure 2.11.2 Investigating the effect of the colour of a surface on the rate of cooling

KEY POINTS

1   All objects are constantly absorbing or emitting infra-red (IR) radiation.

2   The hotter an object is the more IR radiation it emits.

3   The temperature of dark coloured objects changes rapidly as they are good emitters and absorbers of IR radiation.

4   The temperature of silver coloured objects changes slowly as they are poor emitters and absorbers of IR radiation.

5   Rough surfaces are better emitters and absorbers of IR radiation than smooth surfaces.

SUMMARY QUESTIONS

1   In many tropical countries buildings are painted in light colours. How do these colours help to keep the building cool during the day and warm during the night?

2   In the Arctic, polar bears are white. How does this help them keep warm?

3   In Antarctica, penguins huddle together in large numbers. How does this help them keep warm?

Applying thermal energy transfer principles

At the end of this topic you should be able to:

• describe how an understanding of the methods of thermal energy transfer can be used to reduce or increase the flow of heat energy in a wide range of circumstances.

Understanding the processes which cause thermal energy transfer allows us to design devices to increase or decrease the rates of heating and cooling of objects. Sometimes we need to dispose of large amounts of thermal energy into the surroundings quickly and sometimes we need to prevent the loss or gain of thermal energy.

Vacuum flasks

A vacuum flask is designed to prevent as much thermal energy transfer as possible. To do this it has features that reduce conduction, convection, radiation and evaporation processes (Figure 2.12.1).

• The main chamber is constructed of glass (a very poor conductor) with a vacuum between the two layers. As the vacuum contains no particles there can be no conduction or convection to transfer thermal energy between the layers. Thermal energy can be transferred around the glass layer by conduction but this is a very slow process.

• The inside surfaces of the glass layers are coated in silver to reduce radiation. The surfaces are very poor emitters and absorbers of radiation so there is very little transfer of energy between them.

• A hollow plastic cap is used to prevent evaporation.

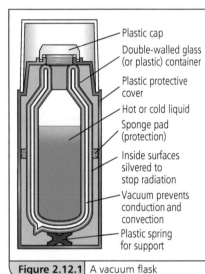

Plastic cap

Double-walled glass (or plastic) container

Plastic protective cover

Hot or cold liquid

Sponge pad (protection)

Inside surfaces silvered to stop radiation

Vacuum prevents conduction and convection

Plastic spring for support

Figure 2.12.1 | A vacuum flask

Solar water heaters

Many houses heat water using solar energy. Cool water is either pumped or driven by convection currents through pipes in panels on the roof (Figure 2.12.2). The pipes are painted black so that they absorb energy from the sunlight and this energy is transferred to the water passing through them.

Designs for cooling

Car radiators

The engine in a car produces a large amount of thermal energy when the fuel is burnt. If this energy were allowed to build up then the temperature of the engine would increase rapidly. Expansion of the engine parts would soon cause the engine to seize up.

To prevent this, water is pumped through pipes which pass through the engine. The water absorbs some of the thermal energy by conduction and is then pumped through a radiator mounted on the front of the car (Figure 2.12.3). As the car moves, air travels between the radiator pipes and thermal energy is transferred from the water to the air.

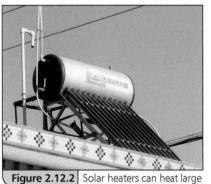

Figure 2.12.2 | Solar heaters can heat large amounts of water. They are used for washing or to keep the house warm at night.

Cooling panels on refrigerators

The back panels on refrigerators are painted black to allow heat energy taken from the inside to be radiated away quickly.

Heat sinks

Microprocessors can produce very large amounts of heat energy during their operation. This energy will reduce the efficiency or even damage the processor if it is not transferred away rapidly. To make sure that this happens, a heat sink is mounted on the top of the microprocessor (Figure 2.12.4). A highly conductive 'thermal paste' is used as the glue between the processor and heat sink. The heat sink is designed to have many fins so that the heat energy can be carried away by convection currents (sometimes assisted with fans) and also radiated away.

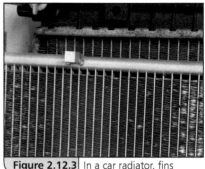

Figure 2.12.3 In a car radiator, fins increase the surface area and both pipes and fins may be painted black to increase the rate of emission.

The greenhouse effect and global warming

The Earth absorbs energy radiated by the Sun and this energy warms the planet. The Sun's energy arrives as visible light and short wavelength infra-red radiation which passes through the atmosphere. The surface of the Earth re-emits this energy as longer wavelength infra-red radiation. Some of this is reflected back to the surface of the Earth by greenhouse gases such as carbon dioxide and methane. The process, known as the **greenhouse effect**, tends to maintain a balance (Figure 2.12.5). The Earth has remained at constant temperature for several thousand years.

However, human activity such as burning fossil fuels, increased crop production, deforestation and keeping livestock is increasing the amount of greenhouse gases in the atmosphere. This causes more heat energy to be trapped and results in an overall increase in atmospheric and ocean temperatures.

Figure 2.12.4 A heat sink mounted on a microprocessor

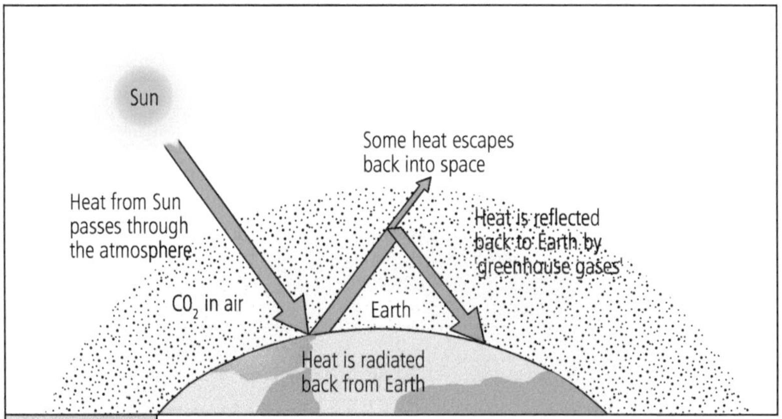

Figure 2.12.5 The increase in greenhouse gases may lead to catastrophic climate change.

Sun

Some heat escapes back into space

Heat from Sun passes through the atmosphere

Heat is reflected back to Earth by greenhouse gases

CO_2 in air

Earth

Heat is radiated back from Earth

SUMMARY QUESTIONS

1 Describe how a vacuum flask can keep its contents cold.

2 How can the effects of global warming be slowed?

KEY POINT

1 Careful selection of materials can be used to control heat flow.

SECTION 2: Practice exam questions

1 During an investigation into cooling by evaporation, 20 cm³ of ethanol was placed into each of five circular beakers that had different diameters. The mass of the beakers and ethanol was measured with a top-pan balance. The ethanol samples were allowed to evaporate for 30 minutes and then the mass of the beakers was recorded again.

Diameter/cm	4	5.5	6	7	10
Area/cm²					
Start mass/g	75.5	95.5	121.0	141.0	180.5
End mass/g	67.9	81.2	104.0	117.9	133.3
Change in mass/g					

a Calculate the surface area of each of the beakers.

b Calculate the mass loss for each of the beakers.

c Plot a graph comparing the mass loss and the surface area of the beakers.

d Describe the mathematical relationship between the surface area and the rate of evaporation for ethanol.

e Use the graph to find the rate of evaporation per centimetre squared per minute for ethanol during the experiment.

2 Describe how a liquid-in-glass thermometer can be calibrated.

3 Describe and explain the key features of a clinical thermometer as shown in the diagram.

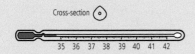
Cross-section
35 36 37 38 39 40 41 42

4 Copy and complete this table converting temperatures between degrees Celsius and kelvin.

Celsius/°C		0	100		−50	−127
Kelvin/K	0			234		

5 Compare the behaviour and spacing of the particles in solids, liquids and gases. Use these concepts to explain the compressibility and fluidity of the three states of matter.

6 Describe the changes in particle behaviour and the changes in energy during the following changes of state:

a from solid to liquid

b from liquid to gas.

7 A metal block of mass 0.8 kg is heated strongly until its temperature reaches 200 °C. The block is then placed into a bucket containing 4.0 kg of cold water and the water is stirred until the temperature of the water stops rising. The temperature of the water rises from 10 °C to 19 °C. (The specific heat capacity of water is 4200 J kg⁻¹ K⁻¹.)

a Calculate the temperature rise of the water.

b Calculate the energy gained by the water.

c State the heat energy loss of the metal block.

d Calculate the specific heat capacity of the metal.

8 Two metal plates are placed an equal distance from an electrical heater. One plate is shiny, silver-coloured and the other matt black. The temperature of each plate is recorded over a period of five minutes as shown in the following results table.

Time/min	0	1	2	3	4	5	6	7	8	9	10
Temperature of shiny plate/°C	30	40	48	55	61	66	70	74	77	80	82
Temperature of black plate/°C	30	45	58	65	70	75	78	79	81	82	82

a Plot a graph comparing the rise in temperature of the plates.

b Describe and explain the pattern in the rise in temperatures.

c Why do the plates stop rising in temperature?

9 Liquid nitrogen is used in rapid cooling systems, absorbing energy when it changes state from a liquid to a gas. How much liquid nitrogen is required to absorb 500 kJ of heat energy as it changes state? (The latent heat of vaporisation for liquid nitrogen is $2.0 \times 10^5 \, J\,kg^{-1}$.)

10 How much energy is required to convert 3.0 kg of ice with a starting temperature of $-5\,°C$ into 3.0 kg of steam with a final temperature of $105\,°C$?
   - Specific heat capacity of ice: $2100 \, J\,kg^{-1}K^{-1}$
   - Specific heat capacity of water: $4181 \, J\,kg^{-1}K^{-1}$
   - Specific heat capacity of steam: $2080 \, J\,kg^{-1}K^{-1}$
   - Specific latent heat of fusion for ice: $3.3 \times 10^5 \, J\,kg^{-1}$
   - Specific latent heat of vaporisation for water: $2.3 \times 10^6 \, J\,kg^{-1}$

11 Describe how a group of students could determine the specific latent heat of vaporisation of ethanol. You must include:
   - the equipment required
   - an assessment of the risks involved
   - an explanation of the measurements and calculations required.

12 Explain the following in terms of infra-red radiation:
   a Some firefighters wear silvered clothing when entering burning buildings.
   b Solar water heaters on roofs are painted black.
   c Dark-coloured clothing dries faster on a washing line than light-coloured clothing.

13 Some students are investigating the rate of evaporation of different liquids: water, ethanol and ether. The experiment is carried out in a fume cupboard. The students pour the liquids into identical rectangular trays measuring 4 cm by 5 cm.
   a What is the surface area of the liquids in the trays?

The students measure the mass of the liquids and trays at the start of the experiment and after 10 minutes. Their results are shown in the table.

Liquid	Starting mass/g	End mass/g	Change in mass/g	Rate of evaporation /g min^{-1}
water	14.4	14.2		
ethanol	13.4	12.4		
ether	17.8	12.6		

   b Which liquid has evaporated at the fastest rate?
   c What is the rate of evaporation per cm^2 for each of the liquids?

At the end of the experiment the students notice that they did not turn on the fume cupboard extractor fan as they were supposed to.

   d In what way would the results have been different if the fan had been turned on?

Wave motion

Wave motion transfers energy from place to place without the transfer of material (matter). There may be a single wave pulse caused by a single **oscillation** or a series of oscillations producing a progressive wave train.

Waves in springs

Wave motion can be demonstrated with springs. Vibrations in one part of the spring will produce vibrations in the rest of the spring. Observing the behaviour of the coils will allow us to describe wave motion.

Wave pulses

When the end of a long spring is moved sideways and back once, a **wave pulse** is generated. The coils move in turn along the length of the spring until the pulse reaches the end (Figure 3.1.1a). If the spring is stretched slightly with one end pushed in and out rapidly another type of wave motion is produced. The spring has regions where the coils are compressed closer together and these regions move along the length of the spring (Figure 3.1.1b).

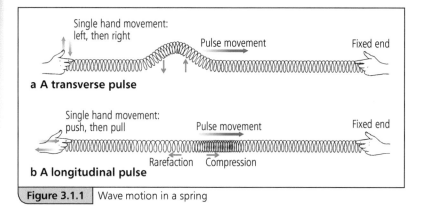

Single hand movement: left, then right — Pulse movement — Fixed end

a A transverse pulse

Single hand movement: push, then pull — Pulse movement — Fixed end

Rarefaction   Compression

b A longitudinal pulse

Figure 3.1.1 | Wave motion in a spring

Continuous waves

Continuous waves are produced if the source of the vibration continues to oscillate. A continuous series of pulses form a **wave train** moving along the spring. The particles oscillate in a regular motion over a period of time, repeating the same pattern.

Classes of waves

There are two classes of waves: **transverse** and **longitudinal**.

Transverse waves

Transverse waves form when the oscillations of the particles are perpendicular to the direction of **propagation** (direction of the energy transfer). The movement of one particle causes the neighbouring particle to oscillate and this oscillation is passed along the wave (Figure 3.1.2).

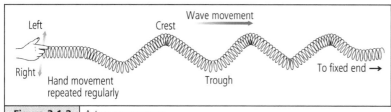

Figure 3.1.2 A transverse wave

Ripples on the surface of water are transverse waves. A disturbance causes the water molecules to oscillate vertically while the water waves spread out horizontally from the source.

Light is another example of a transverse wave. Light waves consist of oscillating electric and magnetic fields which vibrate at right angles to each other and to the direction in which the wave propagates.

Longitudinal waves

In longitudinal waves the particles oscillate parallel to the direction of propagation. The particles move back and forth about their rest positions forcing their neighbours to follow the same pattern of oscillations (Figure 3.1.3).

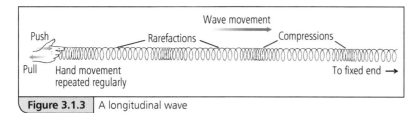

Figure 3.1.3 A longitudinal wave

Sound waves are longitudinal.

Observing wave motion with ripple tanks

Ripple tanks are used to investigate transverse wave motion in water (Figure 3.1.4). A motor causes a horizontal beam to dip in and out of the water, producing parallel plane waves. Circular waves are generated when a round 'dipper' is used in place of the horizontal beam.

The crests of the wave form **wavefronts** and these travel in the direction of propagation of the wave. Observation of the wavefronts allows us to see when the waves reflect, change speed or change direction.

Figure 3.1.4 Circular and plane waves in a ripple tank

SUMMARY QUESTIONS

1 Figure 3.1.5 shows a wave pulse in a rope. The pulse is traveling at $40\,\mathrm{cm\,s^{-1}}$.

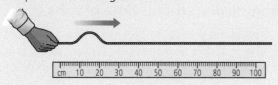

Figure 3.1.5

a Which type of wave is shown?

b Redraw the diagram showing the position of the pulse 0.5 second later.

2 Sketch the pattern of wavefronts that you would see if a pebble were dropped into the centre of a calm pond.

3.2

Describing waves

At the end of this topic you should be able to:

* describe waves in terms of frequency, wavelength, speed, period and amplitude
* use the wave speed equation in a range of contexts
* interpret displacement–position and displacement–time graphs for waves.

Progressive waves can be represented by two different kinds of graph:

* A **displacement–position graph**
* A **displacement–time graph**

Understanding displacement–position graphs

A displacement–position graph represents the position of all of the particles in a wave at a fixed time during its movement. The positions of a large number of particles are shown at a single instant, like a snapshot photograph (Figure 3.2.1).

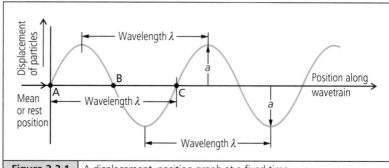

Figure 3.2.1 A displacement–position graph at a fixed time

The **wavelength**, λ, of a wave is the distance between one wave crest and the next. As it is a distance, the wavelength is measured in metres. In fact, the wavelength is the distance between a particle and another particle that is exactly at the same point in its motion (having the same displacement and moving in the same direction). This means that all of the troughs on a transverse wave are also one wavelength apart.

For longitudinal waves the wavelength is a measure of the distance between adjacent compressions or rarefactions.

The **amplitude**, a, of a wave is the maximum displacement a particle can have from its rest (undisturbed) position. It is the height of a crest or the depth of a trough. In high amplitude waves the particles oscillate a greater distance from their rest position.

Understanding displacement–time graphs

A displacement–time graph shows the behaviour of a single particle over a period of time. It shows how the displacement of the particle changes as a wave passes. Figure 3.2.2 represents the motion of a particle at point C from the displacement–position graph.

EXAM TIP

Remember that hertz (Hz) is the same as the unit s⁻¹.

The amplitude of a wave is the maximum displacement from the rest position of a particle, not the distance from a peak to a trough.

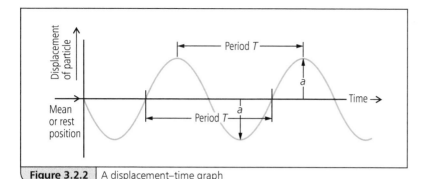

Figure 3.2.2 A displacement–time graph

The **period**, T, of a wave is the length of time taken for a particle to complete one full oscillation. The particle moves from the rest position to maximum positive displacement back through the rest position to the maximum negative displacement and then back to the rest position.

The **frequency**, f, of a wave is the number of oscillations per second. Frequency has the unit hertz (Hz) which is identical to the unit s^{-1}.

Period and frequency are related by the equation:

$$period = \frac{1}{frequency} \quad or \quad T = \frac{1}{f}$$

Therefore the greater the frequency of the wave the shorter the period will be.

Wave speed (v)

Different waves travel at different speeds. For example, a water wave may travel at $5.00\,m\,s^{-1}$ whereas a light wave may be travelling at $3.00 \times 10^8\,m\,s^{-1}$. The speed of a wave is related to the frequency and wavelength by the equation:

$$wave\ speed = frequency \times wavelength \quad or \quad v = f\lambda$$

a What is the wavelength of a water wave with a frequency of 5.0 Hz and a speed of $25\,cm\,s^{-1}$?

Original equation:

$$v = f\lambda$$

Transpose the equation:

$$\lambda = \frac{v}{f}$$

Substitute in values:

$$\lambda = \frac{25\,cm\,s^{-1}}{5.0\,Hz}$$

Answer:

$$\lambda = 5.0\,cm$$

b What is the frequency of a light wave which travels at $3.00 \times 10^8\,m\,s^{-1}$ and has a wavelength of $4.00 \times 10^{-7}\,m$?

$$v = f\lambda$$

$$f = \frac{v}{\lambda}$$

$$f = \frac{3.00 \times 10^8\,m\,s^{-1}}{4.00 \times 10^{-7}\,m}$$

$$f = 7.50 \times 10^{14}\,Hz$$

1 A sound wave has a period of 0.04 s. What is the frequency of this wave?

2 Sketch a displacement–time graph for a particle at point B in Figure 3.2.1 if the frequency of the wave is 2 Hz.

3 Copy Table 3.2.1. Then calculate the missing values and fill them in. You must include the appropriate units.

Table 3.2.1

	v	f	λ
a		500 Hz	0.2 m
b	$340\,m\,s^{-1}$	3.5 kHz	
c	$3.00 \times 10^8\,m\,s^{-1}$		$5.00 \times 10^{-3}\,m$

1 The speed of a wave is given by the equation
wave speed = frequency × wavelength ($v = f\lambda$)

2 A displacement–position graph can be used to represent the positions of the particles in a wave at a fixed time.

3 A displacement–time graph can be used to represent the motion of a single particle (or point) in a wave over a period of time.

3.3 Electromagnetic waves

LEARNING OUTCOMES

At the end of this topic you should be able to:

- state the properties which all electromagnetic waves share
- differentiate electromagnetic waves by their wavelength or frequency
- specify sources and uses for each of the regions of the electromagnetic spectrum.

ACTIVITY

- Produce a summary poster about the properties and uses of electromagnetic waves. Make sure that you include some examples of the wavelengths and frequencies involved.
- Find out how different parts of the EM spectrum can be used for communication systems including the subcategories of radio waves.

Visible light is a form of electromagnetic radiation but it only forms a very small part of the whole electromagnetic spectrum. Waves in the **electromagnetic spectrum** are grouped into six major regions based on their wavelengths or how they are produced (Figure 3.3.1).

Common properties of electromagnetic radiation

All electromagnetic (EM) radiations share some common properties and behaviours:

- EM radiation travels as a transverse wave.
- EM radiation travels at $3.00 \times 10^8\,m\,s^{-1}$ in a vacuum. Different parts of the spectrum travel at different speeds in other materials.
- The wave does not require a medium (material) to pass through. The wave motion consists of oscillating electric and magnetic fields and no particles are required.

The sources, detectors and uses of electromagnetic waves are shown in Table 3.3.1.

Ionisation

Some forms of EM radiation carry enough energy to ionise atoms. This means that electrons are removed from the atoms which become charged particles called ions. These ions are highly reactive and can damage living tissue, causing mutations or cancers.

SUMMARY QUESTIONS

1 What is the relationship between the frequency of a part of the EM spectrum and the damage it can cause to living cells?

2 Copy Table 3.3.2. Then, for each of the electromagnetic waves given, calculate the missing frequency or wavelength and then identify which region of the EM spectrum the wave belongs in.

Table 3.3.2

	f/Hz	λ/m	Region
a	8.8×10^{15}		
b	1.4×10^{7}		
c		2.2×10^{-8}	
d		1.3×10^{-2}	

Table 3.3.1   Sources, detectors and uses of electromagnetic waves

	Sources	Uses
Radio waves	Electron movements in transmitter circuits of TV and radio systems.	Communications such as radio or television. Microwaves are used to cook food as their energy is absorbed easily by water and fat molecules.
Infra-red radiation	Any warm or hot object. The higher the temperature of the object the shorter the wavelength.	Infra-red cameras (often used for seeing during night-time). IR thermometers to measure temperature without contact.
Visible light	Very hot objects. Some chemical reactions.	Photography. Lasers. Sight.
Ultraviolet light	Very hot objects such as the Sun. Fluorescent lamps containing mercury.	Forensic science. Chemical analysis. Sterilisation of equipment.
X-rays	X-ray tubes which propel fast electrons into metal blocks.	Forming images of bones in the body. High-energy X-rays can be used to find damage in other materials.
Gamma rays	Decay of radioactive materials. Nuclear explosions. Gamma ray bursts from cosmic events such as formation of black holes.	Cancer treatment (radiotherapy). Gamma emitters are used as radioactive tracers in medicine or other applications. Sterilisation of equipment or some foods.

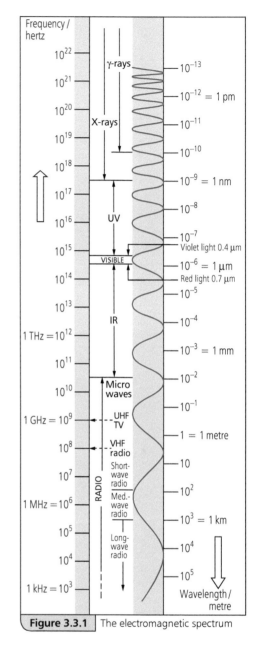

Figure 3.3.1 | The electromagnetic spectrum

Figure 3.4.1 Light cannot pass through the boy and so a shadow is formed.

A light source such as a lamp radiates light energy in all directions. We say that the light energy is being **emitted**. This light energy can be **absorbed** (taken in) when it reaches surfaces. For example, light energy is absorbed by the retina at the back of the eye.

Ray boxes and rays

A ray box uses a lamp to produce light. Narrow beams of light can be produced by placing a 'stop' with a single slit (or series of slits) next to the lamp. We can see these light rays because some of the light is scattered off surfaces into our eyes.

A **laser** can also produce very narrow light rays. It is harmful to the eye to look directly at a laser beam. These rays are not usually visible but spraying some aerosol or sprinkling talcum powder into the path of the laser beam causes scattering and allows us to see the straight path of the laser beam.

The formation of shadows

Light travels in a straight line from the source. If an opaque object is in the path of the light then there will be a region where the light cannot reach. This region will be in shadow.

A point source of light will produce a very sharp shadow behind an opaque object.

An extended light source will produce a less sharp shadow. The regions where all of the possible ray paths are blocked will be completely dark. The regions where some of the ray paths are blocked will be partially shaded.

Eclipses

Eclipses demonstrate that light travels in straight lines. The Sun is the only source of visible light in the solar system. The planets and moons are visible only because they reflect some of this sunlight.

Solar eclipse

The Sun is very much larger than the Moon but it is much further away. This means that they appear to be almost exactly the same size when viewed from the Earth. A solar eclipse occurs when the Moon passes directly between the Sun and the Earth (Figure 3.4.2). Because the Sun is not a point source of light there are regions on the Earth for which only some of the sunlight is blocked by the Moon. These regions lie within the **penumbra** and experience a partial eclipse. A small region on the Earth's surface lies within the **umbra** and so is in total darkness during an eclipse. This dark region moves across the surface of the Earth as the Earth rotates.

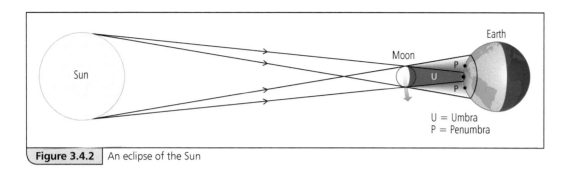

Figure 3.4.2 An eclipse of the Sun

Lunar eclipse

We can see the Moon when sunlight reflects off its surface. A lunar eclipse occurs when the Earth blocks sunlight travelling to the Moon and so the Moon appears dark (Figure 3.4.3). During a lunar eclipse the Moon sometimes appears to be dark red, this is because some red light passes through the Earth's atmosphere and reaches the Moon.

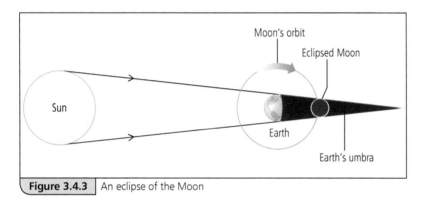

Figure 3.4.3 An eclipse of the Moon

The pinhole camera

A pinhole camera is a simple optical instrument used to produce an image on a screen (Figure 3.4.4). A pin is used to make a very small hole in an opaque sheet such as aluminium foil. The foil is placed in front of a brightly lit object. Rays of light from the object travel through the pinhole. An image of the object can be formed on a sheet of translucent paper.

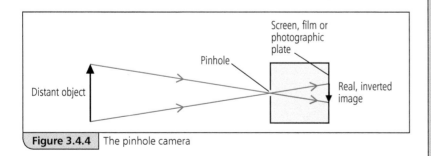

Figure 3.4.4 The pinhole camera

SUMMARY QUESTIONS

1 The International Space Station is approximately 100 metres long and orbits at a height of 200 km from the surface of the Earth. Use a diagram to explain why it causes no obvious shadow as it passes between the Earth and the Sun.

2 Explain how the equipment shown in Figure 3.4.5 can be used to show that light rays travel in straight lines.

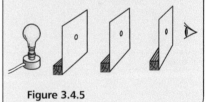

Figure 3.4.5

KEY POINTS

1 Light rays travel in straight lines and are detected when the ray reaches our eyes.

2 Shadows are formed when an opaque object blocks the path of light rays.

3 Solar eclipses occur when the Moon passes between the Earth and the Sun.

4 Lunar eclipses occur when the Earth prevents sunlight from reaching the Moon.

At the end of this topic you should be able to:

- state and apply the laws of reflection
- describe how images are formed in a mirror and the properties of those images.

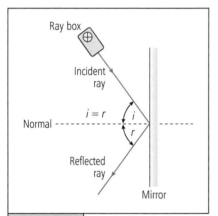

Figure 3.5.1 Investigating the laws of reflection using a ray box

When light rays strike a surface they may be absorbed, transmitted or reflected. Reflections all follow specific laws.

Describing reflection

Reflection occurs when a ray of light reaches a surface or boundary between materials. For example, a reflection occurs when the light ray strikes a mirror. The ray that strikes the mirror is called an **incident ray**. This ray reflects off the silvered surface and is called a **reflected ray**.

At the point where the incident ray touches the mirror we can draw a **normal**. The normal is a line perpendicular (at right angles) to a surface. When measuring angles during reflection all angles must be measured relative to the normal, not to the surface itself.

The laws of reflection

For any reflection at a surface two laws apply:

- the angle of reflection is equal to the angle of incidence
- the incident ray, reflected ray and normal are all in the same plane.

Figure 3.5.1 shows a simple reflection in a plane (flat) mirror. Experiments show that the **angle of incidence**, i, and the **angle of reflection**, r, are *always* equal, proving the first law.

The second law of reflection states that the two rays and the normal all lie on a plane (a flat surface like a piece of paper). This means that the reflected ray does not twist upwards or downwards during reflection.

Regular and diffuse reflection

Reflections from a mirror produce an image (a picture we can see). This is because the reflective surface of the mirror is very smooth. Parallel rays of light will be reflected and will remain parallel and so the observed size and shape of the image will match that of the original object. This is **regular reflection** (Figure 3.5.2a).

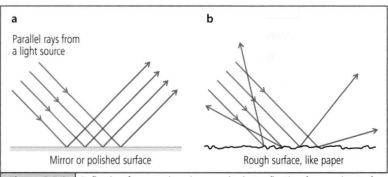

Figure 3.5.2 Reflection from a mirror is **a** regular but reflection from a sheet of paper is **b** diffuse.

Most surfaces are not smooth. When parallel rays of light hit these surfaces the rays will be reflected according to the laws of reflection but the roughness of the surface causes these reflected rays to travel in different directions. This means that no clear image will be formed. This is **diffuse reflection** (Figure 3.5.2b).

Images in plane mirrors

The image we see when we look into a mirror is a **virtual image**. A virtual image cannot be projected onto a screen or surface because no rays of light actually pass through the image. The image is the same distance behind the mirror as the object is in front. In Figure 3.5.3 the distances x and y are the same.

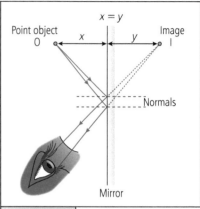

Figure 3.5.3 | The image formed in a plane mirror

ACTIVITY

Design a method to prove that the image in a mirror is the same distance behind the mirror as the object is in front of it.

EXAM TIP

In exam questions, mirrors may not be positioned horizontally or vertically, but at an angle as in Summary question 1. If you make sure you measure angles to the normal they shouldn't give you any problems.

KEY POINTS

1 Angles are always measured from the normal.

2 The angle of reflection is equal to the angle of incidence for all reflections.

3 The image in a plane mirror is virtual and the same distance behind the mirror as the object is in front of the mirror.

Light travels at approximately $3.00 \times 10^8 \, \text{m s}^{-1}$ in air but slows to $2.00 \times 10^8 \, \text{m s}^{-1}$ in glass. This change of speed causes the ray of light to change direction at the boundary between the two materials. This change in direction is always measured relative to the normal at the point of refraction.

Refraction in a rectangular block

When the light ray enters the glass block it slows down and this causes the ray to refract, to change its path towards the normal (Figure 3.6.1). When the light ray leaves the glass block it speeds up and refracts away from the normal. Because the two boundaries are parallel, the ray ends up travelling in the same direction as it was originally but it is **laterally displaced**.

Refraction in a semi-circular block

If the incident ray enters a new material along the normal then the ray cannot 'turn towards the normal' and it continues along the same path. The ray still slows down or speeds up. This can be demonstrated with a semi-circular glass block where the ray can be directed along the normal to the curved surface (Figure 3.6.2).

Refraction in a prism

Triangular prisms are also used to refract light. As the ray enters the prism it refracts towards the normal and as it leaves it refracts away from the normal. As the two refracting surfaces are not parallel the emergent ray is not parallel to the incident ray.

Dispersion

All electromagnetic radiation travels at the same speed in a vacuum but will travel at different speeds in other mediums. In particular different colours of light travel at different speeds in glass or other transparent materials. The size of the change in direction during refraction depends on the change in the speed of light at the boundary (see 3.7) and so different colours of light will refract by different amounts. For example, violet light refracts to a greater degree than red light as it has a greater change in speed. This effect is called **dispersion** (Figure 3.6.4).

Rainbows are caused when light from the Sun passes through raindrops. The light is dispersed and a coloured spectral pattern is produced.

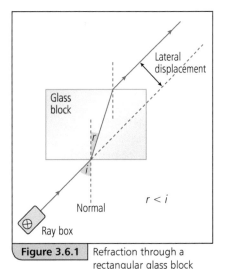

Figure 3.6.1 | Refraction through a rectangular glass block

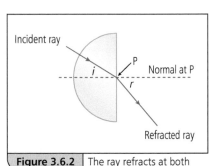

Figure 3.6.2 | The ray refracts at both boundaries but does not change direction when it enters the block as it is travelling normal to the surface.

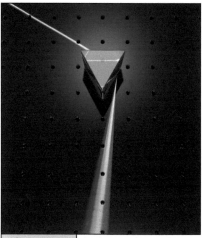

Figure 3.6.3 | The pool is deeper than it appears due to refraction.

Refraction in water

When rays of light travel from water into air the rays refract away from the normal. If a ray travels from the bottom of a pool then the path of the ray will change such that the ray appears to come from closer to the surface. This causes the pool to look shallower that it actually is (Figure 3.6.3).

SUMMARY QUESTIONS

1 Copy Figures 3.6.5 and 3.6.6 and then complete the ray path for the incident rays.

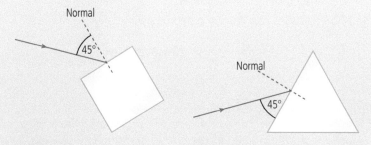

Figure 3.6.5   Figure 3.6.6

2 Which colour of visible light slows by the least amount when it enters glass from air?

3 Which of these statements is/are correct?

- The higher the frequency of light the greater the change in speed as it enters glass from air.
- The longer the wavelength of light the smaller the change in speed as it leaves glass and enters air.

Figure 3.6.4 | A prism can be used to disperse white light.

KEY POINTS

1 When a ray of light travels from one medium to another it changes speed.

2 If the ray slows down, its path will turn towards the normal at the point of refraction.

3 If the ray speeds up, its path will turn away from the normal at the point of refraction.

4 White light will disperse during refraction and separate into its constituent colours.

3.7 Refractive index and total internal reflection

LEARNING OUTCOMES

At the end of this topic you should be able to:

- apply Snell's law to refractions to calculate change in angle or speeds
- find the critical angle for a boundary
- describe total internal reflection
- explain how total internal reflection is used in optical fibres.

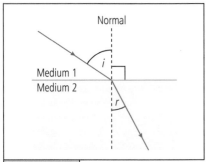

Figure 3.7.1 The refractive index of the boundary is the ratio of $\sin i$ to $\sin r$. This is also the ratio of the speeds of light in the materials.

Table 3.7.1 Examples of refractive indices for a ray of light entering the material from a vacuum (or air)

Material	Refractive index, n
glass	1.50
water	1.33
Perspex	1.50
diamond	2.42

Snell's law

Snell's law states that the ratio of the sines of the angle of incidence and angle of refraction at a boundary is a constant (Figure 3.7.1). This constant is the **refractive index** of the boundary. Table 3.7.1 shows the refractive index of different materials.

$$\frac{\sin i}{\sin r} = \text{refractive index, } n$$

The same form of relationship also applies to the ratio of the speed of light in the two materials. For a boundary between air and another transparent material:

$$\frac{\text{speed of light in air, } v_1}{\text{speed of light in material, } v_2} = \text{refractive index, } n$$

The two equations can be combined to give:

$$\frac{\sin i}{\sin r} = \frac{v_1}{v_2} = \text{refractive index}$$

WORKED EXAMPLE 1

A ray of light is refracted at the boundary from air into glass (refractive index 1.50). The angle of incidence is 30°. What is the angle of refraction?

$$\frac{\sin i}{\sin r} = \text{refractive index}$$

$$\sin r = \frac{\sin i}{\text{refractive index}} = \frac{\sin 30°}{1.50} = 0.33$$

$$r = \sin^{-1} 0.33 = 19.5°$$

Total internal reflection

When light reaches a boundary between a material of high refractive index and one with lower refractive index (e.g. glass to air) then the light can be reflected by the surface instead of being refracted. This occurs if the angle of incidence is greater than an angle called the **critical angle** (Figure 3.7.2). The critical angle, C, for a boundary is given by the relationship:

$$\sin C = \frac{1}{\text{refractive index of boundary}}$$

During this process all of the light is reflected back into the first material and so the process is called total internal reflection. During this process there is no loss of light energy.

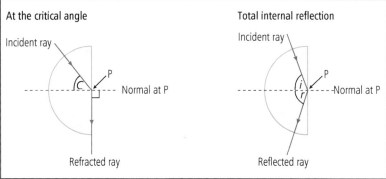

At the critical angle

Incident ray

C
P
Normal at P

Refracted ray

Total internal reflection

Incident ray

P
i
r
Normal at P

Reflected ray

Figure 3.7.2 Total internal reflection occurs if the angle of incidence is greater than the critical angle C. The reflected ray follows the laws of reflection ($r = i$).

ACTIVITY

- Next time you are swimming in a pool go to the bottom and look towards the surface. Try to explain the effects that you see. Note: only do this if you are being supervised.

- Flash a light into one end of a long fibre optic cable. You should see the flashing at the other end even when the cable is coiled up.

WORKED EXAMPLE 2

The refractive index of an air to Perspex boundary is 1.50. What is the critical angle for this boundary?

$$\sin C = \frac{1}{\text{refractive index of boundary}} = \frac{1}{1.50} = 0.66$$

$$C = \sin^{-1} 0.66 = 41.8°$$

Optical fibres use the process of total internal reflection to transmit signals (Figure 3.7.3). A ray of light (more usually infra-red radiation) enters the fibres and travels along it by being reflected at the surface of the glass. The ray can travel for several kilometres through the glass even when the fibre is coiled in loops.

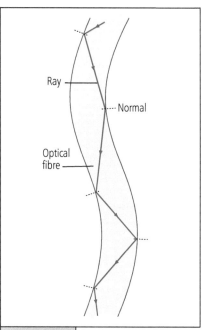

Ray

Normal

Optical fibre

Figure 3.7.3 Rays in an optical fibre

SUMMARY QUESTIONS

1 Copy Table 3.7.2 and then complete it using Snell's law for rays entering a material from air.

Table 3.7.2

Angle of incidence/ degrees	Angle of refraction/ degrees	Refractive index of boundary	Speed of light in material/m s^{-1}
30		1.33	
	20	1.45	
50	30		
45			1.5×10^8

2 Draw a diagram showing a ray of light travelling from the bottom of a pond so that it just escapes from the surface of the water. Calculate the critical angle for this boundary.

KEY POINTS

1 The ratio of the sines of angles of incidence and refraction is a constant called the refractive index.

2 The refractive index is also the ratio of the speed of light in the two materials.

3 When a ray of light passes along an optical fibre it totally internally reflects many times but little energy is lost at these reflections.

Converging lenses

At the end of this topic you should be able to:

• describe the path of rays through a converging (convex) lens

• describe the images formed by converging lenses.

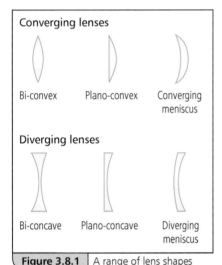

Figure 3.8.1 | A range of lens shapes

Types of lens

Lenses are curved blocks of glass or plastic which cause refraction of light (Figure 3.8.1). Lenses usually have two curved surfaces and each surface causes refraction. In order to simplify diagrams, we assume that a single refraction takes place for each ray and this happens in the centre of the lens.

There are many shapes of lens but there are only two main effects:

• A converging lens brings rays of light, parallel to the principal axis, together.

• A diverging lens spreads rays of light, parallel to the principal axis, apart. See 3.9.

The **principal axis** is an imaginary line which passes through the centre of the lens and is perpendicular to it.

The principal focus lies on the principal axis and the distance between it and the centre of the lens is the **focal length**, f, of the lens. Strong lenses cause more refraction than weak lenses and so have shorter focal lengths.

Converging lenses

Figure 3.8.2 shows a set of rays passing through a converging lens. These rays are parallel to the principal axis and they are refracted by the lens so that they all meet at a point called the **principal focus** (marked F). Each lens has two **principal foci**.

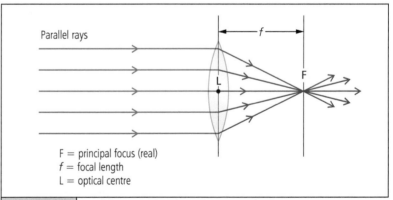

F = principal focus (real)
f = focal length
L = optical centre

Figure 3.8.2 | Parallel rays passing through a converging lens

The **focal plane** is a plane perpendicular to the principal axis that passes through the principal focus. Parallel rays from a distant object would be brought to a focus on a screen placed in the focal plane.

Images from converging lenses

We can find the properties of the image by analysing the ray paths from an object. In Figure 3.8.3 three rays are drawn from the top of the object.

- Ray 1 travels to the lens parallel to the principal axis. The ray is refracted so that it passes through the principal focus.
- Ray 2 passes through the **optical centre** of the lens and as no refraction takes place there is no change of direction.
- Ray 3 passes through the principal focus on the left of the lens. When it reaches the lens it is refracted so that it becomes parallel to the principal axis.

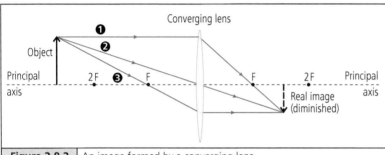

| **Figure 3.8.3** | An image formed by a converging lens |

The three rays meet and form an image on the right of the lens. You should be able to see that, in this case, the image is smaller than the original object (**diminished**), it is upside down (**inverted**) and that rays of light really pass through the image and so it is a **real image**.

ACTIVITY

Place a converging lens in front of a ray box producing parallel rays of light and describe what happens to the rays. Find the principal focus and measure the focal length of the lens.

Draw two more versions of Figure 3.8.3 but place the object:

a between F and 2F

b between F and the lens.

For each case, draw the three rays and describe the image.

SUMMARY QUESTIONS

1 Define the key terms: focal length, focal plane, principal focus and principal axis.

2 Draw a scale diagram showing five rays parallel to the principal axis each 0.5 cm apart as they pass through a converging lens of focal length 5 cm.

KEY POINTS

1 A converging lens refracts rays, parallel to the principal axis, so that they are brought together at the focal point.

2 A diverging lens refracts rays, parallel to the principal axis, so that they appear to come from the focal point.

Diverging lenses and the eye

At the end of this topic you should be able to:

• describe the path of rays through a diverging (concave) lens

• describe the images formed by diverging lenses.

Figure 3.9.2

Figure 3.9.1 shows a set of rays passing through a diverging lens. The rays spread out (diverge) in such a way that they appear to all come from one point. As for a converging lens, this point is called the principal focus and the distance between the lens and the principal focus is the focal length.

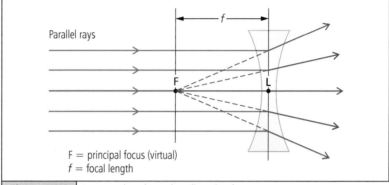

F = principal focus (virtual)
f = focal length

Figure 3.9.1 | Rays passing through a diverging lens

Images in diverging lenses

To find the properties of an image produced by a diverging lens draw three rays as for a converging lens (Figure 3.9.3):

• Ray 1 is parallel to the principal axis and is refracted so that it appears to come from the principal focus (the dotted line shows this).

• Ray 2 passes straight through the optical centre without a change in direction.

• Ray 3 is the ray which would pass through the principal focus beyond the lens. This ray is brought parallel to the principal axis when it passes through the lens.

ACTIVITY

Place a diverging lens in front of a ray box producing parallel rays of light and describe what happens to the rays. Find the principal focus and measure the focal length of the lens.

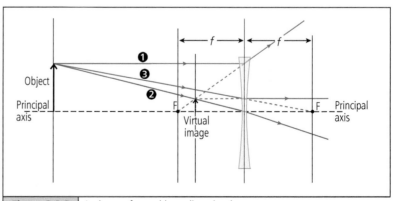

Figure 3.9.3 | An image formed by a diverging lens

As before, the three rays appear to come from a point. The image is formed between this point and the principal axis. You should see that the image is diminished and upright. The image is also virtual. This means that the rays do not actually pass through that point and so you could not place a screen there and see the image.

Human vision

Our eyes contain two surfaces which act as lenses. The eye's lens is a converging lens with a variable focal length (Figure 3.9.4). Small *ciliary muscles* are used to stretch the lens to allow us to focus on objects at different distances. The outer layer of the eye, the *cornea*, also acts as a lens with a fixed focal length.

Correcting vision

Both converging and diverging lenses are used to correct defects of vision (Table 3.9.1).

• A short-sighted (near-sighted) person suffers from *myopia*. The lens in their eye cannot become thin enough to focus on distant objects. The rays of light from a distant object would be brought to a focus in front of the eye's *retina* instead of clearly on its surface. This poor focusing leads to blurred vision of distant objects. A diverging lens can be used to correct myopia by diverging the rays of light before they reach the cornea.

• A long-sighted (far-sighted) person suffers from *hyperopia*. They cannot focus objects (such as the words on a page) that are close to the eye. Rays of light from the object would be focused behind the retina so a blurred image is formed. A converging lens can be used to correct this problem by increasing the overall converging power of the eye.

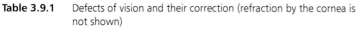

Figure 3.9.4 | The human eye

Table 3.9.1 Defects of vision and their correction (refraction by the cornea is not shown)

	Myopia	Hyperopia
Before		
After correction		

Magnification

LEARNING OUTCOMES

At the end of this topic you should be able to:

- calculate the magnification produced by a magnifying glass or other lens
- determine the focal length of a converging lens experimentally.

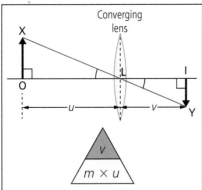

Figure 3.10.1 Linear magnification

WORKED EXAMPLE 1

A lens forms an image of a candle with a height of 10.0 cm. If the magnification of the lens is 1.60 what is the actual size of the candle?

Linear magnification =

$$\frac{\text{height of image}}{\text{height of object}}$$

Height of object =

$$\frac{\text{height of image}}{\text{linear magnification}}$$

$$= \frac{10.0\,\text{cm}}{1.60} = 6.25\,\text{cm}$$

As you have seen, the images of an object are not always the same size as the object. The image may be magnified (larger than the object) or diminished (smaller than the object).

Magnification and image height

Magnification of the images is defined by an equation comparing the image height to the object height:

$$\text{linear magnification, } m, = \frac{\text{height of image}}{\text{height of object}}$$

Magnification and object distance

The **linear magnification** of a converging lens can also be found using the object distance and image distance. Figure 3.10.1 shows the formation of an image by a converging lens. The triangles LIY and LOX are similar triangles and so the ratios of OX (object height) to IY (image height) is the same as the ratio of u to v.

$$\text{Linear magnification, } m, = \frac{\text{image distance, } v}{\text{object distance, } u}$$

A magnifying glass

A magnifying glass uses a single converging lens to produce a magnified image of an object (Figure 3.10.2). For the magnifying glass to work effectively the object needs to be closer to the lens than the focal length. This arrangement will produce a magnified, virtual image.

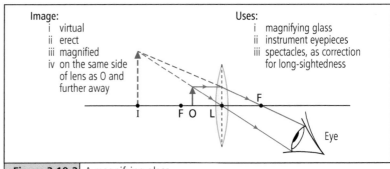

Figure 3.10.2 A magnifying glass

The lens formula

The relationship between the focal length of a lens, the image distance, v and the object distance, u is given by:

$$\frac{1}{f} = \frac{1}{u} + \frac{1}{v}$$

When using the lens formula the distances are positive for real images but are negative for virtual images. For example, a diverging lens may produce a virtual image 0.1 m from the lens and so v would be -0.1 m.

The lens formula can be used to determine the focal length of a lens by illuminating an object and positioning the lens to form a clear image on a screen (Figure 3.10.3). The distance between the lens and the object is measured as is the distance between the lens and the screen. These two distances can be substituted into the formula to find the focal length of the lens.

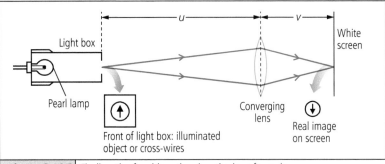

Figure 3.10.3 Finding the focal length using the lens formula

WORKED EXAMPLE 2

A lens used in a simple camera has a focal length of 0.10 m. To produce a clear image on a CCD the image must be formed 0.20 m behind the lens. How far from the lens should the object be positioned to produce this clear image?

$$\frac{1}{f} = \frac{1}{u} + \frac{1}{v}$$

$$\frac{1}{0.10\,\text{m}} = \frac{1}{u} + \frac{1}{0.20\,\text{m}}$$

$$\frac{1}{u} = \frac{1}{0.10\,\text{m}} - \frac{1}{0.20\,\text{m}}$$

$$\frac{1}{u} = 10 - 5 = 5$$

$$u = \frac{1}{5} = 0.20\,\text{m}$$

SUMMARY QUESTIONS

1 In which of these three situations is the magnification the largest?
   - An object of height 5.0 cm producing an image of 20 cm.
   - An object of 13 cm producing an image of 1.0 cm.
   - An object of 3 cm producing an image of 7 cm.

2 Copy Table 3.10.1. Then use the lens formula and magnification equation to complete the table for a range of converging lenses.

Table 3.10.1

Object distance	Image distance	Focal length	Magnification
2.00 m		0.25 m	
15 cm	6 cm		
	14 cm		0.2

ACTIVITY

- Perform an investigation to find the focal length of a range of lenses. Compare your results to the curvature of the lens. Describe the relationship between the curvature of the lens and the focal length.

- Use a magnifying glass to see what happens when the object is positioned beyond the focal length of the lens. Describe the image produced.

KEY POINTS

1 The magnification of an image is the ratio of the height of an image to the height of the original object.

2 The magnification is also the ratio of the image distance to the object distance.

3 The focal length of a lens can be found from the object distance and image distance using the lens formula.

EXAM TIP

Take care when using the lens formula, as you are dealing with reciprocals.

Diffraction, interference and theories about the nature of light

Scientists have studied the behaviour of light for centuries and have debated whether it is behaving as a stream of particles or as waves.

A very brief history…

Christiaan Huygens formulated a theory that light travelled as a wave and used this concept to describe reflection and refraction in terms of wavefronts.

Isaac Newton believed that light consisted of a stream of particles he called corpuscles. He used this model to describe the behaviour of light and his ideas were generally accepted.

Thomas Young devised experiments which demonstrated the wave behaviour of light. The results of these experiments could not be explained if light were a stream of particles and so the particle theory was abandoned and replaced with the wave theory. These experiments are described in more detail below.

Albert Einstein used a particle model of light to explain the experimental result called the 'photoelectric effect'. This could not be explained using wave theory.

Today it is accepted that light has both wavelike properties and particle behaviours in different situations.

Diffraction of waves

When a water wave passes through a gap we can see that the wave spreads out. This process is **diffraction** and occurs for all types of waves. The amount of diffraction that takes place depends on the size of the gap (Figure 3.11.1). Maximum diffraction takes place when the wave passes through a gap roughly the same size as the wavelength of the wave.

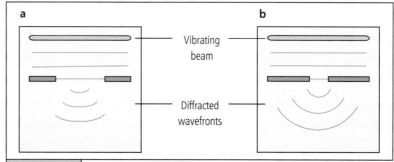

Figure 3.11.1 Diffraction of water waves **a** at a wide gap **b** at a narrow gap

Light diffracts when it passes through a gap. As the wavelength of light is very small (around 0.5×10^{-6} m), this process is only noticeable when the gaps are very narrow. This diffraction gives evidence that light is behaving like a wave.

Interference and the two-slit experiment

When two waves meet and pass through each other, the waves superimpose (Figure 3.11.2). The two displacements caused by the separate waves are simply added together.

At some points where the waves overlap the superposition of the waves cancel each other out (for example, when a crest meets a trough). This is **destructive interference**.

At other points a crest will meet a crest and the displacements will increase. This is **constructive interference**.

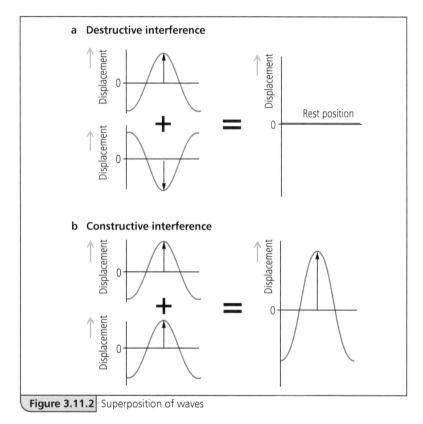

a **Destructive interference**

Rest position

b **Constructive interference**

Figure 3.11.2 Superposition of waves

The resulting pattern formed by the waves is an **interference pattern** (Figure 3.11.3).

Thomas Young investigated what happened when light passed through two very narrow gaps. He found that the light produces clear interference patterns in the same way as water waves passing through two gaps (Figure 3.11.4). A stream of particles would not produce this effect. The patterns could only be explained if light was travelling as a wave.

The particle nature of light

Some effects, however, cannot be explained by the wave model of light. Digital cameras and photovoltaic cells behave as if they are collecting light energy in small packets, similar to particles. These small packets of light energy are called **photons**.

Figure 3.11.3 Two water waves produce an interference pattern as the waves superimpose.

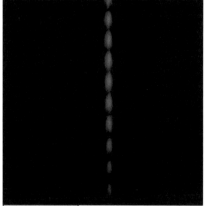

Figure 3.11.4 An interference pattern

SUMMARY QUESTIONS

1 Sketch a diagram showing what happens to water waves as they pass through a harbour entrance.

2 Why do we not normally see diffraction of light waves?

3 Summarise the evidence found in this topic that indicates that light behaves as a wave.

KEY POINTS

1 There have been several theories about the particle or wave behaviour of light.

2 Diffraction and interference experiments provide evidence for the wave behaviour of light.

Sound waves

At the end of this topic you should be able to:

• describe how sound waves are produced

• compare sounds in terms of frequency and amplitude

• relate amplitude to loudness and frequency to pitch.

Sound is produced by vibrating objects. Typical sources include:

• the vibrating strings on a guitar

• the skin on a drum

• moving columns of air in a woodwind instrument

• vibrating vocal chords when you speak

• a drill being used to dig up a road.

Propagation of sound waves

Sound waves propagate (travel) as longitudinal waves through a medium. A medium is necessary because the vibrations must be passed on from particle to particle. This can be demonstrated by placing an electric bell inside a glass bell jar and using a vacuum pump to remove the air (Figure 3.12.1). As the air is removed, the sound of the bell becomes quieter until it cannot be heard at all. This is because there is no longer a medium for the sound waves to pass through.

Sound waves are composed of a series of **compressions** and **rarefactions** which spread out from the source (Figure 3.12.2). The compressions are regions of air (or another medium) where the particles have been compressed more closely together while the rarefactions are regions where the particles are further apart.

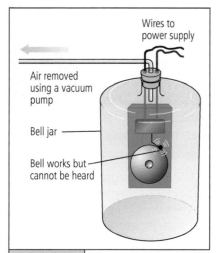

Wires to power supply

Air removed using a vacuum pump

Bell jar

Bell works but cannot be heard

Figure 3.12.1 When the air is removed from the jar the bell can no longer be heard.

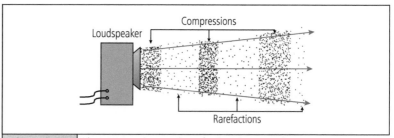

Compressions

Loudspeaker

Rarefactions

Figure 3.12.2 The compressions and rarefactions in a sound wave

Describing and displaying sounds

Just like all other waves, sound waves have amplitude and frequency.

• The greater the **amplitude** of a sound the *louder* it is.

• The higher the **frequency** of the sound the higher the **pitch**.

Representing sound waves on an oscilloscope

Sound waves can be represented on the screen of an oscilloscope connected to a microphone. The microphone converts the sound energy into an electrical signal and this signal controls the display on the oscilloscope. The oscilloscope then displays the 'shape' of the sound wave as a trace on the screen.

Table 3.12.1 Sound travels at different speeds in different media

Medium	Approximate speed of sound/m s^{-1}
air	340
water	1500
steel	6100

On the oscilloscope display:

- The *height* of this waveform is related to the *amplitude* of the wave. Taller waves show louder sounds.
- The *distance between the peaks* on the wave represents the *period* of the sound wave. The closer the peaks are together the shorter the period of the sound wave.

This period is inversely proportional to the frequency (frequency = $\frac{1}{period}$) and so the closer together the peaks, the higher the frequency of the sound. Figure 3.12.3 shows oscilloscope traces of simple sound waves.

Most sounds are much more complex than these single frequencies. They are composed of waves of different frequencies superimposed on each other. This produces more complicated waveforms as shown in Figure 3.12.4.

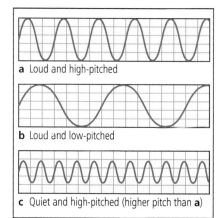

a Loud and high-pitched

b Loud and low-pitched

c Quiet and high-pitched (higher pitch than **a**)

Figure 3.12.3 Sound waves represented on an oscilloscope screen

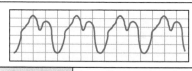

Figure 3.12.4 An oscilloscope trace for a note played on a flute

SUMMARY QUESTIONS

1 Why do you hear distorted sounds when you are swimming underwater?

2 Sketch a diagram showing how these two sounds would be represented on an oscilloscope screen:

   a A high frequency sound with low amplitude.

   b A sound with half the frequency and twice the amplitude of sound in part **a**.

3 Use the wave speed equation to find the frequency of a sound wave of wavelength 1.0 cm:

   a in air

   b in water

   c in steel.

   (The speed of sound in the different media is shown in Table 3.12.1.)

ACTIVITY

Use an oscilloscope to compare the waveforms produced by different musical instruments or tuning forks.

KEY POINTS

1 Sound waves are produced by vibrating objects including loudspeakers.

2 Sound waves travel as longitudinal waves through a medium composed of a series of compressions and rarefactions.

3 The higher the frequency of a sound the higher the pitch of the sound.

4 The greater the amplitude of a sound the louder the sound.

WORKED EXAMPLE

The period of a sound wave is 4.0×10^{-3} s.

What is the frequency of the wave?

$$f = \frac{1}{T}$$

$$= \frac{1}{4.0 \times 10^{-3}\,\text{s}}$$

$$= 250\,\text{Hz}$$

Experimenting with sound waves

At the end of this topic you should be able to:

- describe how sound can be reflected, refracted and diffracted
- describe interference of sound waves
- describe how sound can be used in pre-natal scans and materials testing.

The behaviour of sound waves

Reflection

Sound waves can be reflected just like any other wave. Smooth and rigid surfaces cause the strongest reflections. The reflected sound waves are called **echoes** (Figure 3.13.1).

Refraction

Sound waves will change direction when they move from one material to another because they change speed. The speed of sound in air also increases as the temperature of the air increases. This means that sound waves can bend as they travel through layers of air at different temperatures (Figure 3.13.2). This effect is most noticeable at night when the air near the ground is cooler than the air above it.

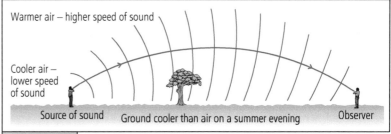

Warmer air – higher speed of sound

Cooler air – lower speed of sound

Source of sound   Ground cooler than air on a summer evening   Observer

Figure 3.13.2 Sound waves can follow a curved path through a temperature gradient.

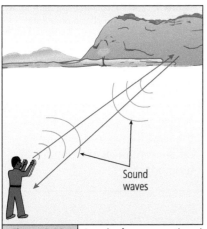

Sound waves

Figure 3.13.1 An echo from a smooth and rigid surface

Diffraction

Sound waves have a much greater wavelength than light waves and so they are diffracted easily by larger gaps. Sound waves will spread as they pass through doorways or around corners as their wavelength is similar to the size of these gaps.

Interference

When two sound waves meet they interfere. The waves are superimposed on top of each other. If two sources producing an identical signal are used then this effect can be detected. Two loudspeakers connected to the same source will form an interference pattern in front of them. This pattern will have regions where the waves destructively interfere and no sound will be heard. There will also be regions where the two waves constructively interfere and the sound will be louder than normal.

Using sound waves

If the speed of sound is known then we can measure distances by recording the time taken for sound to reach us. For example, during a

- Investigate whether sound waves follow the laws of reflection using some cardboard tubes to direct the sound waves.
- Find out about the hearing frequency range of bats and dolphins. Produce a report about how they sense prey and predators.

storm, light from a lightning strike reaches us almost instantly but the sound takes a measureable amount of time allowing us to calculate how far away the lighting struck.

A lightning strike hits a tree and the thunder is heard 4 seconds later. How far away did the lightning strike?

$$\text{Speed (m s}^{-1}) = \frac{\text{distance (m)}}{\text{time (s)}}$$

$$\text{distance} = \text{speed} \times \text{time} = 340\,\text{m s}^{-1} \times 4\,\text{s} = 1360\,\text{m}$$

Figure 3.13.3 A lightning strike

Ultrasound

High frequency sounds (above 20 kHz) are not detectable by humans and so are classed as **ultrasound**. Animals such as bats or dolphins produce ultrasound pulses to detect obstacles.

Because ultrasound pulses can be directed in narrow beams more easily than audible sound, they can be used to make measurements or produce images.

In pre-natal care, ultrasound pulses are used to form an image of the foetus (Figure 3.13.4). The pulses reflect off the different tissues and the echoes of these pulses are processed by a computer to form an image. Unlike X-rays, ultrasound does not cause ionisation and so is much safer to use.

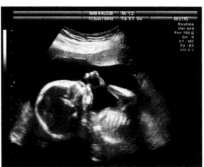

Figure 3.13.4 An ultrasound image of a foetus

An ultrasound pulse can also be used to 'see' into solid materials such as pipework, to measure the depth of the sea-bed or to detect shoals of fish near a boat (Figure 3.13.5).

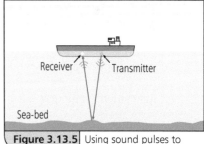

Figure 3.13.5 Using sound pulses to measure depth

An ultrasound pulse is used to detect a crack in a metal pipe. The pulse travels at 6000 m s⁻¹ in the metal and the echo is received 4.0 μs after the pulse is sent. How deep within the pipe is the crack?

$\text{Distance} = \text{speed} \times \text{time} = 6000\,\text{m s}^{-1} \times 4.0 \times 10^{-6}\,\text{s} = 0.024\,\text{m}$

The pulse has travelled to the crack and back and so the crack is 0.012 m within the pipe.

1 While walking along a road you hear an ambulance siren from around the corner but you cannot see the ambulance. Draw a diagram and explain how this can happen.

2 A dolphin produces a sound pulse which reflects off a fish it is hunting. The echo of the pulse is detected by the dolphin 0.4 second after the pulse was sent. The speed of sound in water is 1500 m s⁻¹. How far apart are the dolphin and the fish?

SECTION 3: Practice exam questions

1 The relationship between the refractive index and the angles of incidence and refraction for a ray crossing the boundary between air and glass is given by:

$$\text{refractive index} = \frac{\sin i}{\sin r}$$

During an experiment to measure the refractive index of a glass block the following results were obtained.

Angle of incidence, i/degrees	10	15	20	25	30	35
Angle of refraction, r/degrees	7.0	10.8	14.3	17.6	21.2	24.2
$\sin i$						
$\sin r$						

a Copy and complete the table by calculating the values for $\sin i$ and $\sin r$.

b Plot a suitable graph using the values for $\sin i$ and $\sin r$ which allows you to obtain a value for the refractive index for the glass block.

2 Diagram A shows a distance–displacement graph for a water wave and diagram B shows a displacement–time graph for a particle in the same wave.

a State:

   i   the wavelength of the wave

   ii   the amplitude of the wave

   iii the period of the wave.

b Calculate the speed of the wave.

A

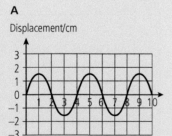

Displacement/cm

Distance/cm

B

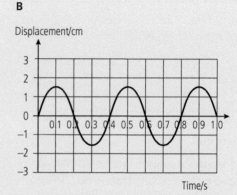

Displacement/cm

Time/s

3 On a calm day you can see your reflection when looking into a pond. When the pond's surface is disturbed you can no longer see a reflection. Why is this?

4 The electromagnetic (EM) spectrum consists of a series of waves.

a State two properties which all electromagnetic waves have in common.

b Copy and complete this table showing the EM spectrum in order of increasing wavelength.

Gamma rays			Visible light		Radio waves

c Which of the regions of the electromagnetic spectrum:

   i   has the lowest frequency?

   ii   is a major cause of skin cancers?

   iii is used in radiotherapy to treat cancers?

5 An oscilloscope is used to display signals received from a microphone when two different tuning forks, A and B, are struck nearby. These signals are shown in the diagrams opposite. The oscilloscope has been adjusted so that each horizontal division represents a time period of 2 ms.

a Which of the tuning forks produced the louder sound?

b Which of the tuning forks produced the higher pitch?

c   Find the frequency of tuning fork A.

d   Without further calculation, state the frequency of tuning fork B.

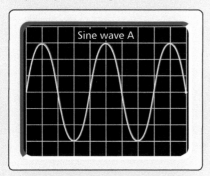

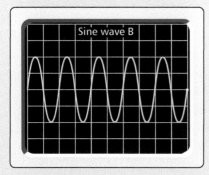

6   During an experiment to measure the speed of sound in metal, two microphones are attached to a long, thin steel bar. The first microphone starts the stopclock when it detects sound in the bar. The second microphone is 50 cm further along the bar and stops the stopclock when it detects sound. The measurement on the stopclock is 0.2 ms.

   a   What type of wave is sound?

   b   What is the speed of sound in the steel bar?

   c   The sound source produces a sound wave with a frequency of 1000 Hz. The speed of sound in air is 340 m s^{-1}.

      i   What is the wavelength of the sound in air?

      ii   What is the wavelength of the sound in the metal bar?

7   During a medical examination an ultrasound pulse is used to measure the thickness of a fat layer in a patient's skin. Sound travels at 630 m s^{-1} in this tissue. The echo from the pulse is received 0.3 μs after the pulse is sent.

   a   How thick is the fat layer?

   b   Why are ultrasound frequencies used instead of lower frequencies?

   c   Why are ultrasound scans used instead of X-rays in pre-natal care?

8   A student investigated the law of reflection using a ray box and a curved mirror as shown.

   a   State the two laws of reflection.

   b   Copy and complete the diagram showing the reflected ray.

   c   Mark on the angle of reflection and state its value.

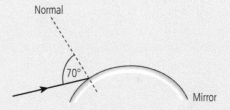

9   A group of scientists investigating optical properties have constructed a triangular prism from diamond. Diamond has a refractive index of 2.40.

   a   The speed of light in air is 3×10^8 m s^{-1}. What is the speed of light in diamond?

   b   Explain why the diamond disperses white light to a much greater extent than a glass prism would.

10 Borosilicate glass and a type of baby oil are both transparent and have **exactly** the same refractive index. When a block of the glass is placed into a beaker of the baby oil the block becomes invisible. Why is this?

11 A ray of light passes into the side of a thick-walled glass beaker containing water as shown in the diagram.

   a Calculate the angle of refraction at the air to glass boundary.

   b State the angle of incidence at the glass to water boundary.

   c Calculate the angle of refraction at the glass to water boundary.

   d Complete the ray diagram showing the ray reaching the centre of the beaker.

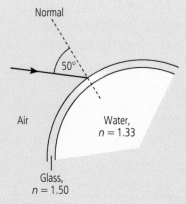

Normal

50°

Air

Water, $n = 1.33$

Glass, $n = 1.50$

12 Rays of light are shone into two prisms, A and B, as shown in the diagram. Prism A is constructed of a standard glass with refractive index 1.50. Prism B is constructed from a plastic with a significantly lower refractive index of 1.2.

   a Calculate the critical angles for both of the prisms.

   b Use the results of the calculations to complete the ray paths until the rays leave the blocks.

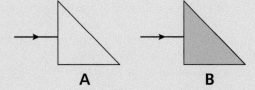

A   B

13 An optical fibre is constructed from a glass with a refractive index of 1.60. The fibre is curved as shown in the diagram.

   a Copy the diagram and draw the path of the ray from entry into the fibre until it leaves at the far end.

   b What is the critical angle for the glass to air boundary?

   c When bending the fibre a small crack forms at the surface. Explain why this may prevent light from reaching the end of the fibre.

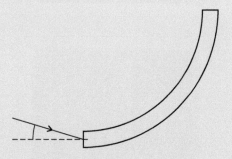

14 A slide projector produces a magnified image of slides when light is shone through them. The slides are placed 14 cm from a converging lens which has a focal length of 8.0 cm.

   a Draw a ray diagram showing how the image is produced.

   b Describe the properties of this image.

   c Calculate the distance to this image.

   d Calculate the magnification of this image.

15 The lens in a human eye is converging and can form a focussed image on the retina at the back of the eye. The retina lies 5 cm behind the lens and the eye can form a clear image when an object is placed a minimum distance of 20 cm from the eye.

An object of height 4.0 cm is placed at this minimum distance from the lens as shown in the simplified ray diagram.

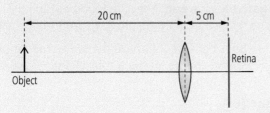

a Draw three rays on a copy of this diagram showing how the image would be formed on the retina.

b Describe the properties of the image formed.

c Calculate the magnification of the image.

d Calculate the vertical size of the image on the retina.

Static electricity

Atoms are composed of three types of particles: protons, neutrons and electrons (Figure 4.1.1). Protons and electrons have a property called electric charge.

• Protons are said to be **positively charged** and are bound into the nucleus of the atom. They cannot be removed easily.

• Neutrons are also found bound in the nucleus but have no electrical charge.

• Electrons are **negatively charged**. They are found outside the nucleus and can be removed if they are provided with some energy.

Atoms are neutral particles because they have the same amount of positive charge and negative charge, giving a total charge of zero.

Separating charges

Most materials are uncharged because they are composed of neutral atoms. When some materials are rubbed together the frictional forces can cause electrons to be transferred from one material to another. Because the protons are tightly bound in the nucleus they cannot move from place to place.

This transfer of electrons results in both of the materials becoming electrically charged:

• When extra electrons enter an object the object becomes negatively charged.

• When electrons leave an object the object becomes positively charged.

Rubbing a polythene rod with a dry cloth will cause electrons to move from the cloth to the polythene rod. The rod will become negatively charged because it has extra electrons and the cloth will become positively charged because it has fewer electrons than protons (Figure 4.1.2).

Rubbing a Perspex rod will cause electrons to move from the rod to the cloth leaving the rod positively charged and the cloth negatively charged.

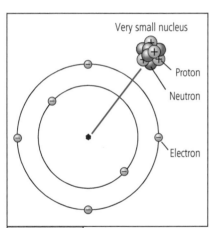

| Figure 4.1.1 | The structure of an atom |

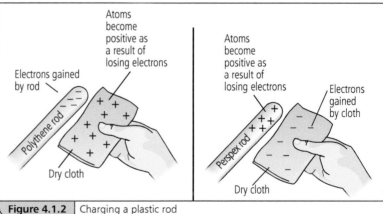

| Figure 4.1.2 | Charging a plastic rod |

Forces between charged objects

Charged particles produce a force on each other in a similar way to magnets:

* Opposite charges attract each other. (Positive and negative charges attract each other.)
* Similar charges repel each other. (For example, positive charges repel positive charges.)

Induced charge

A neutral object can become charged when a charged object is placed nearby (Figure 4.1.3). The electrons in the object will be attracted by a positively charged rod and move towards it causing one part of the object to become negatively charged and leaving the other part of the object positively charged. If we touch the positively charged area then electrons can move into the object from the Earth. Removing the original charged rod will then cause the excess electrons to distribute themselves on the object leaving it charged. This process is referred to as charging by **induction**.

The same effect can be seen when a charged rod is placed near to some uncharged chalk dust. The electrons in the dust are able to move slightly and cause the dust particles to become charged on one side. This means that the dust particles become attracted to the charged rod.

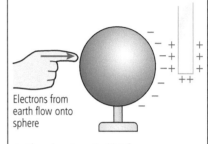

a The charged rod is held near the sphere

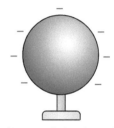

Electrons from earth flow onto sphere

b The sphere is earthed briefly

c The rod is removed. The sphere is left with an opposite charge to the rod.

Figure 4.1.3 Charging by induction

SUMMARY QUESTIONS

1 A student walks along a nylon carpet and then reaches out to a door handle. A tiny spark is produced and the student feels an electric shock. Explain why this happens.

2 Dust particles are uncharged but they often stick to electrical equipment such as television screens. Why does this happen?

KEY POINTS

1 Atoms have no overall charge because they contain an equal number of protons and electrons.

2 Electrons can be transferred between objects by frictional forces.

3 Oppositely charged objects attract each other while similarly charged objects repel.

4 Charges can be induced in neutral objects.

Electric fields and the Van de Graaff generator

At the end of this topic you should be able to:

• describe an electric field and its effect on charged particles

• explain how a Van de Graaff generator separates charges

• explain how buildings are protected from damage by lightning.

Electric fields

An electric field is a region of space in which a charged object will experience a force.

The field shows the direction of force acting on a positively charged particle placed in the field (Figures 4.2.1 and 4.2.2). A negatively charged particle experiences a force in the opposite direction.

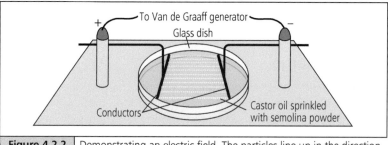

Figure 4.2.2 Demonstrating an electric field. The particles line up in the direction of the field.

The Van de Graaff generator

Rubbing a rod with a cloth can only separate a small amount of charge. To produce a larger build-up of charge a **Van de Graaff (VdG) generator** can be used (Figure 4.2.3).

• A large, hollow, metal dome is insulated from the ground by a plastic tower.

• Inside the tower a rubber belt is moved by an electric motor and passes over two rollers made of different plastic materials.

• As the belt passes over the lower roller electrons are transferred from the inner part of the belt to the roller, making the roller negatively charged.

• Positively charged ions are attracted to the roller from the metal comb but are trapped on the belt as it moves upwards. This leaves the outer surface of the belt positively charged.

• At the top of the generator the positively charged belt draws electrons from the dome through the second metal comb. The dome becomes positively charged by induction.

• As the rubber belt rotates, more electrons are removed from the dome and positive charge can build up on the surface of the dome.

Some effects of the VdG generator

The effectiveness of the VdG generator depends a great deal on the weather conditions. In humid conditions the charges can be carried away on water molecules in the air.

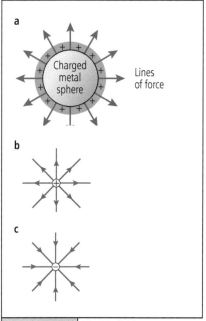

Figure 4.2.1 Electric fields near **a** a charged sphere, **b** a positive point charge and **c** a negative point charge

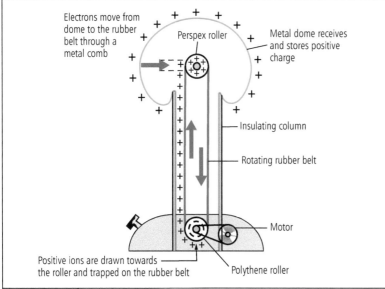

Electrons move from dome to the rubber belt through a metal comb

Perspex roller

Metal dome receives and stores positive charge

Insulating column

Rotating rubber belt

Motor

Positive ions are drawn towards the roller and trapped on the rubber belt

Polythene roller

Figure 4.2.3 A Van de Graaff generator

Lightning

Lightning is a very large spark. Clouds can become highly charged by frictional forces acting inside them. Droplets of water and ice crystals brush against each other and charges are separated. Eventually the charge separation is so large that a lightning bolt is produced.

A lightning bolt is often a flow of electrons to earth. A very large electric current is produced and this heats the air around it rapidly causing a bright white glow. The air is heated so quickly that a sound shockwave, thunder, is produced.

Protection from lightning

Lightning conductors are placed on tops of tall buildings, to protect the building in two ways:

• The pointed end of the conductor allows induced charge, which builds up in the building, to leak away into the air making it less likely that the building will be struck.

• Sometimes the lightning will strike the building anyway. The large current could cause fire or even an explosion. Lightning conductors have thick metal cables or bars that allow the electric current from lightning to pass through to earth safely without generating too much heat.

Figure 4.2.4 Very large amounts of charge can be created by forces in the atmosphere.

Uses and dangers of static electricity

Figure 4.3.1 Aircraft can build up static charge as they fly. These thin spikes on the wing are designed to help reduce the build-up of static electricity.

Figure 4.3.2 This electronic engineer is connected to the Earth through a wristband as he repairs a computer. Any static build-up in his body will discharge through the lead instead of damaging the delicate circuitry.

Dangers of static electricity

You have already seen that the build-up of large charges can be dangerous, resulting in lightning, for example. Even small sparks or currents can sometimes be dangerous or damaging.

Refuelling explosions

Large electrical charges can build up on vehicles when they move. Air resistance or other frictional forces cause the transfer of electrons (Figure 4.3.1).

Car tyres can transfer charge to the car's metal body. If enough charge builds up on the car a spark can be produced. When refuelling a car, a small spark can ignite petrol vapour and cause an explosion. Modern car tyres have been designed to help reduce this dangerous build-up of charge.

When aircraft are refuelled, the moving fuel could cause a build-up of charge in the aircraft's fuel tanks and a spark could cause an explosion. To prevent this build-up of charge the aircraft and refuelling tanker are connected together by a conducting cable to allow the charge to dissipate safely.

Sparks can even cause explosions when there is dry powder in the air such as in flour mills.

Damage to electronics

Microprocessors and other integrated circuits are extremely sensitive to static electricity and can be ruined if there is a build-up of charge.

Uses of static electricity

Static electricity can also be useful in photocopiers, in reducing air pollution and in spray painting surfaces.

Photocopiers

Photocopiers use careful control of static charge to produce images on paper (Figure 4.3.3).

- A rotating drum is negatively charged by a brush.
- A bright light is shone onto an image on a sheet of paper.
- The bright light is reflected onto the charged drum.
- The negative charge can escape from the drum in areas that receive the reflected light. The areas that do not receive light remain negatively charged. This means that the charges on the drum are arranged in the same pattern as the image on the original sheet of paper.

- A positively charged 'toner' powder is applied to the drum. This powder is attracted to the negatively charged areas but not to the uncharged areas.
- A negatively charged piece of paper is pressed against the rotating drum. The toner remaining on the drum is attracted to the paper.
- The paper is heated and the toner melts onto it creating a permanent copy of the original image.

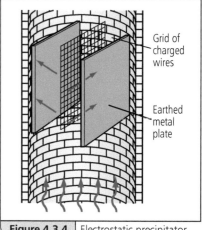

Figure 4.3.4 Electrostatic precipitator

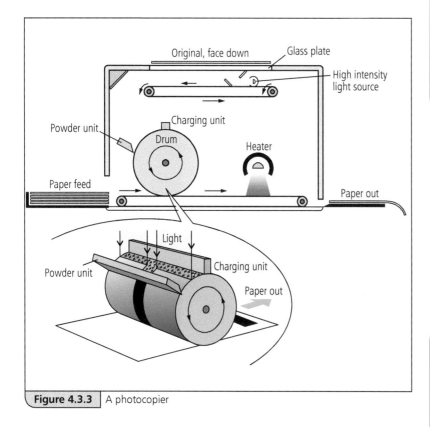

Figure 4.3.3 A photocopier

Laser printers operate in a similar way. Instead of using reflected light to create the image on the drum, a laser beam draws a pattern so that any image can be created.

Reducing air pollution

Power stations produce soot that would normally escape through the chimney. To prevent this pollution a charged metal grid can be used to collect the soot particles. As the soot particles rise up the chimney and past the metal grid they gain positive charge and are attracted to earthed metal plates on the side of the chimney. The soot can then be collected. This process is called **electrostatic precipitation**.

Improving painting

To improve the quality of painted surfaces the paint can be charged as it is sprayed. The surface is oppositely charged and so the paint is attracted to the whole surface. This gives a very even coating of paint.

Electric current

At the end of this topic you should be able to:

- describe an electric current in terms of charge transfer
- describe the current in a metal wire
- describe the current in an ionic solution.

Current and charge

The flow of electric charge is a **current**. This flow of charge is caused by a potential difference between two points.

Defining current

The size of a current is the rate of flow of charge and this is measured in a unit called the ampere (A). The relationship is normally written as:

charge transferred = current × time or $Q = It$

Quantities of charge are measured using a unit called the coulomb (C) and 1 coulomb = 1 ampere second (A s).

WORKED EXAMPLE

What is the current in a wire if a charge of 360 C is transferred in one minute?

$$Q = It$$

$$I = \frac{Q}{t} = \frac{360\,C}{60\,s} = 6.0\,A$$

Current in circuits

Electrical charges move around circuits in a current. In an electrical circuit a current is used to transfer energy to electrical devices.

In a simple circuit the current is a flow of electrons through metal wires and components. The current is not used up as it travels around the circuit. All of the electrons complete the whole journey releasing energy in the components as they pass through them.

Conventional current

Conventional current is described in terms of a flow of positive charge. In circuits the energy is actually carried by a flow of negative charges. This means that the particles carrying charge are actually moving in the opposite direction to the conventional current.

EXAM TIP

It is important to always state that conventional current travels from positive to negative even when discussing circuits.

Conductors and insulators

Metals are composed of a lattice of positive ions surrounded by a 'sea' of free electrons which can move about. This means that it is easy for charges to move freely through metals so they are good **conductors** of electricity.

Most other solid materials do not have free electrons or other charge carriers and so it is difficult for a current to flow. These materials are called **insulators**.

Semiconductors

Some materials lie between the two extremes of conductivity. They can conduct under the right circumstances. These are classed as **semiconductors**. Silicon is a semiconductor and its ability to conduct can be altered by adding atoms of other semiconductors such as germanium. Some semiconductors are made to conduct in one direction and only if the potential difference across it is high enough. This effect is used in diodes and transistors.

Current in ionic solutions

When sodium chloride is dissolved in water an ionic solution is formed. This contains two different types of ions: Na^+ and Cl^-.

If electrodes are placed in the solution and connected to a battery, both of these charged particles can flow because of the potential difference between the two electrodes.

- The sodium ions are positively charged and so are attracted to the negative electrode. When they reach the electrode they obtain electrons and form sodium. This rapidly reacts with the water to form sodium hydroxide and hydrogen gas and so bubbles can be seen on the electrode.
- The chlorine ions are negatively charged and are attracted to the positive electrode. When they reach the electrode they lose an electron and form chlorine gas.

This process is called electrolysis and can be carried out on an industrial scale to produce useful chlorine gas and sodium hydroxide solution. Electrolysis of other ionic solutions can produce other useful chemicals.

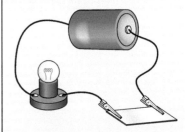
SUMMARY QUESTIONS

1 Copy and complete Table 4.4.1 relating current, charge and time.

Table 4.4.1

Current/A		2.5	0.05
Charge/C	100		0.2
Time/s	40	300	

2 A current of 150 mA flows through a circuit for 4 minutes. How much charge has been transferred?

3 Molten electrolytes can also conduct electricity. Molten lead bromide contains Pb^{2+} and Br^- ions. Explain what happens when electrodes are placed in molten lead bromide and connected to a battery.

KEY POINTS

1 The current in a metal wire is caused by a flow of electrons from a negative terminal to a positive terminal.

2 Conventional current is a flow of positive charge from a positive terminal to a negative terminal.

Electrical energy and transformations

At the end of this topic you should be able to:

- calculate the potential difference between two points
- calculate the energy transferred by an electrical device.

Potential difference

Potential difference is the cause of the movement of charge. A charged particle will move to a position where it will have less potential energy and so will move to a 'lower' point in an electric field.

This is a little like a mass in a gravitational field. As the mass falls through the gravitational field it loses potential energy. The energy loss depends on the distance moved through the field, the strength of the field and the size of the mass. In electricity the energy change depends on the size of the charge and the potential difference it moves through.

Potential difference is therefore defined by the equation:

$$\text{potential difference} = \frac{\text{energy transferred}}{\text{charge}} \text{ or } V = \frac{E}{Q}$$

WORKED EXAMPLE 1

How much energy is transferred when a charge of 3.2 C passes through a potential difference of 5.0 V?

$$V = \frac{E}{Q}$$

$$E = VQ = 5.0\,V \times 3.2\,C = 16\,J$$

In circuits the positive terminal of a battery or power supply is at higher potential than the negative terminal.

Voltage, potential difference and electromotive force

The voltage produced by an electrical power source is called the **electromotive force (e.m.f.)** and the voltage across an electrical component is usually called the potential difference (p.d.). Both are measured in volts and are often referred to simply as voltages.

EXAM TIP

Electrical power is measured in the unit watt (W) in the same way as mechanical power is. One watt is one joule per second.

Electrical power

Just as in mechanical energy transfer, the power of an electrical device is the rate at which it transfers energy. This can be linked to the definitions of potential difference and current as follows:

$$V = \frac{E}{Q} \text{ and } Q = It, \text{ therefore } V = \frac{E}{It}$$

$$IV = \frac{E}{t} \text{ and, as power is defined by } P = \frac{E}{t}, P = IV$$

Electrical power is measured in watts (W).

How much energy is transferred by a bulb in 20s if it operates with a potential difference of 6.0 V and a current of 0.5 A?

$P = IV = 0.5\,A \times 6.0\,V = 3.0\,W$

$E = Pt = 3.0\,W \times 20\,s = 60\,J$

Electrical transformations

Electrical energy can be transformed in many useful ways. Here are some examples:

- Electrical motors transform electrical energy into kinetic energy, allowing a wide range of objects to move.
- Electricity can be converted into light using filament bulbs, LEDs or fluorescent tubes.
- Loudspeakers convert electrical energy to sound.

Conservation of energy

Electrical energy is very useful as it can be transferred and transformed easily but most of the production of electricity relies on burning fossil fuels. These fuels are only available in limited quantities and so reducing their use is important. We can conserve some of these resources by using more efficient electrical devices (Figure 4.5.1) or by using alternative sources of energy where possible (Figure 4.5.2).

Figure 4.5.1 Light emitting diodes or fluorescent tubes are much more efficient than filament bulbs.

Figure 4.5.2 Electricity can be generated using photovoltaic solar cells.

ACTIVITY

Use a voltmeter and an ammeter to measure the current in and potential difference across a lamp. Use your readings to find its power rating.

SUMMARY QUESTIONS

1 What is the power of an electrical device which operates with a current of 12.4 A and potential difference of 12 V?

2 How much charge is transferred when a torch with a power rating of 4.0 W and operating voltage of 6.0 V operates for one minute?

3 What potential difference is required to provide a charge of 40 mC with 10 J of energy?

KEY POINTS

1 The potential difference across a component is defined by
$$V = \frac{E}{Q}$$

2 The power of an electrical device is given by $P = IV$

Simple circuits and components

At the end of this topic you should be able to:

• draw simple circuit diagrams containing a range of components

• interpret circuit diagrams and use them to construct real circuits

• explain why a standard set of symbols is used for circuits.

A simple circuit consists of a source of electromotive force (a cell, a battery or a power supply), connecting leads and some electrical components.

Circuit diagrams

Drawing realistic diagrams of the components is not necessary and can be confusing, so a standard set of symbols is used.

• The same symbols are used around the world allowing all engineers to understand them.

• A circuit diagram shows the important connections between components very clearly.

The key circuit symbols are shown in Table 4.6.1.

Table 4.6.1   Standard electrical symbols

Component	Symbol	Use	Component	Symbol	Use
earth		point of lowest potential	wires passing	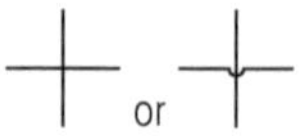 or	indicates that wires are not connected together
cell	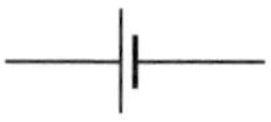	provides an electromotive force in the circuit	lamp or bulb	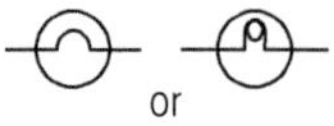 or	transforms electrical energy into light
battery		provides an electromotive force in the circuit	voltmeter	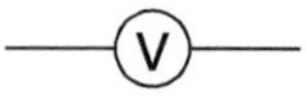 (V)	measures the potential difference between two points
d.c. power supply	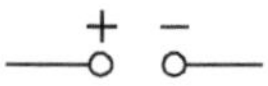 + −	provides an electromotive force in the circuit	ammeter	 (A)	measures the current at that point in the circuit
a.c. power supply		provides a changing electromotive force in the circuit	galvanometer	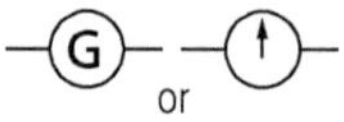 (G) or	measures very small currents
switch	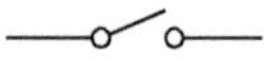	connects or disconnects components	semiconductor diode		allows current only in direction of the arrow
junction		indicates that wires are connected together	electrolytic cell		produces a precise electromotive force

Component	Symbol	Use	Component	Symbol	Use
fuse	—□— ∞ or	melts and cuts off the circuit if the current is too large	loudspeaker		transforms electrical energy into sound
fixed resistor	—▭— or —ⱲⱲⱲ—	reduces the current in a branch of a circuit	transformer		changes the p.d. of an alternating current
variable resistor		a resistor whose value can be manually altered	generator	—(GEN)—	transforms kinetic energy into electrical energy
electric motor	—○—	transforms electrical energy into kinetic energy			

ACTIVITY

Draw a circuit diagram for the two circuits in Figure 4.6.1.

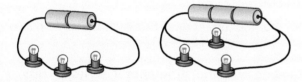

Figure 4.6.1

To draw a circuit clearly follow these simple rules:

- Start by drawing the cell, battery or power supply.
- Use a ruler to draw all of the connecting leads and wires and any other straight lines.
- Work around the circuit in a logical order. Start from the positive terminal.
- Draw one component at a time working towards the negative terminal of the battery.
- If the circuit has any branches then complete one branch before moving on to the next.
- If necessary mark the direction of the conventional current on the circuit using small arrows.
- There should be no gaps in the circuit.

SUMMARY QUESTIONS

1 Draw the correct circuit diagram for the two circuits shown in Figure 4.6.2.

Figure 4.6.2

2 A student has drawn a circuit diagram poorly (Figure 4.6.3). Describe and correct the mistakes the student has made.

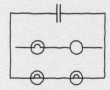

Figure 4.6.3

KEY POINTS

1 Circuit diagrams show the connections between components clearly.

2 Standard symbols must be used for circuit diagrams.

Series and parallel circuits

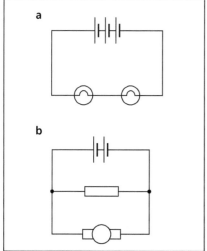

Figure 4.7.1 Circuit **a** shows two bulbs in series and circuit **b** shows a resistor in parallel with an electric motor.

There are two categories of circuits: **series** and **parallel** (Figure 4.7.1). To analyse these circuits we need to understand the behaviour of the current in the circuit and the changes in energy provided to the components.

Series circuits

Series circuits are the simplest type of circuit. There is only one pathway connecting the positive and negative terminals.

Understanding current in series circuits

In the circuit the current is composed of a flow of charge, in the form of electrons, moving through the wires. The electrons pass through each component in turn but they cannot be created or destroyed. They can only release some of the energy they carry. The electrons also cannot stay in a component. The same number has to leave as enter and at the same rate.

This means that the current must be exactly the same in all of the components in series with each other.

Understanding potential difference in series circuits

The source of electromotive force in the circuit can be a cell, a battery or a power supply. In this description we will assume a cell is being used but the principle is the same for all sources.

Electrons passing through the cell gain potential energy as they pass through. When the electrons move through a component in the circuit they transfer some of the energy they gained when passing through the cell. After moving through all of the components the electrons will have the same amount of potential energy as they first started with, before they passed through the cell.

As energy must always be conserved the electrons have to lose exactly the same amount of energy when they pass through the components as they gained from the cell. This means that the sum of the potential difference drops around the circuit must match the electromotive force of the cell.

Parallel circuits

Parallel circuits have branches where the current can divide and re-join.

Understanding current in parallel circuits

The current into any junction must exactly match the current out of that junction. This is because the rate of electrons entering the junction must be the same as the rate of electrons leaving the junction. They can't stay at the junction.

If current divides to follow different branches then the current will recombine when the branches re-join. The current entering the cell, or other power supply, has to match the current leaving it.

Understanding potential difference in parallel circuits

The potential difference across each branch must be the same. Electrons following one path have to lose the same amount of energy as electrons following a different path before they re-join.

What is the current and potential difference across the bulbs in the circuit shown in Figure 4.7.2?

The potential difference across the branches must be the same as the electromotive force of the battery. This means there is a p.d. of 12.0 V across bulbs D and E.

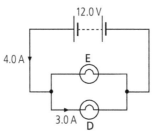

The current from the battery is 4.0 A. The current into bulb D is 3.0 A and so the current into bulb E must be 1.0 A.

Figure 4.7.2

More complex circuits

A circuit does not have to be purely series or parallel. Many are combinations of both. The rules for parallel and series circuits apply to the appropriate parts of the circuit.

The circuit shown in Figure 4.7.3 contains both parallel and series elements. Find the current and potential difference across each of the bulbs.

The current from the battery is 2.0 A. This means that the current through bulb P must be 2.0 A and so must the current through bulb S. The total current through bulb Q and bulb R must be 2.0 A and so the current through R must be 2.0 A − 1.5 A = 0.5 A.

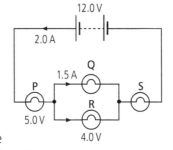

Figure 4.7.3

The p.d. across bulb Q must be the same as the p.d. across bulb R so it is 4.0 V.

The total p.d. around the circuit must be 12.0 V.

This means that the p.d. across bulb S must be 12.0 V − 5.0 V − 4.0 V = 3.0 V.

1 Sketch all of the possible circuits that can involve five bulbs. Include series, parallel and combined circuits.

2 Find the current in and the p.d. across the resistors Y and Z in Figure 4.7.4. X and Y are equal resistances.

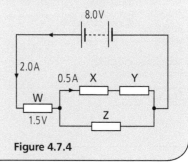

Figure 4.7.4

1 The current into any junction is equal to the current out of it.

2 The potential difference around any closed loop in a circuit is zero.

Cells and batteries

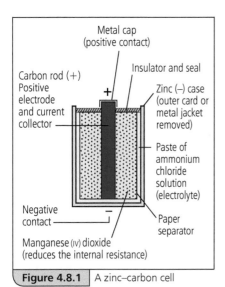

Figure 4.8.1 | A zinc–carbon cell

Figure 4.8.2 | A car battery is a secondary cell. It can be recharged.

Chemical reactions in cells

The electromotive force (e.m.f.) required to drive a current can be produced by chemical reactions between acids and metals. Each cell has two terminals or electrodes: the positive and the negative.

Cells are restricted in the size of the current they can provide by their internal resistances which are due to their physical and chemical composition.

A battery is simply a collection of cells placed in series with each other. The e.m.f. of the battery will be the sum of the e.m.f.s of the cells, assuming all of the cells are placed the same way around.

Primary cells

In a **primary cell** the chemical reaction which produces the e.m.f. cannot be reversed. This means that, once the reaction has taken place, the cell cannot be recharged and reused. There are several types of primary cells. One common example is the zinc–carbon dry cell (Figure 4.8.1).

In a zinc–carbon cell a metal case of zinc acts as the negative electrode and a carbon rod acts as the positive electrode. A reaction occurs between the zinc and carbon and an ammonium chloride paste and this reaction produces an e.m.f. of 1.5 V initially.

Zinc–carbon cells have a relatively high internal resistance and so they cannot provide large currents, the maximum being around 1 A. This means that they are not suitable for providing energy to high power devices.

Chemical reactions take place inside zinc–carbon cells even when they are not in use. This means that the cells discharge over time and become useless. They can also corrode inside equipment if not replaced regularly.

Secondary cells

A **secondary cell** also relies on a chemical reaction to produce an e.m.f. but this time the reaction can be forced to reverse by applying a potential difference in the opposite direction to the cell. This means that a secondary cell can be recharged repeatedly.

The most common type of secondary cell is the lead–acid cell used in car batteries. In this cell the reaction between lead plates (negative electrode) and lead oxide plates (positive electrode) and dilute sulfuric acid produces an e.m.f. of 2 V. Inside a car battery six cells are placed in series and so a total e.m.f. of 12 V is produced.

Lead–acid cells have very low internal resistance and can provide the large currents required to power a starter motor. They also contain significant quantities of lead and so are very heavy and have corrosive sulfuric acid inside.

WORKED EXAMPLE

A car battery produces an e.m.f. of 12 V. What size current is required to turn a starter motor with a power rating of 4.8 kW?

$$P = IV$$

$$I = \frac{P}{V} = \frac{4.8 \times 10^3 \, W}{12 \, V} = 400 \, A$$

Recharging secondary cells

A single lead–acid cell can be recharged using a power supply or a battery with an e.m.f. greater than 4.0 V. This applied e.m.f. is greater than the e.m.f. of the cell to be recharged and will force the chemical reaction to happen in the reverse direction (Figure 4.8.3).

A car battery is recharged by an alternator driven by the car engine. This provides a reverse e.m.f. to the battery while the car is in motion and so the battery remains fully charged.

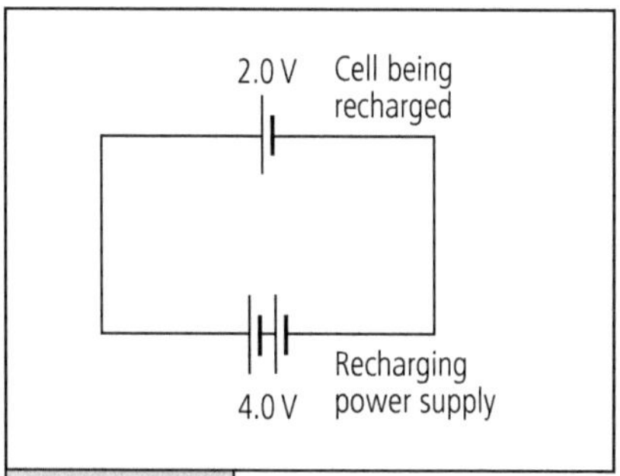

Figure 4.8.3 Recharging a lead–acid cell. Note how the negative electrode of the cell is connected to the negative electrode of the power supply forcing the current to travel in the opposite direction to that when the cell is discharging.

(diagram labels: 2.0 V — Cell being recharged; 4.0 V — Recharging power supply)

ACTIVITY

Use a lead–acid cell to power a low voltage bulb. Monitor the condition of the plates over several hours and use data logging equipment to measure the current and e.m.f. provided by the cell.

Recharge the cell using a power supply and repeat the test. Does the cell behave in the same way?

SUMMARY QUESTIONS

1 Draw a table summarising the characteristics of primary and secondary cells.

2 A zinc–carbon battery provides a maximum current of 1.2 A with an e.m.f. of 1.5 V. What is the maximum power that can be provided by this cell?

KEY POINTS

1 Cells produce an electromotive force through a chemical reaction.

2 Primary cells use irreversible reactions and cannot be recharged.

3 Secondary cells use reversible reactions and can be recharged.

4.9 Resistance

Using electrical meters

Electrical meters are used to measure both current and potential difference but the meters must be placed carefully in order to operate correctly (Figure 4.9.1).

- An **ammeter** is used to measure the current at a point in a circuit. The current has to pass through the ammeter for its magnitude to be measured and so the ammeter needs to be placed in series with the other components. Placing the ammeter in this way could reduce the current and so ammeters need to have very low resistances.

- A **voltmeter** measures the potential difference between two points in the circuit. It has to be placed in parallel with the components it is measuring the potential difference across. Voltmeters need to have very high resistance so that almost no current will pass through them.

Resistance

In 4.8 it was mentioned that cells have an internal resistance which restricts the current in them. All components have a resistance to a current. Metals wires have low resistance while glass rods have very high resistance.

The **resistance** of a component is defined as the ratio of the p.d. to the current through it:

$$\text{resistance} = \frac{\text{p.d.}}{\text{current}} \text{ or } R = \frac{V}{I}$$

Resistances are measured in a unit called the ohm (Ω).

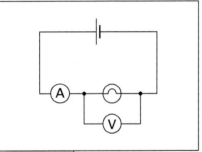

Figure 4.9.1 Using an ammeter and voltmeter to measure the current through, and p.d. across, a bulb.

> **WORKED EXAMPLE 1**
>
> What is the resistance of a length of metal wire if there is a current of 2.5 A when a p.d. of 3.0 V is across it?
>
> $$R = \frac{V}{I} = \frac{3.0\,\text{V}}{2.5\,\text{A}} = 1.2\,\Omega$$

Ohmic conductors

A simple metal wire will have a constant resistance as long as its physical properties and conditions do not change. This relationship was discovered by Georg Ohm and so is called Ohm's law:

The current through a conductor is directly proportional to the potential difference across it

$$I \propto V$$

LEARNING OUTCOMES

At the end of this topic you should be able to:

- use an ammeter and voltmeter correctly
- calculate the resistance of a component
- state Ohm's law and the conditions under which it applies.

The constant of proportionality is the resistance of the wire. Materials which obey Ohm's law (have constant resistance) are called ohmic conductors. For some other components the resistance does not remain constant (as you will see in 4.10) and their behaviour is classed as 'non-ohmic'.

Resistor components

In circuits a resistor is sometimes used to limit the maximum size of the current. This prevents other components from being damaged by large currents. The resistors are usually small devices placed in series with the other components.

WORKED EXAMPLE 2

The maximum current through a diode needs to be restricted to 0.2 A, when it is operated by a battery supplying a potential difference of 6.0 V. What resistor should be placed in series with the diode to ensure that the current can never be greater than 0.2 A?

$$R = \frac{V}{I} = \frac{6.0\,V}{0.2\,A} = 30\,\Omega$$

ACTIVITY

Build a simple circuit using a variable resistor so that the brightness of a bulb can be adjusted.

Variable resistors

Variable resistors can also be used to adjust the current in a branch of the circuit (Figure 4.9.2). The resistance of the variable resistor can be altered by turning a dial or moving a sliding contact. In laboratories variable resistors are often called rheostats.

Other resistors

A **light dependent resistor (LDR)** has a resistance which varies with the light level it is exposed to. LDRs have low resistance in bright light and very high resistance in low light. They can be used to build light sensors and switch on lighting systems automatically when it gets dark.

Temperature sensitive resistors are called **thermistors** and their resistance changes depending on the temperature. They can be used to control heating or cooling systems.

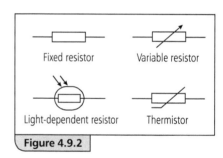

Fixed resistor   Variable resistor

Light-dependent resistor   Thermistor

Figure 4.9.2

KEY POINTS

1 The resistance of a component is defined by the equation $R = \dfrac{V}{I}$

2 Ohmic conductors have a fixed resistance while the resistance of non-ohmic conductors changes due to factors like light or temperature.

SUMMARY QUESTIONS

1 What current will there be in a 12 V bulb with a resistance of 1.5 Ω?

2 Explain how a variable resistor can be used to adjust the brightness of a bulb using the ideas of potential difference, resistance and current.

Investigating current and potential difference characteristics

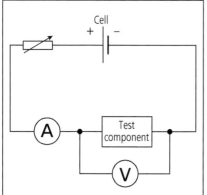

Figure 4.10.1 Finding the current–voltage characteristics of a component

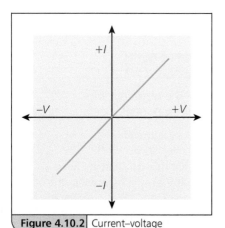

Figure 4.10.2 Current–voltage characteristic of an ohmic conductor

Investigating the resistance of components

To investigate the behaviour of different components we measure the current in the component when different voltages are applied to it. For this investigation the circuit shown in Figure 4.10.1 is used. The variable resistor is used to control the current in the wire.

Once the data is collected a current–voltage (or I–V) graph can be drawn and this reveals the characteristic of the resistance. The shape of the graph is referred to as the I–V characteristic of the component.

Metal wires

As shown in 4.9 a metal wire is an ohmic conductor. We can see evidence for this in the graph (Figure 4.10.2). A straight line is produced demonstrating that $I \propto V$. We can find the resistance of the wire by finding the gradient of this graph:

$$\text{gradient} = \frac{\Delta y}{\Delta x} = \frac{I}{V} \therefore R = \frac{1}{\text{gradient}}$$

The graph also shows that the direction of the current is not relevant to the resistance. This is as we would expect because the electrons can travel just as freely in either direction.

Filament lamps

Filament lamps are simply very thin metal wires kept inside an inert gas. When there is a small current in the filament its temperature does not increase significantly and so the resistance of the filament is constant just as for an ohmic conductor.

When the current increases sufficiently it will cause the wire to heat up, increasing the resistance of the wire as it is more difficult for the electrons to travel through a hot wire. This causes the characteristic line to curve below that for an ohmic conductor (Figure 4.10.3). The relationship $I \propto V$ no longer holds, as a progressively larger increase in V is required to increase the current.

The characteristic for a filament lamp is symmetrical.

Semiconductor diodes

The conduction mechanism in semiconductor diodes is very different from that in metals and is beyond the scope of this course. The I–V characteristic graph, as shown in Figure 4.10.4, has an unusual shape and the currents involved are usually very small so a microammeter is recommended for the investigation.

When a negative voltage is applied the diode has a very large resistance and therefore there is a very small current, a few microamps. The diode is said to be 'reverse biased'.

In the forward bias direction the diode has an even higher resistance with almost no current at all for voltages up to 0.7 V. Beyond this voltage the diode becomes a much better conductor allowing larger currents through.

Ionic solutions

To investigate the *I–V* characteristics of ionic solutions two electrodes need to be placed into the solution a fixed distance apart.

The resulting graph shows that the ionic solution behaves as an ohmic conductor. However, the resistance is large when compared to metal wires and it depends on the concentration of the solution. Instead of electrons there are two different charge carriers, for example, copper ions (Cu^{2+}) moving to the cathode and sulfate ions (SO_4^{2-}) moving to the anode.

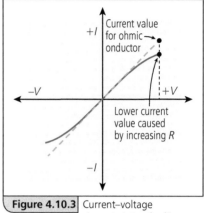

Figure 4.10.3 Current–voltage characteristic of a filament lamp

ACTIVITY

Use the method described to investigate the characteristics of an ionic solution over an extended period of time. How does the resistance of the solution change?

KEY POINTS

1 Ohmic conductors (wires and ionic solutions) have constant resistances.

2 The resistance of filament lamps increases at high currents as the temperature of the wire increases.

3 Semiconductor diodes have very high resistance below a threshold voltage and low resistance beyond it.

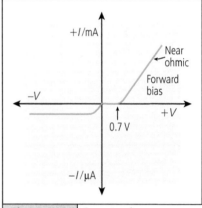

Figure 4.10.4 Current–voltage characteristic of a semiconductor diode

SUMMARY QUESTION

1 A class of students investigated a range of components collecting the data shown in Table 4.10.1. Plot graphs of the current and voltage characteristics and identify the component.

Table 4.10.1

Component A	Voltage /V	−5	−4	−3	−2	−1	0	1	2	3	4	5
	Current /A	−0.8	−0.76	−0.69	−0.48	−0.24	0	0.24	0.48	0.69	0.76	0.8
Component B	Voltage /V	−1	−0.8	−0.6	−0.4	−0.2	0	0.2	0.4	0.6	0.8	1
	Current /mA	−0.01	−0.01	−0.01	−0.01	−0.01	0	0	0	0.2	2.1	4.2

At the end of this topic you should be able to:

• find the resistance of resistors in series and parallel

• find the power output of resistor combinations.

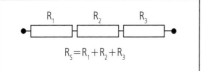

$$R_s = R_1 + R_2 + R_3$$

Figure 4.11.1 Resistors in series

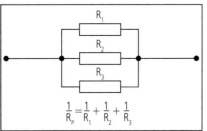

$$\frac{1}{R_P} = \frac{1}{R_1} + \frac{1}{R_2} + \frac{1}{R_3}$$

Figure 4.11.2 Resistors in parallel

Most circuits contain a range of components usually including groups of resistive components in series and parallel. We can combine the resistances to fully analyse the circuit.

Resistor combinations

There is often more than one source of resistance in a circuit and we need to find the total resistance of combinations.

Resistors in series

The total resistance of components in series is simply the sum of their respective resistances. This is exactly as you would expect. If you connect a wire with $5\,\Omega$ resistance to a wire with $6\,\Omega$ resistance you would expect the complete wire to have a resistance of $11\,\Omega$.

More formally this is written as:

$$R_s = R_1 + R_2 + R_3 + \dots$$

Resistors in parallel

Finding the total resistance of resistors in parallel is a little more complicated. Using the fact that the resistors all have the same voltage acting across them, this equation can be derived:

$$\frac{1}{R_P} = \frac{1}{R_1} + \frac{1}{R_2} + \frac{1}{R_3} + \dots$$

Power and resistance

To find the power output of a combination of resistors we could find the power output of the individual resistors and then use the electrical power equation. However, it is usually much easier to find the equivalent resistance and the current and use these two values to find the power output.

WORKED EXAMPLE 1

The heating element of a car rear window contains eight metallic strips each with a resistance of $120\,\Omega$. The heater operates using the car's 12 V battery. The strips are connected in parallel.

a What is the total resistance of the rear window heater?

$$\frac{1}{R_P} = \frac{1}{120} + \frac{1}{120} + \frac{1}{120} + \frac{1}{120} + \frac{1}{120} + \frac{1}{120} + \frac{1}{120} + \frac{1}{120}$$

$$R_P = \frac{120}{8} = 15\,\Omega$$

b What is the power of the heater?

Find the current through the heating element using the total resistance:

$$I = \frac{V}{R} = \frac{12\,V}{15\,\Omega} = 0.8\,A$$

Finally find the power of the heater:

$$P = IV = 0.8\,A \times 12\,V = 9.6\,W$$

Analysing circuits

Using the resistance equations we can analyse complex circuits. This worked example will lead you through one of these analyses.

WORKED EXAMPLE 2

Analyse this circuit, shown in Figure 4.11.3, to find the currents I_1 and the potential differences V_1 and V_2.

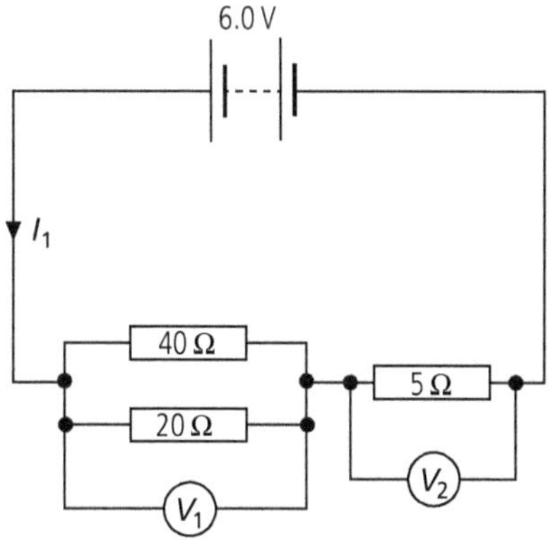

First find the total resistance of the circuit. This means finding the resistance of the parallel section (R_p).

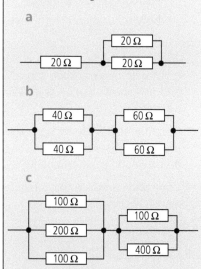

$$\frac{1}{R_p} = \frac{1}{40} + \frac{1}{20} = \frac{3}{40}$$

$$R_p = \frac{40}{3} = 13.3\,\Omega$$

Figure 4.11.3

The total resistance (R_T) of the circuit is given by:

$$R_T = R_p + 5\,\Omega = 18.3\,\Omega$$

Now find I_1, the total current from the battery, using the battery voltage and the total resistance:

$$I_1 = \frac{V}{R_T} = \frac{6\,V}{18.3\,\Omega} = 0.33\,A$$

We can find V_2 because we know the current through the resistor and its resistance:

$$V_2 = I_1 R = 0.33\,A \times 5\,\Omega = 1.65\,V$$

Finally we know that the total voltage drop around the circuit must be 6.0 V and so the voltage V_1 can be found:

$$V_1 = 6.0\,V - 1.65\,V = 4.35\,V$$

We could continue to find the current through each of the parallel resistors using their resistances and the voltage across them.

SUMMARY QUESTIONS

1 Find the resistance of the three resistor arrangements shown in Figure 4.11.4.

a

b

c

Figure 4.11.4

2 Find the current in each of the two parallel resistors in Worked example 2.

KEY POINTS

1 The resistance of components in series is the sum of the individual resistances
$$R_s = R_1 + R_2 + \ldots$$

2 The resistance of components in parallel is given by the equation
$$\frac{1}{R_p} = \frac{1}{R_1} + \frac{1}{R_2} + \ldots$$

3 The power output of a combination of resistors is the sum of the power outputs of the individual resistors.

SECTION 4: Practice exam questions 1

1 A plastic rod is rubbed with a dry cloth until they both become charged. The rod is found to have a positive charge.

   a   What is the charge on the cloth?

   b   Describe, in terms of particle movement, how the rod and cloth have become charged.

2 Sometimes, when clothing is taken out of a tumble drier, a crackling sound can be heard and tiny sparks can be seen. Why does this happen?

3 Describe how a photocopier uses the principles of static electricity to reproduce accurate copies of an image.

4 Copy and complete this table showing electrical circuit symbols.

Component	Symbol	Component	Symbol
lamp		semiconductor diode	
	⎯⊏◯⊐⎯		⎯(A)⎯
battery			⎯▱⎯

5 The dome of a Van de Graaff generator is charged until it holds a total charge of 0.01 C. The dome is then discharged by connecting it to earth with a grounding wire.

   a   What type of particles travel in the wire during the discharge?

   b   What is the average current in the wire during the discharge if the process takes 0.02 second?

6 A 6.0 V battery is connected to a resistor of resistance 5 Ω.

   a   How much charge passes though the resistor in one minute?

   b   What is the power output of the resistor?

7 What are the differences between a primary cell and a secondary cell?

8 Why must a voltmeter have very high resistance while an ammeter must have very low resistance?

9 A filament lamp operates with a potential difference of 12.0 V across its terminals. The lamp transforms 4000 J of electrical energy into heat and light energy in one minute.

   a   What is the power rating of the lamp?

   b   What is the current in the lamp?

   c   What is the resistance of the lamp?

10 A student investigates the current–voltage characteristics of a semiconductor diode. The data gathered are shown in the table.

Voltage/V	−0.3	−0.2	−0.1	0	0.1	0.2	0.3	0.4	0.5	0.6	0.7
Current/mA	0	0	0	0	0	0	0	0.01	0.1	0.2	0.3

a Draw a diagram of a circuit suitable for this investigation.

b Plot a graph of the results.

c Describe the results shown in the graph.

11 Magnesium chloride dissolves in water to form a solution containing magnesium (Mg^{2+}) and chloride (Cl^-) ions.

a Describe the process which allows this solution to conduct.

b What is meant by an ohmic conductor?

c Is the solution an ohmic conductor?

12 Calculate the resistance of these three resistor combinations:

a

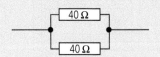

b

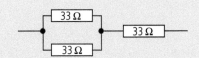

c

13 Three resistors each of resistance $66\,\Omega$ can be connected to a 2.0 V cell in a variety of ways.

a Draw a circuit diagram showing the arrangement of the resistors when they form a circuit with the highest resistance.

b Calculate the current through one of the resistors.

c Calculate the total power of the resistor combination.

d Repeat a, b and c for the configuration with the lowest resistance.

14 Determine the readings on the four ammeters and two voltmeters in this circuit.

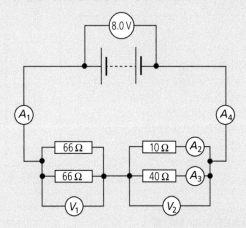

Direct current and alternating current

ACTIVITY

In the 19th century, Nikola Tesla and Thomas Edison disagreed about whether to use direct or alternating current for mains supplies. Research the background to this 'war of the currents' and find out why alternating current was eventually selected.

WORKED EXAMPLE

What is the frequency of the a.c. supply shown in Figure 4.12.1?

$$f = \frac{1}{T} = \frac{1}{0.04\,s} = 25\,Hz$$

Direct current

Cells and batteries produce direct current (d.c.). This is a current that travels only in one direction (from positive to negative) and has a fixed magnitude.

Alternating current

Alternating current (a.c.) is used in mains supplies. The direction of the current reverses rapidly, many times each second, and the magnitude varies.

Alternating current is caused by an alternating voltage source such as a generator. These will be discussed in 4.23. The magnitude of the voltage varies sinusoidally from a positive peak value to a negative peak value.

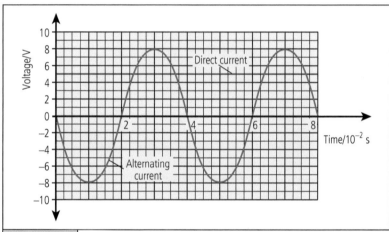

Figure 4.12.1 Comparing alternating current to direct current

The alternating voltage shown in Figure 4.12.1 is for a low voltage a.c. power supply. From the diagram you can measure the maximum voltage and the period of one complete oscillation.

- The peak voltage is the highest voltage reached over the cycle. In the example this is ±8.0 V.
- The period (T) of the alternating current is the time taken for one complete cycle. In the example this is 0.04 s.

Finding the frequency

The frequency of the a.c. source is the number of complete cycles per second. This is related to the period by:

$$\text{frequency} = \frac{1}{\text{period}} \text{ or } f = \frac{1}{T}$$

The unit of frequency is s^{-1} or hertz (Hz).

Exploring waveforms

In 3.12 you saw that an oscilloscope could be used to investigate sound waves and their frequency. The sound energy was converted to an electrical signal which could then be displayed on the oscilloscope screen. The oscilloscope can also be used to measure the properties of alternating currents.

The two most important controls used on the oscilloscope are the volts per division and the time base:

- The volts per division (volts/div) control allows you to measure the peak-to-peak voltage of an alternating source. If the wave occupies six vertical boxes when the volts per division is set to 0.5 V/div then the peak-to-peak voltage is 3.0 V.
- The time base determines the time represented by a horizontal division. For example, if one complete wave occupies four divisions when the time base is set to 0.2 s/div, the period is 0.8 s.

To analyse an alternating source follow this procedure:

- Connect the source to the a.c. input terminals of the oscilloscope.
- Adjust the vertical volts per division until the peak and trough of the waveform can clearly be seen on the screen.
- Adjust the time base so that at least one full wave can be seen and the period can be measured.
- Measure and note the peak or peak-to-peak voltage.
- Measure the period of the source and calculate the frequency.

The oscilloscope can also be used to measure the voltage of a direct current source, which would be displayed as a horizontal line.

Digital oscilloscopes

Cathode-ray oscilloscopes are expensive and can be difficult to operate. Most waveform analysis is now carried out using digital oscilloscopes which can be connected directly to a computer.

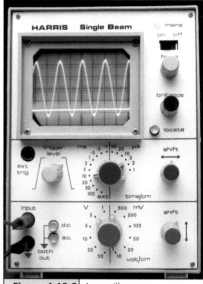

Figure 4.12.2 An oscilloscope

KEY POINTS

1 Direct current travels in only one direction.

2 Alternating current switches direction and magnitude.

3 Oscilloscopes can be used to investigate the properties of a.c. signals.

SUMMARY QUESTIONS

1 Find the peak voltage, period and frequency of the a.c. source shown in Figure 4.12.3.

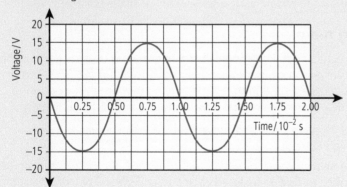

Figure 4.12.3

2 Sketch appropriate graphs of the following a.c. waveforms:

a an a.c. source with a peak voltage of 110 V and a frequency of 50 Hz

b an a.c. source with a peak voltage of 20 mV and a frequency of 2 kHz.

Mains electricity in the Caribbean

Table 4.13.1 Mains supply in some Caribbean islands

Island	Voltage /V	Frequency /Hz
Barbados	115	50
Cuba	110	60
Jamaica	110 or 220	50
St Kitts and Nevis	110 or 230	60
St Martin	120 or 230	50
Trinidad and Tobago	115	50

Mains supply voltage and frequency

Mains electricity is supplied as alternating current. The mains supply voltage and frequency vary from island to island in the Caribbean for historical reasons (Figure 4.13.1).

As the voltage is varying continuously over a cycle the effective average voltage is used to describe the mains supply. This is called the root mean square (r.m.s.) voltage as shown in Table 4.13.1.

Higher voltage supplies can provide the same power using smaller currents allowing thinner wires to be used. However, higher voltages are more dangerous.

Mains supplies are often slightly 'noisy'. The smooth curves have slight spikes as the supply picks up interference from other electrical devices. Some equipment can be sensitive to this noise.

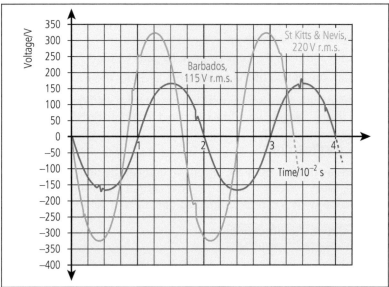

Figure 4.13.1 Mains supply varies between islands in the Caribbean

Ring mains

An electrical configuration called a ring main is used as the basis for the connection of domestic power sockets (Figure 4.13.2). Two or three wires are used in the ring main and they are thick enough to provide a current to several devices at once without overheating.

- The live wire (coloured brown) provides the power and operates at a high voltage.
- The neutral wire (coloured blue) completes the circuit, allowing the current to flow in a closed circuit.
- Many devices are also connected to an earth wire (coloured green and yellow).

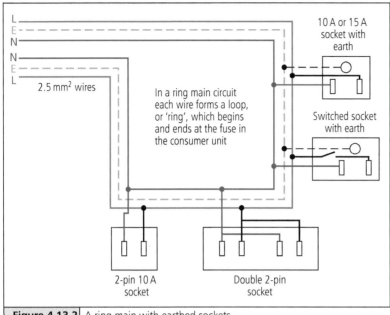

Figure 4.13.2 A ring main with earthed sockets

Figure 4.13.3 Make sure that you match your plugs and sockets correctly.

Plugs and sockets

Some electrical devices, such as ovens, are wired directly into the mains supply, but most are connected by a plug so that they can be disconnected easily and moved. In the Caribbean there are two main plugs and sockets used and these are referred to as type A and type B (Figure 4.13.3).

- Type A plugs have only two pins which connect to the live and neutral wires.
- Type B plugs have three pins. The additional pin is connected to the earth wire.

The different plugs are matched by different sockets and a type A plug should not be inserted into a type B socket.

Connecting to the wrong supply

As there are several different mains voltages in use it is possible to accidently connect a device to the wrong supply.

- Connecting a 110 V device to a 220 V supply will cause the device to take a large current. This will most likely melt the wires in the device causing severe damage.
- Connecting a 220 V device to a 110 V supply will result in the device receiving too low a current. The device will not operate correctly or won't work at all.
- Connecting a device designed to operate with a 50 Hz supply to a 60 Hz supply, or the reverse, is also likely to damage the device as its electrical components will not function correctly.

SUMMARY QUESTIONS

1 Why shouldn't you change the plug on an electrical device from a type B to a type A?

2 What advantages does a ring main provide?

KEY POINTS

1 Mains electricity can be supplied at different voltages and at 50 Hz or 60 Hz.

2 Always connect a device to the correct type of supply using the correct kind of plug.

Mains electricity is dangerous because the voltages are large enough to force a current through your body. The currents can also be large enough to start electrical fires if there is a fault in the device. Because of this, safety features need to be incorporated to protect the device and the user.

Fuses

If there is a fault in an electrical device where the live wire short circuits and connects to the neutral wire then the resistance of the device will be small and a large current will flow. This large current would heat the wires in the device and could cause a fire. A fuse prevents this by being the 'weakest' point in the circuit and melting before any other part. The fuse consists of a thin piece of wire, often held inside a glass or ceramic tube.

Fuses need to be selected so that they will not melt in normal operation but only if there is an excess current.

Figure 4.14.1 Fuses have specific current ratings, such as 1 A, 3 A, 5 A, 13 A.

WORKED EXAMPLE

An air-conditioning unit is designed to operate at 220 V with a power rating of 1.0 kW. What size fuse should be used with this unit?

First find the normal operating current of the unit:

$$P = IV \text{ so } I = \frac{P}{V} = \frac{1000\,\text{W}}{220\text{V}} = 4.55\,\text{A}$$

Then select a fuse that is slightly larger than the normal operating current. In this case, a 5 A fuse is appropriate.

It should be noted that fuses alone do not protect the operator of a device. A current of only a few milliamps is enough to kill a human and this small increase in current would not cause a fuse to melt.

Circuit breakers

Circuit breakers operate in a similar manner to fuses but they rely on the excess current opening a magnetic switch and cutting off the circuit. This process is faster and more sensitive than a fuse. Circuit breakers also have the advantage of being able to be reset without having to replace the part (Figure 4.14.2).

A residual current circuit breaker (RCCB) is an even more sensitive device. It compares the current in the live wire and the neutral wire which should be exactly the same. If there is even a very small current leak (through the user of a device) then the circuit breaker opens and the current is cut off.

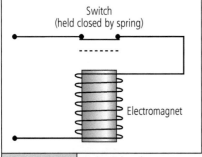

Figure 4.14.2 A circuit breaker uses an electromagnet to break the circuit when the current is too large.

The earth wire

An electrical device becomes very dangerous to the user if its case becomes live (is connected to the live wire). This can happen if the live wire breaks inside the device.

Some devices automatically protect the user because they are made from insulating materials such as plastic. Even if the live wire becomes loose it cannot electrocute the user. Devices with this safety feature are double insulated and should carry the symbol shown in Figure 4.14.3.

If the case is metal and is in contact with the live wire, a user can receive a fatal electric shock on touching it. A fuse alone would not prevent this, as no additional current would flow until the user touches the device.

To prevent these accidents the case can be connected to an additional wire: the earth wire. This wire provides a low resistance route for the current to pass to earth and so the current will not pass through the user. Also, the large current will cause the fuse to melt or circuit breaker to trip, breaking the circuit (Figure 4.14.4).

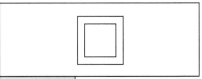

Figure 4.14.3 This symbol indicates that an appliance is double insulated.

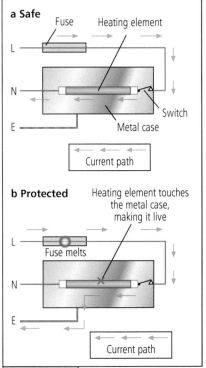

Figure 4.14.4 The earth wire protects the user from electrocution.

ACTIVITY

Inspect the plugs and electrical information on a range of electrical devices to find out their power rating, operating voltage and the type of mains supply they require. Work out which type of fuses the devices need. Don't try to carry out any rewiring yourself without expert supervision!

SUMMARY QUESTIONS

1 Why should you use the correct fuse in an electrical device?

2 What should you do if the circuit breaker in your house keeps tripping?

3 What fuses do the devices in Table 4.14.1 require?

Table 4.14.1

Device	Power rating/W	Mains voltage/V
washing machine	800	110
tumble drier	1200	230
electric lamp	80	120

KEY POINTS

1 Fuses and circuit breakers break circuits if the current in the live wire becomes too large due to a fault.

2 The earth wire protects the user from electrocution in case of an electrical fault.

Conversion of a.c. to d.c.

LEARNING OUTCOMES

At the end of this topic you should be able to:

- explain why a.c. sources sometimes need to be converted to d.c.
- draw a circuit diagram showing how a.c. can be converted to d.c.

The need for direct current

It is much easier to increase the voltage of alternating current so that electrical energy can be transmitted efficiently over long distances. Alternating current is also much easier to produce from the generators in power stations.

For many devices an alternating current will provide the energy they need to work properly. However, some devices, including computers, require direct current at very steady voltage levels to operate correctly.

Rectification

The process of converting an alternating current to a direct current is called **rectification**. Rectification relies on the properties of diodes as shown in 4.10. A diode will only allow current in one direction and so if one is connected to an alternating supply there will only be a current half of the time.

Half-wave rectification

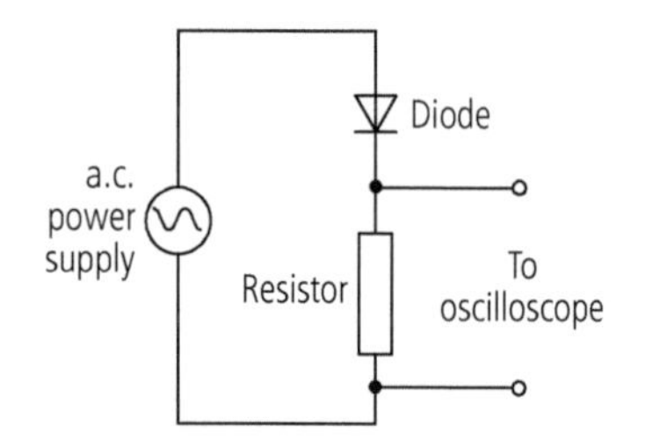

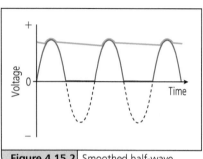

Figure 4.15.1 Simple half-wave rectification

Figure 4.15.1 shows a circuit which can be used to produce direct current from an alternating supply. The diode only allows a current in one direction and so the output current is direct. The load resistor represents the resistance of the device the power supply is connected to.

If we use an oscilloscope to measure the voltage across the load, we can see what happens in the circuit.

The current provided by half-wave rectification is direct in the sense that it is only in one direction. However the voltage is still varying from maximum to a zero value and for periods of time there is no current at all. This is very inefficient and does not provide the type of current required by electronic devices.

Improving rectification

Figure 4.15.2 Smoothed half-wave rectification

One way to improve the profile of the current is to use a capacitor (Figure 4.15.2). A capacitor is a simple device which stores charge for a short period of time. Adding it on to the simple half-wave rectifier produces a smoothed d.c. output as shown by the blue line.

When the voltage is rising and there is a current in the load some charge will be stored on the capacitor.

When the voltage is decreasing there would normally be a decreasing current in the load. However the capacitor will release charge from its plates and provide a current. This current will decrease more slowly than the current provided by the a.c. source.

During the sections where there is no voltage the capacitor will continue to discharge and provide a current.

If the frequency of the source were low, the capacitor would discharge almost completely. At high frequency, the capacitor only has to discharge slightly and the current provided is therefore fairly constant.

Full-wave rectification

In half-wave rectification you can see that only half of the alternating current is actually producing a useful direct current. A more complicated circuit involving four diodes can be used to produce a positive potential difference even when the alternating supply is producing a negative voltage. This gives full-wave rectification which supplies a much steadier d.c. supply (Figure 4.15.3).

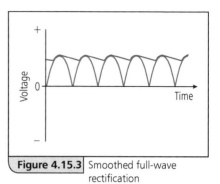

Figure 4.15.3 Smoothed full-wave rectification

SUMMARY QUESTIONS

1 Sketch the oscilloscope trace you would expect to see when the a.c. source in Figure 4.15.4 is:

  a half-wave rectified

  b full-wave rectified.

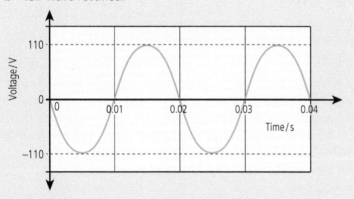

Figure 4.15.4

2 Redraw the traces as they would appear if the output had been smoothed by a capacitor.

EXAM TIP

Although you do not have to know how capacitors work or full-wave rectification operates, remember that a.c. can be transformed into a steady and continuous d.c. supply fairly easily.

KEY POINTS

1 Alternating current can provide electrical energy for most, but not all, electrical devices.

2 Rectification is used to convert a.c. into d.c.

3 Rectification relies on the properties of diodes.

Binary

Computer systems operate using digital information represented as a binary system. The binary system only contains two digits represented by 0 and 1 unlike our decimal system which contain ten digits. Numbers are represented as a string of digits just as in any other number system but only 1s and 0s are used. Table 4.16.1 shows some example decimal numbers represented as four binary digits.

Binary numbers can be represented physically in a number of ways. In electronics they are represented as two voltage levels:

• **high** which represents the digit 1 and is called logic 1

• **low** which represents the digit 0 and is called logic 0.

The exact voltage levels vary from system to system depending on what type of semiconductor is being used.

Table 4.16.1 Examples of decimal numbers represented as four binary digits

Decimal	Binary	Decimal	Binary
0	0000	6	0110
1	0001	7	0111
2	0010	8	1000
3	0011	9	1001
4	0100	10	1010
5	0101	11	1011

Logic gates

A logic gate is an electronic component which processes a binary input and produces a binary output based on a set of rules.

Examples:

• A NOT gate produces an output which is **not** the same as the input. This means that when there is a logic 0 input there is a logic 1 output but when there is a logic 1 input there is a logic 0 output. As the output is always the opposite of the input these gates are sometimes called inverters.

• An OR gate produces a logic 1 output if one **or** other of its inputs is logic 1.

• An AND gate produces a logic 1 output if its first input **and** its second input are both logic 1.

The complete list of the five logic gates you are required to know is shown in Figure 4.16.1.

Truth tables

Truth tables show the output states of a logic gate for all of the possible inputs to the gate. These allow us to easily determine what the output would be when the gates are connected to input sources. When in doubt about what a logic gates does, you should always consult the truth table. For example the truth table shows that an OR gate will still produce a logic 1 output even if both of the inputs are logic 1.

Gate	Symbol	Function (high voltage = 1, low voltage = 0)	Truth table INPUTS A B	OUTPUT
OR	A—⊐ OUTPUT B—	OUTPUT = 1 if A OR B = 1	0 0 0 1 1 0 1 1	0 1 1 1
AND	A—⊐ OUTPUT B—	OUTPUT = 1 if A AND B = 1	0 0 0 1 1 0 1 1	0 0 0 1
NOR	A—⊐o OUTPUT B—	OUTPUT = 0 if A OR B = 1	0 0 0 1 1 0 1 1	1 0 0 0
NAND	A—⊐o OUTPUT B—	OUTPUT = 0 if A AND B = 1	0 0 0 1 1 0 1 1	1 1 1 0
NOT	▷o OUTPUT INPUT	OUTPUT = 1 if INPUT = 0 OUTPUT = 0 if INPUT = 1	0 1	1 0

Figure 4.16.1 Logic gates and their truth tables

Combining logic gates

Logic gates have limited use individually but when they are combined together they can be used to process information and cause actions to be taken.

To work out the output for any collection of gates draw up a truth table representing all of the possible input combinations. For each set of inputs in turn work your way through the logic combinations and find the output. Keep on going until you have found the outputs for all of the possible input combinations.

SUMMARY QUESTIONS

1 Draw up a truth table for the logic gate systems shown in Figures 4.16.3 and 4.16.4.

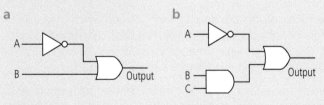

a

A —▷o—⊐ B — Output

b

A —▷o—⊐ B —⊐ Output C —

Figure 4.16.3   **Figure 4.16.4**

2 Design a logic gate system to match the following:

   a Three inputs A, B and C which produce an output of 1 when any one of the inputs is 1.

   b Three inputs D, E and F which produce an output of 1 when all of the inputs are 0.

WORKED EXAMPLE

What are the input conditions required for the logic gate system shown in Figure 4.16.2 to produce an output of 0?

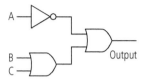

A —▷o—
B —⊐
C —   Output

Figure 4.16.2

Draw up the truth table for the logic gate system working in a sensible order and making sure all of the possible input combinations are covered (Table 4.16.1).

Table 4.16.1

Input A	Input B	Input C	Output
0	0	0	1
1	0	0	0
0	1	0	1
1	1	0	1
0	0	1	1
1	0	1	1
0	1	1	1
1	1	1	1

From the truth table we can see that the output of the logic gate system is logic 0 only when A is 1, B is 0 and C is 0.

KEY POINTS

1 Binary digits can be represented by high and low voltage levels.

2 Logic gates process binary inputs and produce binary outputs.

3 Simple logic gates can be combined to provide additional processing.

Figure 4.17.1 A data logging device connected to a computer

Logic gates are often combined with digital sensors which detect environmental conditions and produce logical signals. These signals are then processed through a sequence of logic gates and output devices are triggered. The logic gates are designed so that the output device activates only when the required environmental input conditions are met.

| Sensors produce logic level outputs | → | Logic gates process signals | → | Output devices are triggered by results of processing |

Sensors

The sensors connected to the logic system can be represented by symbols as shown in Table 4.17.1. The table also shows the outputs produced by these sensors in different environmental conditions.

Table 4.17.1

Sensor	Symbol	Produces logic 0 when	Produces logic 1 when
switch	S ⊗	open	closed
temperature	T ⊗	temperature is low	temperature is high
light	L ⊗	in darkness	in light
pressure	P ⊗	not under pressure	under pressure

In reality these sensors are devices such as mechanical switches, thermistors or light dependent resistors (LDRs) connected to voltage supplies. The point at which the sensor switches from a logical output of 0 to a logical output of 1 can be finely tuned.

• A temperature sensor could be designed to switch from 0 to 1 when the temperature rises above 40 °C.

• A pressure sensor can switch output from 0 to 1 when a large force is applied to it such as somebody stepping on a mat.

Many other sensors are possible such as tilt switches, pH sensors, infra-red sensors, sound level sensors and even radioactivity sensors.

An alarm signal may need to be triggered only when it is dark and a door is opened. How could this system be implemented?

The alarm must be triggered when it is dark **and** a door is opened. This indicates that an AND gate will be required and this will trigger the alarm when both of its inputs are logic 1.

To check if the door is open, a mechanical switch is needed. This would produce a logic 0 if the door and thus the switch were open so this input needs to be inverted using a NOT gate before the input goes into the AND gate.

To check if it is dark, a light sensor is needed. This produces a logic zero in the dark so this input needs to be inverted with a NOT gate too.

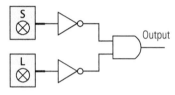

Figure 4.17.2

This gives the logic circuit shown in Figure 4.17.2. The output would be logic 1 only when the door is opened and it is dark. This could be connected to an alarm system or be used to switch on a light.

Complete a survey of the devices you use every day that rely on electronics and write a short report about how life would be different without this technology.

Computers

Digital computers contain millions of logic gates in integrated circuits. They process binary operations at very high speeds, controlled by a 'clock' which stops the signals getting mixed up. The developments in electronics and microelectronics have had a massive impact on society over the past fifty years. For example, computer systems and mobile phones around the world are linked together through the internet providing almost instant access to information for billions of people.

1 A bank vault needs to have an alarm system which activates when a sound is heard or somebody steps on the floor of the vault. This should only happen when the alarm has been primed by a switch. Design a logic system to accomplish this task.

2 Design a logic circuit which could activate an alarm if it is raining at night.

SECTION 4: Practice exam questions 2

1 Describe the differences between alternating current and direct current.

2 An oscilloscope is used to analyse an a.c. power supply producing the trace shown. The time base has been set to 0.05 s per division and the volts/div has been set to 2 V/div.

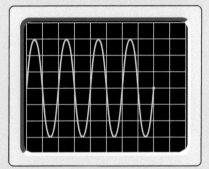

   a What is the peak voltage of the power supply?

   b What is the period of the power supply?

   c What is the frequency of the a.c. source?

3 Explain why a ring main circuit is used for wall sockets in houses.

4 Select the appropriate fuse for each of the following devices from the range 1 A, 3 A, 5 A and 12 A.

Device	Operating voltage/V	Power
filament lamp	110	80 W
portable air-conditioning unit	110	500 W
kettle	220	2 kW
electric drill	220	300 W
electric grill	110	1.5 kW

5 How does an earth wire protect the user of a faulty electrical device?

6 Explain why the core of an electrical cable is made from copper but the outer sheathing is made from flexible plastic.

7 What is the function of a fuse and how does it operate?

8 What are the advantages of a circuit breaker when compared to a fuse?

9 Draw a circuit diagram showing how an alternating current can be half-wave rectified to produce a direct current. How can this rectification system be improved?

10 Sketch voltage–time graphs showing:

   a a d.c. source of voltage 10 V

   b an a.c. source with a period of 0.2 seconds and peak voltage of 8 V

   c a half-wave rectified a.c source with a period of 0.2 seconds and peak voltage of 8 V

   d a half-wave rectified a.c source with a period of 0.2 seconds and peak voltage of 8 V with the output smoothed using a large capacitor.

11 Copy and complete this table of logic gates describing their functions.

Logic gate	Symbol	Description
		Inverts the input symbol (changes a logic 0 to logic 1 and vice versa)
AND		Produces an output of logic 1 when input A and input B are both logic 1
	(symbol)	
NAND	(symbol)	
NOR		Produces a logic 1 output when both inputs are logic 0

12 Copy and complete this truth table for all of the possible inputs for this arrangement of logic gates.

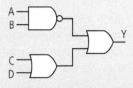

Input A	Input B	Input C	Input D	Output Y
0	0	0	0	
1	0	0	0	
0	1	0	0	
1	1	0	0	
0	0	1	0	
1	0	1	0	
0	1	1	0	
1	1	1	0	
0	0	0	1	
1	0	0	1	
0	1	0	1	
1	1	0	1	
0	0	1	1	
1	0	1	1	
0	1	1	1	
1	1	1	1	

13 How can an AND gate be constructed from a NOR gate and two NOT gates?

14 Design the logic circuit for an alarm which only sounds during daylight and when it is raining.

Permanent magnets

Figure 4.18.1 The poles of magnets are often coloured: red for north and blue for south.

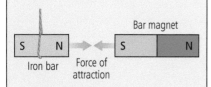

Figure 4.18.2 Testing the forces between magnets

Magnetic materials experience forces when placed near a **magnet**. Magnets themselves are made from these same magnetic materials. Only a few materials are magnetic. These include iron, nickel, cobalt and magnadur. Alloys, such as steel, that contain these metals may also be magnetic. Magnets will not attract non-magnetic materials, even metals (unless there is a current in them as we will see later).

All magnets have two poles which are referred to as the north (or north seeking) and south (or south seeking) poles. In a simple bar magnet these poles are at either end but magnets can be made in several shapes and so the poles may be found in other locations.

Magnetic interactions

The interactions between magnets can be summarised by these rules:

- Opposite poles attract each other: south poles attract north poles.
- Like poles repel each other: south poles repel south poles, and north poles repel north poles.
- The closer the magnets are to each other, the stronger the force between the magnets.

Magnetic materials placed near either pole of a magnet will be attracted towards it.

Magnetic induction

When an iron nail is placed on the end of a bar magnet it can be used to attract other iron nails. We say that magnetism has been **induced** in the iron nail. The nail is temporarily acting as a magnet but will stop acting this way when it is removed from the permanent magnet.

If we try the same process with a steel nail the nail will act as a magnet but may also retain some of its magnetic properties after it has been removed from the permanent magnet.

- Iron and mumetal are classed as **soft magnetic** materials and are used to make temporary magnets. They are easy to magnetise but do not retain magnetism well.
- Steel is classed as a **hard magnetic** material. It is more difficult to magnetise but it will retain its magnetism for longer. It is used to make permanent magnets. Magnadur magnets are also permanent.

Making magnets

A new permanent magnet can be made from a steel bar by rubbing a permanent magnet along its length as shown in Figure 4.18.3. The permanent magnet must only be moved in one direction.

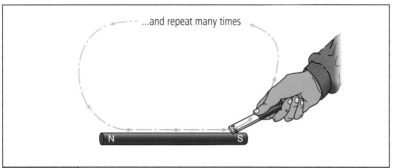

...and repeat many times

N   S

Figure 4.18.3 Making a permanent magnet

ACTIVITY

Make your own magnet using the technique shown in Figure 4.18.3. Can the magnet be made stronger if it is rubbed for a longer time?

Breaking magnets

A magnet will lose some of its strength if it is struck. Repeatedly dropping a permanent magnet onto the floor will weaken its magnetism.

EXAM TIP

Only a few materials are magnetic. Don't make the mistake of thinking all metals are.

SUMMARY QUESTIONS

1 Copy and complete Table 4.18.1 showing the interactions between the poles of two magnets.

Table 4.18.1

North to north	North to south	South to south	South to north

2 Why is steel rather than iron used to make small permanent bar magnets?

KEY POINTS

1 Magnets produce forces which act on other magnets or magnetic materials.

2 Permanent magnets are made from magnetic materials such as steel.

3 Like poles repel and unlike poles attract.

4 The size of the force between magnets decreases with their distance apart.

Magnetic fields

At the end of this topic you should be able to:

- draw and plot the magnetic field around a bar magnet
- describe the magnetic field produced by the Earth
- explain how a compass works.

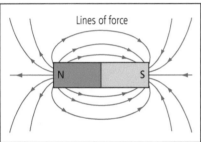

Lines of force

Figure 4.19.1 The magnetic field around a bar magnet

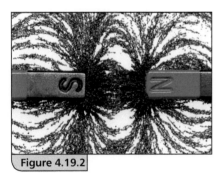

Figure 4.19.2

Magnetic fields

You have already seen that the forces acting between charged objects are produced by electric fields. Similarly, the forces acting between magnets are caused by magnetic fields.

A magnetic field is a region of space in which a magnetic material will experience a force.

The shape of a magnetic field is not as simple as that of an electric field as there are always two poles involved.

The field is represented as a series of lines which show the direction an imaginary north pole would be pushed by the field. This means that the field lines point away from the north pole of the magnet and towards the south pole (Figure 4.19.1).

Finding the shape of a magnetic field

There are two common ways of finding the shape of a magnetic field around magnets.

Iron filings

Iron filings can be sprinkled around the magnet. These filings will align with the field lines and the shape of the field will be seen clearly (Figure 4.19.2). This technique is particularly useful for looking at the shape of the field when more than one magnet is involved.

To prevent the filings sticking to the magnet the magnet can be placed under a piece of paper or wrapped in plastic film.

A plotting compass

A plotting compass can be placed against the north pole of a bar magnet. The needle of the compass will point along the direction of the field line and a dot can be placed where the compass is pointing.

The compass is moved repeatedly until a trail of dots is formed. This will curve back to the south pole of the magnet. The dots can be joined with a curve to form a field line. The whole process is repeated starting at several different points near the poles until the shape of the field is revealed.

The Earth's magnetic field

The Earth produces a magnetic field around itself (Figure 4.19.4). This is due to the rotation of its metallic core. The magnetic field envelops the whole planet as if there were a bar magnet within the Earth. The south pole of this imaginary bar magnet lies near, but not at, the geographic north pole.

The Earth's magnetic field has been used for navigation for thousands of years. Lodestone is a naturally magnetic material and a thin slice of lodestone can be made to float on water. The lodestone will align itself to the Earth's magnetic field.

Magnetised steel pins are used in compasses and follow the same principle but these are suspended inside a case so that they may rotate freely. The 'north seeking' pole will point towards the north pole of the Earth because it is attracted to the magnetic south pole.

The Earth's magnetic field is also useful as it deflects charged particles from the Sun and protects the Earth's surface from potentially harmful effects.

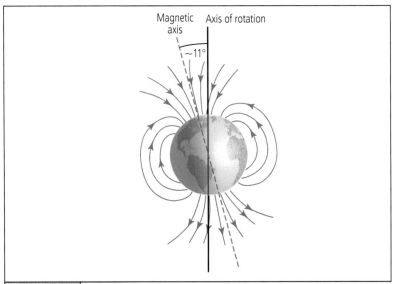

Figure 4.19.4 The Earth's magnetic field

ACTIVITY

Use the techniques described on page 146 to find the shapes of the magnetic fields surrounding two permanent magnets arranged as shown in Figure 4.19.3.

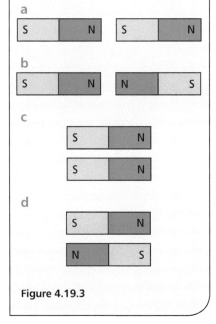

Figure 4.19.3

EXAM TIP

When drawing magnetic field lines always remember that they come out of the north pole and go into the south pole.

The terminology about the Earth's poles can be a bit confusing. Make sure you understand it clearly.

SUMMARY QUESTIONS

1 How can iron filings be used to reveal the shape of magnetic fields?

2 An iron nail is seen to attract a paper clip. Comment on whether this proves that the bar is a magnet.

KEY POINTS

1 Magnets have magnetic fields around them which affect magnetic materials.

2 The shape of the fields can be found with a compass or iron filings.

3 Field lines come out of the north pole and enter the south pole.

4 The Earth has a magnetic field which assists with navigation and protects us from some cosmic rays.

ACTIVITY

Find out about the aurora borealis and aurora australis and what causes these phenomena.

Currents and magnetic fields

The charges moving in a wire produce a magnetic field around the wire. This was first demonstrated by Hans Christian Ørsted when he placed a compass near a wire. The compass would point northwards until there was a current in the wire. This caused the compass to point in a different direction.

Demonstrating the shape of the field

To demonstrate the shape of the magnetic field we can use iron filings or plotting compasses in a similar way to the techniques used with bar magnets.

The current-carrying wire is made to pass perpendicularly through a sheet of horizontal card (Figure 4.20.1). A set of plotting compasses is placed on the card and the current is turned on. The compasses will show that there is a circular field around the wire. Iron filings can also be sprinkled onto the card and these will form a pattern of circles confirming the shape of the field.

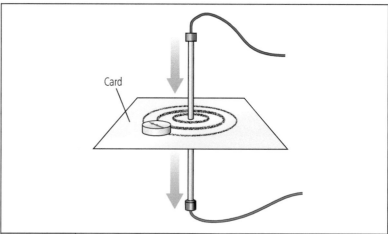

Figure 4.20.1 An updated version of Ørsted's experiment

To determine which way the field lines loop you can use the 'right-hand grip rule' as shown in Figure 4.20.2.

Solenoids

The magnetic field around a single wire is not strong and so coils of wire called solenoids are used. The magnetic field outside the solenoid is similar in shape to that of a bar magnet but there is a field inside the coil too. This internal field is almost uniform. The field lines are all parallel to each other. One end of the coil acts as a north pole and the other acts as a south pole (Figure 4.20.3).

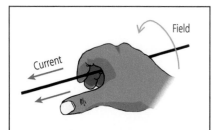

Figure 4.20.2 Using your right hand, imagine curling your fingers around the wire while sticking your thumb out in the direction of the conventional current. The curved direction of your fingers shows you which way the magnetic field loops.

Increasing the strength of the magnetic field

The strength of the field produced by a solenoid is increased by:

- using more loops (turns) of wire
- increasing the current in the wire
- placing an iron core inside the solenoid (this has the effect of concentrating the field lines creating a strong field at the end of the core).

Powerful electromagnets can be produced by using all of these measures.

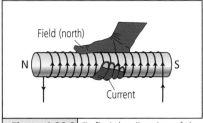

Figure 4.20.3 To find the direction of the field from the direction of the current, we can use our right hand again. This time your fingers follow the direction of the current curving around the coil. Your thumb will point in the direction of the magnetic field (northwards).

ACTIVITY

Build your own electromagnet using a large iron nail, a low-voltage power supply and a length of insulated wire. Wrap the wire around the nail in a tight coil and test the power of your electromagnet. Be careful not to use large currents. You can add a variable resistor to control the current.

Using electromagnets

Electromagnets can be very useful. They can be turned on and off and their strength can be controlled by adjusting the current in them. They are used for a wide range of applications from heavy industry to medical diagnosis.

- Scrap yards use powerful electromagnets to lift up cars and other objects. Turning off the electromagnet allows them to be put down again.
- An **electromagnetic relay** can be used to operate a switch remotely. A small, and safe, current enters the electromagnet and the electromagnet pulls a switch. The switch is actually part of a high current circuit. Examples of these relays can be found in cars where a small current from the ignition circuit is used to turn on a large current to the starter motor.

Electromagnetic fields are also vital in electric motors as you will see in 4.23.

Figure 4.20.4 A very strong electro-magnet

KEY POINTS

1. A current in a wire produces a circular magnetic field in a plane at right angles to the wire.
2. A solenoid is a coil of wire which produces a magnetic field similar to that of a bar magnet.
3. The strength of the magnetic field of a solenoid is increased by using more loops of wire, increasing the current and adding an iron core.

SUMMARY QUESTIONS

1. What advantages do electromagnets have when compared to permanent magnets?
2. Imagine there was a current-carrying wire coming vertically out of this book. Sketch the magnetic field pattern around this imaginary wire. The current is flowing upwards.

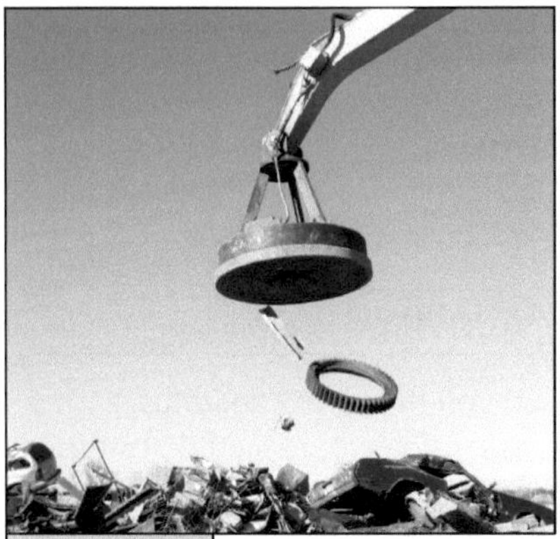

Forces from magnetic fields

When a wire carries a current there will be a magnetic field surrounding the wire. If the wire is placed inside the magnetic field from a permanent magnet then the two magnetic fields will interact with each other. A force will act on the wire and the permanent magnet. This is the **motor effect**.

Demonstrating the motor effect

The motor effect can be demonstrated simply using the apparatus shown in Figure 4.21.1.

• The magnets produce an almost uniform magnetic field between them.

• Two thick wires hold another loose wire, so that a complete circuit is made.

• When the circuit is switched on the current in the loose wire will produce a magnetic field which will interact with the field from the permanent magnets.

• The loose wire will experience a force making it jump to the right.

If the direction of the current or the direction of the magnetic field is reversed then the loose wire will move to the left.

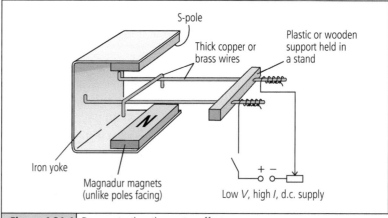

Figure 4.21.1 Demonstrating the motor effect

The size of the force

The size of the force acting on the wire will depend on the following:

• The current in the wire. The larger the current the stronger the magnetic field around the wire and the greater the interaction with the magnetic field from the permanent magnets.

• The strength of the magnetic field from the permanent magnets. A stronger field will produce a greater force.

• The length of wire inside the permanent magnetic field. There will be a greater force if the wire is longer.

Fleming's left-hand rule

It can be difficult to work out the direction of the force acting on a wire in a magnetic field. Fleming's left-hand rule (also known as the motor rule) lets us find the direction of the force acting on the wire when we know the direction of the current and the magnetic field.

Using your left hand:

- Separate your thumb, first and second fingers so that they all point at right angles to each other (see Figure 4.21.2).
- Point your **F**irst finger in the direction of the magnetic **F**ield (north pole to south pole).
- Point your se**C**ond finger in the direction of the **C**urrent (from the positive terminal to the negative terminal). You may have to twist your hand about to do this but always keep the three fingers at right angles to each other.
- Your thu**M**b will show the direction of the force acting on the wire (or **M**ovement).

Understanding the field

The force on the wire arises because of the interaction of the two magnetic fields so it is important to know the shape of the resultant field (Figure 4.21.3).

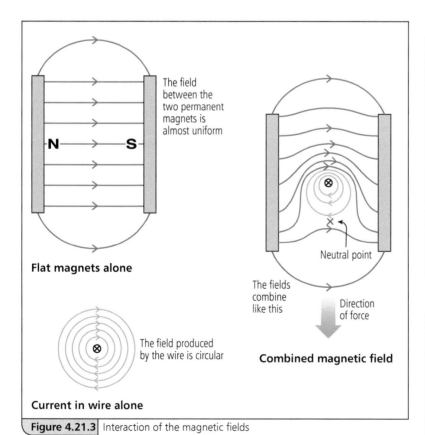

The field between the two permanent magnets is almost uniform

Flat magnets alone

The field produced by the wire is circular

Current in wire alone

The fields combine like this

Neutral point

Direction of force

Combined magnetic field

Figure 4.21.3 Interaction of the magnetic fields

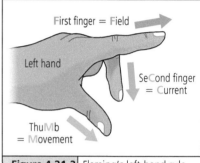

First finger = Field

Left hand

SeCond finger = Current

ThuMb = Movement

Figure 4.21.2 Fleming's left-hand rule

SUMMARY QUESTIONS

1 How can the force acting on a current-carrying wire in a magnetic field be increased?

2 Figure 4.21.4 shows a current-carrying wire. A magnetic field is acting into the paper. In which direction is the force acting on the wire?

Magnetic field into the paper

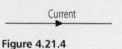

Current

Figure 4.21.4

KEY POINTS

1 A current-carrying wire placed in a magnetic field will experience a force.

2 The direction of the force acting on the wire can be found using Fleming's left-hand rule.

Electromagnetic induction

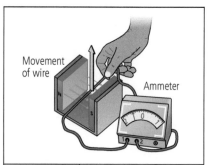

Figure 4.22.1 Demonstrating electromagnetic induction

When a conductor is moved through a magnetic field so that it cuts through the field lines, the electrons in the conductor experience a force which attempts to make them move. This is the electromotive force (e.m.f.). If the conductor is connected to a circuit then the e.m.f. will produce an **induced** current in the circuit.

Demonstrating induction

To demonstrate the effect you can simple move a wire rapidly through a field as shown in Figure 4.22.1. The current induced in the circuit will be very small and so a sensitive ammeter or galvanometer must be used. Note that the current only exists when the wire is moving through the magnetic field. There is no current when the wire is stationary.

Cutting field lines

To understand the reason for the induced current you need to imagine the magnetic field lines around the magnet being cut by the conductor as it moves. It is the cutting of these lines of force which places a force on the electrons. Electromagnetic induction occurs when there is a relative movement between a magnet and a conductor so that the magnetic field lines are being cut.

Investigating induction

It is usually easier to move the magnet than to move the wire and so to investigate the properties of induction you can use a bar magnet and a solenoid (coil of wire) connected to a sensitive ammeter. A solenoid is used so that the field lines cut through the conductors several times and therefore increase the induced current.

- Pushing the magnet (north pole first) into the solenoid so that the magnetic field lines pass through the loops of wire induces a current in the wire.
- Pulling out the magnet induces a current in the opposite direction.
- Reversing the direction of the magnet (pushing in the south pole) will also reverse the direction of the current.
- The faster the magnet is moving relative to the coil the greater the current. This shows that it is the rate that the wire moves through the field lines that is the cause of the increased current.
- The more loops of wire in the solenoid the greater the induced current.
- The stronger the magnet the larger the induced current is.
- Leaving the magnet inside the coil does not produce a current. There is no relative movement between the magnet and the conductor so no field lines are being cut.

The direction of the current

The current induced in the coil will change direction as the magnet is moved in and out of the coil (an alternating current). We need to be able to determine the direction of the current as the magnet moves. To do this we use the following solenoid rule:

The current induced in a solenoid always acts in such a direction as to oppose the change that causes it.

This means that when we push the north end of the magnet into the coil that end of the coil acts as a north pole but when the magnet is withdrawn the magnetic field of the coil reverses. We can use the solenoid rule to work out the direction of the current in the coil (Figure 4.22.2).

This means that a force will be required to push the magnet into the coil and mechanical work must be done in doing so. This mechanical work is transformed into electrical energy and so the law of conservation of energy is observed.

ACTIVITY

Use a magnet, solenoid and coil of wire to investigate induction.

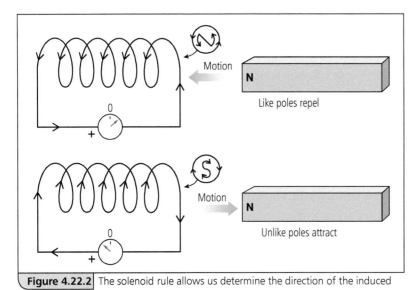

Figure 4.22.2 The solenoid rule allows us determine the direction of the induced current.

SUMMARY QUESTIONS

1 How can you increase the induced current in a solenoid?

2 How does rotating a magnet at the end of a solenoid induce a current?

KEY POINT

1 Electromagnetic induction occurs when there is relative movement between a magnet and a conductor. The induced current depends on the strength and direction of the magnetic field and the speed of the relative movement.

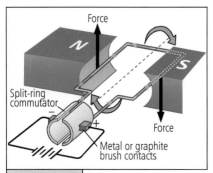

Figure 4.23.1 A d.c. motor

The d.c. motor

A direct current motor uses the motor effect as seen in 4.21 to exert a force on a current-carrying wire. Making a wire move in a straight line is not very useful in most circumstances and so the motor is designed to cause a coil of wire to rotate.

Understanding the d.c. motor

- A coil of wire is mounted on an axle between a pair of magnets. The magnets are arranged so that the opposite poles face each other and produce a strong, uniform, magnetic field between them.
- The coil is connected to a circuit by a pair of connectors called a split-ring commutator. This allows the coil to rotate freely but also allows the direction of the current in the coil to switch every half-turn.
- A current is passed through the coil. The side of the coil near the north pole will experience an upwards force (use Fleming's left-hand rule to check this) while the side of the coil near the south pole will experience a downwards force.
- The two forces will cause the coil to rotate on the axle.
- When the coil has rotated a half-turn the commutator will reverse the current in the coil. This means that the direction of the force on the coil will still cause the left side to be pushed upwards while the right side is pushed downwards.
- As the force remains in the same direction the coil continues to spin, producing a turning moment which can be used to do work.

Applications of motors

Electrical motors are used in a wide range of devices from a small battery-powered fan to a motor which can drive cars.

The a.c. generator

Alternating current generators rely on electromagnetic induction as seen in 4.22. Physically they are similar to the d.c. motor but the energy transformation is the reverse. Kinetic energy is transformed into electrical energy.

Operation of the a.c. generator

The construction of a simple a.c. generator is shown in Figure 4.23.2.

- A coil of wire is mounted on an axle inside a strong magnetic field.
- The coil is rotated.

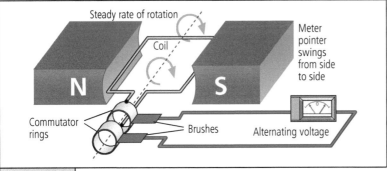

Figure 4.23.2 An a.c. generator

- As the coil rotates it cuts through the magnetic field lines and a current is induced.

  As the coil rotates through the field lines the rate at which it cuts them changes as its alignment changes. This means that the e.m.f. induced in the coil changes with the position of the coil.

- When the coil is horizontal it cuts field lines at a high rate and a large e.m.f. is produced.

- When the coil is vertical it does not cut field lines and so no e.m.f. is induced.

During a full rotation the coil will produce an alternating e.m.f. as shown in Figure 4.23.3.

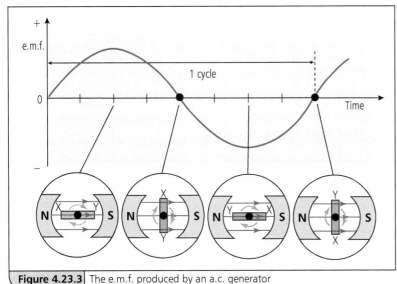

Figure 4.23.3 The e.m.f. produced by an a.c. generator

Changing the rotation speed

Increasing the speed of rotation of the coil will cause it to produce a larger peak e.m.f. It will also increase the frequency of the a.c. supply. Some power station generators are spun 50 times each second providing a frequency of 50 Hz while others are spun 60 times each second (60 Hz).

ACTIVITY

Use a hand powered generator to produce an alternating current. Describe what happens when the generator is spun faster.

SUMMARY QUESTIONS

1 Describe the operation of the motor in Figure 4.23.1 if the battery is reversed.

2 Comparing the a.c. generator to the d.c. motor, what other factors beside the rotational speed will increase the peak e.m.f. produced?

KEY POINTS

1 A d.c. motor transfers electrical energy into kinetic energy using the motor effect.

2 The d.c. motor uses a current-carrying coil of wire which is made to rotate inside a magnetic field.

3 An a.c. generator uses induction to produce a current in a wire by rotating a coil inside a magnetic field.

Transformers

LEARNING OUTCOMES

At the end of this topic you should be able to:

- describe the operation of a transformer
- state the difference between a step-up and a step-down transformer
- use the transformer equation.

The voltage of an alternating current can be changed with a device called a **transformer**. The transformer also changes the size of the current. When electrical energy is transmitted over long distances it is best to do so at high voltage and low current. A lower current in the cable will cause less heating effect and so less energy will be wasted. In power lines the voltages may be several thousand volts.

Transformer operation

A transformer consists of two coils of wire wrapped around opposite arms of a laminated iron core as shown in Figure 4.24.1. These coils are the primary (input) coil and the secondary (output) coil.

- The alternating current in the input coil generates a varying magnetic field in the iron core.
- The magnetic field is focused in the iron core.
- The varying magnetic field induces an alternating current in the output coil.
- The iron core is laminated to reduce currents which would be induced in it. These 'eddy' currents would heat the core and waste energy.
- There is no direct electrical connection between the two coils in the transformer and so no current can pass between them. The coils are said to be **decoupled**.

Note that, because the transformer operates by using changes in magnetic fields, it cannot work with direct current.

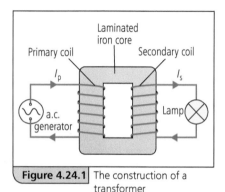

Figure 4.24.1 The construction of a transformer

The transformer equation

There is a relationship between the voltage on the primary coil (V_p) and the voltage on the secondary coil (V_s) and the number of turns of wire on the respective coils (N_p and N_s) given by:

$$\frac{V_s}{V_p} = \frac{N_s}{N_p} = \frac{I_p}{I_s}$$

You can also see that there is relationship between the number of turns and the currents in the coils (I_p and I_s).

If the number of turns on the input coil matches the number of turns on the output coil then there will be no change in voltage or current. If there is a difference in the number of turns then the current and voltage will both change.

Figure 4.24.2

Step-up transformers

Step-up transformers have more turns on the secondary coil than on the primary coil. This has two effects:

- The voltage is increased.
- The current is decreased (compared with primary current) by same factor as voltage is stepped up.

WORKED EXAMPLE 1

A step-up transformer has 50 turns on the input coil and 400 on the output coil. The input voltage is 5.0 V with a current of 2.0 A. What are the output characteristics?

Find the output voltage first:

$$\frac{V_s}{V_p} = \frac{N_s}{N_p}; \; V_s = \frac{N_s \times V_p}{N_p} = \frac{400 \times 5.0\,V}{50} = 40\,V$$

Now find the output current:

$$\frac{I_p}{I_s} = \frac{N_s}{N_p}; \; I_s = \frac{I_p \times N_p}{N_s} = \frac{2\,A \times 50}{400} = 0.25\,A$$

ACTIVITY

Construct a simple transformer from iron cores and investigate the efficiency of the device. Measure the input and output currents and voltages and see if the power ratings ($P = IV$) are the same.

Step-down transformers

A step-down transformer has more turns on the primary coil than on the secondary coil. This also has two effects:

- The voltage is decreased.
- The current is increased by the same factor as the voltage is stepped down.

Step-down transformers are needed to reduce transmission voltages to the 110 V used in homes or even lower for some electrical devices.

WORKED EXAMPLE 2

How many turns of wire are required on the secondary coil of a transformer in order to lower the voltage from 200 V to 6.0 V if the primary coil has 500 turns?

$$\frac{V_s}{V_p} = \frac{N_s}{N_p}; \; N_s = \frac{V_s \times N_p}{V_p} = \frac{6.0\,V \times 500}{200\,V} = 15 \text{ turns}$$

SUMMARY QUESTIONS

1 Why are step-up and step-down transformers used in electricity distribution?

2 What is the output voltage of a transformer if the input voltage is 40 V and there are 400 turns on the primary coil and 2500 on the secondary coil? Is this a step-up or step-down transformer?

Transformer power

The relationship between the primary voltage and current and the secondary voltage and current can be used to find the input and output power of a transformer as follows:

$$\frac{V_s}{V_p} = \frac{I_p}{I_s}; \; V_s I_s = V_p I_p$$

As power is defined as IV we have the relationship:

$$P_{out} = P_{in}$$

The above equation is used for an 'ideal' transformer. However, a transformer is actually a highly efficient device with low power loss and so the equation can be used to find results close to true values.

KEY POINTS

1 A transformer is used to increase or decrease the voltage of an a.c. supply.

2 The transformer equation is:
$$\frac{V_s}{V_p} = \frac{N_s}{N_p} = \frac{I_p}{I_s}$$

3 Transformers are very efficient and so $P_{out} = P_{in}$ provides results close to true values.

1 The resistance of a set of resistors in parallel is given by the relationship:

$$\frac{1}{R_P} = \frac{1}{R_1} + \frac{1}{R_2} + \frac{1}{R_3} + \dots$$

A group of students were asked to verify this relationship by placing a number of $60\,\Omega$ resistors in parallel with each other. They then measured the current through the set and the potential difference across them.

Number of resistors	Theoretical resistance /Ω	Current /A	Potential difference /V	Measured resistance /Ω
1		0.19	12.0	
2		0.38	12.0	
3		0.57	12.0	
4		0.76	12.0	
5		0.95	12.0	

a Sketch the five arrangements of resistors.

b Calculate the theoretical resistance for each set of resistors.

c Calculate the measured resistance of each set of resistors.

d Plot a graph comparing the measured resistance to the theoretical resistance of the combinations.

e Describe the possible causes of the difference between the measured resistance and the theoretical resistance.

2 Describe the effect of placing two bar magnets next to each other in all six possible orientations.

3 Which of these will increase the strength of an electromagnet?

a Increasing the current in the coil.

b Reversing the direction of the current.

c Replacing the iron core with an aluminium core.

d Increasing the number of turns of wire in the coil.

e Switching the electromagnet on and off rapidly.

4 A student tested the relationship between the strength of an electromagnet and the current in it by using the magnet to lift a chain of steel paper clips from a desk. The results are shown in the table.

Current/A	0.2	0.4	0.6	0.8	1.0	1.2	1.4	1.6	1.8
Paper clips lifted	1	3	4	5	7	8	11	13	15

a Plot a graph comparing the number of paper clips lifted to the current in the electromagnet.

b Describe the pattern shown.

5 A group of students was investigating which factor would have the greatest effect on increasing the strength of their electromagnet. The strength of the electromagnet was measured by testing how large a mass it could lift. The students investigated two different factors: increasing the current and increasing the number of loops of wire. They recorded their results in the three tables shown.

Current 0.5 A			
Number of loops of wire	10	15	20	25
Mass lifted/g	1.1	1.3	1.5	1.7

Current 1.0 A			
Number of loops of wire	10	15	20	25
Mass lifted/g	2.2	2.6	3.0	3.4

Current 1.5 A			
Number of loops of wire	10	15	20	25
Mass lifted/g	3.3	3.9	4.5	5.1

a Why should the students use an iron core during all of the experiments?

b What conclusions can be made about the effect of increasing the current?

c What conclusions can be made about the effect of increasing the number of loops of wire?

6 A bar magnet is inserted into a solenoid as shown in the diagram. An ammeter shows there to be a current in the wire as the magnet moves.

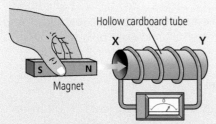
Hollow cardboard tube
Magnet

a What is the name of the process which causes a current in the wire?

b What will happen to the reading on the meter when the magnet is pulled out of the solenoid?

c What will happen to the reading if the magnet is inserted more quickly?

The current in the solenoid causes it to produce a magnetic field when the magnet is being inserted.

d What will be the magnetic polarity of end X of the solenoid?

e What will be the direction of the current in the solenoid (clockwise or anticlockwise)?

7 A d.c. motor is constructed as shown in the diagram.

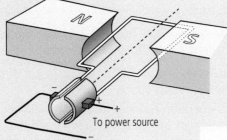
To power source

a Which way will the motor rotate?

b What is the function of the split-ring commutator?

c How can the power of the motor be increased?

8 What are the factors that can be used to increase the e.m.f. of an a.c. generator?

9 An a.c. generator revolves with a frequency of 20 Hz and produces an e.m.f. with a peak voltage of 50 V.

a Sketch a voltage–time graph showing the supply provided by this generator.

The frequency of the generator is increased to 40 Hz.

b Sketch a new voltage–time graph showing how the supply would change.

10 An ideal transformer is used to convert a 110 V a.c. mains voltage to power a 12 V lamp with resistance 5 Ω.

a What is the current in the lamp?

b What is the power of the lamp?

c What is the current in the primary coil?

11 A transformer has 500 turns on the primary coil and 6000 on the output coil. What is the output current when the primary current is 0.2 A.

12 The diagram shows an electrical distribution grid using step-up and step-down transformers. The current in the 132 kV cable is 0.2 A. Assuming all of the transformers are ideal:

a calculate the current from the power station

b calculate the current that can be provided to light industry.

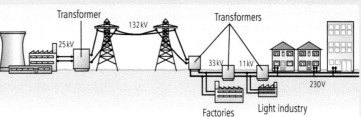
Transformer
132 kV
Transformers
25 kV
33 kV   11 kV
230 V
Factories   Light industry

5 The physics of the atom

5.1   Models of the atom

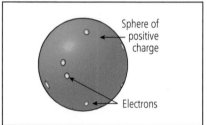

Figure 5.1.1 | The 'plum pudding' model

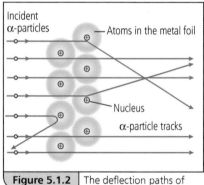

Figure 5.1.2 | The deflection paths of alpha particles fired at gold foil

Initial ideas

Ancient civilisations, such as the Greeks, used the idea of cutting up substances until the simplest components were reached. These simplest substances were 'elemental' and were built from the smallest parts possible: atoms.

The 'plum pudding' model

At the end of the 19th century the British physicist J. J. Thomson discovered that heating metals could release small particles (**electrons**). Thomson proposed that the electrons were released from inside the atoms and therefore the atom was not the smallest possible particle.

As a beam of electrons could be deflected by magnetic and electric fields, Thomson realised that the electrons were charged. As the original atom was uncharged, he proposed a model where the electrons in an atom were trapped inside a positively charged 'sponge'. This was the 'plum pudding' model of the atom (Figure 5.1.1).

Rutherford and the nuclear model

A few years later Ernest Rutherford asked two of his research students, Hans Geiger and Ernest Marsden, to investigate the structure of an atom, using a beam of **alpha particles** (positively charged particles) (Figure 5.1.2). When fired at a thin gold foil:

• most passed straight through the foil with a very small deflection

• some were deflected through large angles

• some bounced straight back.

These results could not be explained by the plum pudding model and so Rutherford proposed a new model 'the nuclear model'.

• As most of the alpha particles pass straight through, most of the atom must be composed of empty space.

• As some alpha particles are deflected they must be repelled by a dense positively charged part of the atom (later named the **nucleus**) which contained **protons** and most of the mass of the atom.

• The apparent radius of atoms was much greater than the measured size of the nucleus. As the electrons were known to be very small, it was suggested that they occupied the space around the nucleus in a way similar to the planets orbiting the Sun.

The Bohr model of the atom

The previous models of the atom could not explain the behaviour of the electrons and why they did not fall into the nucleus due to electromagnetic forces.

Bohr suggested that the electrons could only occupy certain regions (shells or energy levels). Only certain transitions between these shells were possible and this prevented the electrons from falling into the nucleus.

Discovery of neutrons

In 1932 James Chadwick discovered that an uncharged particle (the **neutron**), of similar mass to the proton, existed within the nucleus (Figure 5.1.3).

Our understanding of the structure of the atom continues to develop through the standard model, where the forces binding the nucleus together are explained, and quantum mechanics, where the positions of subatomic particles are described as complex mathematical probabilities.

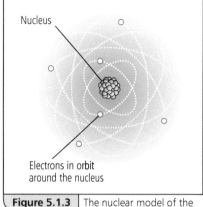

Nucleus

Electrons in orbit around the nucleus

Figure 5.1.3 The nuclear model of the atom

SUMMARY QUESTIONS

1 In the 'plum pudding' model:
   a what charge do electrons have?
   b what is the remainder of an atom composed of?
   c what force holds the electrons in place?

2 During the Geiger–Marsden experiment:
   a why did most of the alpha particles pass through the gold foil without deflection?
   b why were some of the alpha particles directed straight back?

ACTIVITY

Use an online simulator to reproduce the Rutherford scattering experiment.

KEY POINTS

1 The concept that matter is composed of atoms was initially developed in ancient Greece.

2 Scientists developed models of the atom through experimentation and analysis of evidence.

3 The modern view of the atom has a central nucleus containing protons and neutrons, surrounded by electrons in 'shells' or energy levels.

5.2 Electrons, the nucleus and the periodic table

LEARNING OUTCOMES

At the end of this topic you should be able to:

- compare the properties of electrons, protons and neutrons
- identify the constituents of isotopes
- describe the relationship between atomic structure and the periodic table.

The components of atoms

Experiments have now shown that there are three different types of particle that make up all atoms (Table 5.2.1).

Table 5.2.1 Properties of subatomic particles

Particle	Location	Mass	Electric charge
proton	in the nucleus	1 unit $(1.67 \times 10^{-27}\,\text{kg})$	$+1\,e$ $(1.60 \times 10^{-19}\,\text{C})$
neutron	in the nucleus	1 unit $(1.67 \times 10^{-27}\,\text{kg})$	0 $0\,\text{C}$
electron	outside the nucleus in energy levels or 'shells'	$\sim\dfrac{1}{2000}$ unit $9.11 \times 10^{-31}\,\text{kg}$	$-1\,e$ $(-1.60 \times 10^{-19}\,\text{C})$

Neutral atoms have the same number of electrons and protons. As protons and neutrons are found in the nucleus they are referred to as **nucleons**.

Nuclear notation

A nucleus can be described using the number of protons and neutrons in the nucleus.

- The number of protons, the **proton number** (also called the atomic number) is represented by the letter Z.
- The total number of nucleons (protons and neutrons) is called the **nucleon number** (or sometimes mass number) and is represented by the letter A.
- The number of neutrons, the **neutron number**, is represented by the letter N.

$$_{Z}^{A}X$$

The neutron number is not normally recorded because it can be found simply by remembering:

number of neutrons = mass number − atomic number ($N = A - Z$)

Examples

- A nucleus of magnesium with an atomic number of 12 and a mass number of 24 is represented by $_{12}^{24}\text{Mg}$.
- A nucleus of boron containing 5 protons and 5 neutrons is represented by $_{5}^{10}\text{B}$.
- A nucleus of iron containing 26 protons and 30 neutrons is represented by $_{26}^{56}\text{Fe}$.

EXAM TIP

Very specific language is used in nuclear physics. Make sure you understand all of the key words, especially nucleus, nuclide and isotope.

ACTIVITY

Use a periodic table to study the patterns in electron arrangement and the patterns of chemical behaviour of elements in the same group.

Isotopes

Nuclei of a single element always have the same number of protons and so have the same atomic number. However, the nuclei may have a different number of neutrons. For example, most carbon nuclei contain six protons and six neutrons but some carbon nuclei contain seven neutrons or even eight.

Atoms with the same proton number but different nucleon numbers are called **isotopes**.

Three isotopes of carbon are: $_{6}^{12}C$ $_{6}^{13}C$ $_{6}^{14}C$

As the proton number identifies the name of the element it is often more convenient to write isotopes in a simpler format: carbon-12, carbon-13 or carbon-14.

Nuclei that share the same number of protons and neutrons are referred to as **nuclides**.

Patterns in electron shells and the periodic table

The periodic table is arranged in order of proton number from left to right and working down through the periods. Electrons are found in shells (or energy levels) and the periodic table shows a pattern in the behaviour of elements with the same number of electrons in the outermost shell.

Each complete period in the periodic table represents the filling up for an energy level.

- The first shell can contain a maximum of 2 electrons and so there are 2 elements in the first period.
- The second shell can contain up to 8 electrons.
- The third shell can contain up to 8 electrons and the fourth up to 18 electrons.
- For example, a silicon atom has 14 electrons and the electron arrangement is 2,8,4.

WORKED EXAMPLE

Sketch the atomic structure for the two isotopes of boron $_{5}^{10}B$ and $_{5}^{11}B$.

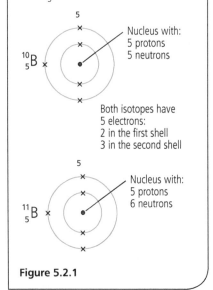

Nucleus with:
5 protons
5 neutrons

Both isotopes have 5 electrons:
2 in the first shell
3 in the second shell

Nucleus with:
5 protons
6 neutrons

Figure 5.2.1

KEY POINTS

1 Atoms are neutral particles because there are an equal number of positive charged protons to negatively charged electrons.

2 Mass number (A) = atomic number (Z) + neutron number (N)

3 Isotopes of elements have the same number of protons in the nucleus but different numbers of neutrons.

SUMMARY QUESTIONS

1 Fluorine has a proton number of 9.

  a How many electrons does a neutral fluorine atom have?

  b Sketch the arrangement of these electrons.

  c In what group of the periodic table is fluorine placed?

2 Copy Table 5.2.2. Then calculate and fill in the missing values.

Table 5.2.2

	Atom	Number of protons, Z	Nucleon number, A	Number of neutrons, N	Number of electrons
a	carbon	6	12		
b	sodium	11		12	
c	gold		197		79
d	osmium	76		114	

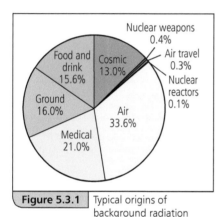

Figure 5.3.1 Typical origins of background radiation

A short history

In 1896 Henri Becquerel noticed that, after leaving a sample containing uranium in a drawer near some photographic film, the film became exposed. He theorised that the uranium was producing 'invisible rays' which caused a chemical reaction in the film. Over the next few years Marie and Pierre Curie investigated other minerals and isolated radium in sufficient amounts to allow the study of its properties.

Background radiation

There is always a small amount of **background radiation** around us from natural and artificial sources (Figure 5.3.1). The level of this radiation varies from place to place. Some locations have more than twenty times the level of radiation as others.

Investigating nuclear radiation

Three different types of nuclear radiation have been discovered: **alpha** (α), **beta** (β) and **gamma** (γ).

As the nuclear radiation interacts with the atoms or molecules of a material it can cause **ionisation**, where some of the electrons are stripped away from their atoms.

Alpha particles are strongly charged and this makes them interact strongly. They are absorbed easily by materials. Beta particles are more penetrating and absorbed less easily and gamma rays are the most penetrating of all, as they interact least with the matter they pass through.

A Geiger counter can be used to detect ionising radiation. A radioactive particle passing through a Geiger–Müller tube produces an electrical pulse which is logged by a counter attached to the tube. By placing different materials between the source and the Geiger counter, the penetrating power can be investigated (Figure 5.3.2).

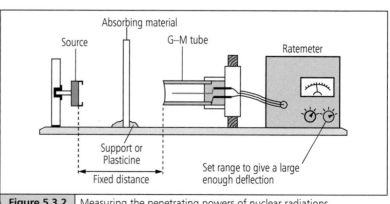

Figure 5.3.2 Measuring the penetrating powers of nuclear radiations

Effect of magnetic and electric fields

Charged particles experience a force when they move through magnetic or electric fields (Figure 5.3.3). The size and direction of the force depends upon the charge of the particle. Alpha particles have more mass than beta particles so do not deflect as easily. Also alpha particles will curve in the opposite direction to beta particles because they have opposite charge. Gamma rays are not affected by the fields as they are not charged.

Table 5.3.1   Properties of alpha, beta and gamma radiation

	Alpha particles	Beta particles	Gamma rays
Symbol	α	β	γ
Nature	A particle consisting of two protons and two neutrons ejected from the nucleus	A fast moving electron ejected from the nucleus	Electromagnetic radiation emitted by the nucleus. A high energy photon.
Electric charge	+2 e (charge of two protons)	−1 e (charge of one electron)	None
Penetrating power	Can travel only a few centimetres in air. Blocked by paper or skin.	Can travel a few metres in air. Blocked by metal foil.	Can travel long distance in air. Intensity reduced by thick metal plating such as lead.
Ionising power	Strongly ionising as it is massive and highly charged	Ionising	Some ionisation
Effect of magnetic and electric fields	Deflects the alpha particle	Deflects the beta particle in the opposite direction to an alpha particle	No effect

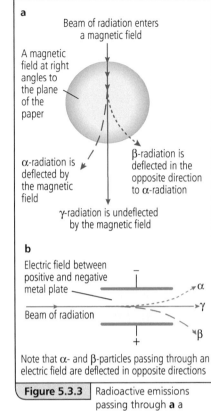

a

Beam of radiation enters a magnetic field

A magnetic field at right angles to the plane of the paper

α-radiation is deflected by the magnetic field

β-radiation is deflected in the opposite direction to α-radiation

γ-radiation is undeflected by the magnetic field

b

Electric field between positive and negative metal plate

Beam of radiation

Note that α- and β-particles passing through an electric field are deflected in opposite directions

| **Figure 5.3.3** | Radioactive emissions passing through **a** a magnetic field and **b** an electric field |

The cloud chamber

Although we cannot see α or β particles or γ-rays, we can see the tracks they make when water droplets condense on ions formed in a cloud chamber.

SUMMARY QUESTIONS

1   Why would these careers possibly lead to you having a higher than average annual dose of radiation?
    • Radiographer in a hospital
    • Airline pilot
    • Miner

2   What type(s) of nuclear radiation:
    a   can penetrate your skin?
    b   causes the most ionisation?
    c   are deflected by a magnetic field?
    d   can travel farthest in air?

Nuclear decays and reactions

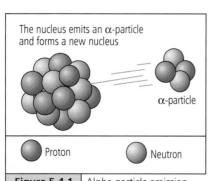

The nucleus emits an α-particle and forms a new nucleus

α-particle

Proton   Neutron

Figure 5.4.1 | Alpha particle emission

WORKED EXAMPLE 1

What is the decay equation for alpha decay of polonium-210 into an isotope of lead?

$$^{210}_{84}Po \longrightarrow ^{4}_{2}\alpha + ^{206}_{82}Pb$$

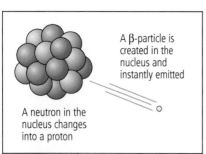

A β-particle is created in the nucleus and instantly emitted

A neutron in the nucleus changes into a proton

Figure 5.4.2 | Beta particle emission

Unstable isotopes

Many nuclides are *stable*. This means that the nucleus has the correct balance of protons and neutrons and does not break apart. However, some nuclides have too many neutrons or too many protons and this makes them unstable causing the nucleus to *decay* (break apart) over time. For example, carbon-12 is a stable nuclide but carbon-14 is not. Carbon-14 nuclei will decay over time changing into nitrogen-14 nuclei.

When a decay occurs it can be described in these simple terms:

parent nucleus $\longrightarrow$ daughter nucleus + α, β, or γ

Alpha decay

During alpha decay an unstable parent nucleus releases two protons and two neutrons bound together forming an alpha particle (Figure 5.4.1). The alpha particle is ejected from the parent nucleus leaving a daughter nucleus with less mass. As two protons have left the nucleus the resulting daughter is a different element than the parent.

The general form of an alpha decay equation is:

$$^{A}_{Z}X \longrightarrow ^{4}_{2}\alpha + ^{A-4}_{Z-2}Y$$

Beta decay

A beta particle is a fast moving electron produced when a neutron converts to a proton inside the nucleus (Figure 5.4.2). The electron was not originally present. After the decay there is an additional proton in the nucleus and so the daughter nuclide is a different element from the parent.

The general form of a beta decay equation is:

$$^{A}_{Z}X \longrightarrow ^{0}_{-1}\beta + ^{A}_{Z+1}Y$$

Gamma decay

An alpha or beta decay may leave the daughter nucleus with some excess energy. The nucleus is said to be in an excited state. This energy may be released by a gamma decay. Gamma decay does not cause any change in the number of protons or neutrons in the nucleus and so the product of the decay is the same element as the parent nuclide.

The general form of a gamma decay equation is:

$$^{A}_{Z}X \longrightarrow ^{0}_{0}\gamma + ^{A}_{Z}X$$

Other nuclear reactions

Nuclear fission

Large nuclei can split into two smaller nuclei, releasing energy. This process is usually caused by hitting the nucleus with a neutron in induced **fission**. The neutron is absorbed and then the nucleus becomes so unstable that it splits up. During fission several neutrons are released alongside the two new nuclei (Figure 5.4.3). In nuclear reactors these neutrons are used to cause further fissions and form a **chain reaction**.

$$^{235}_{92}U + ^{1}_{0}n \longrightarrow ^{141}_{56}Ba + ^{92}_{36}Kr + 3^{1}_{0}n$$

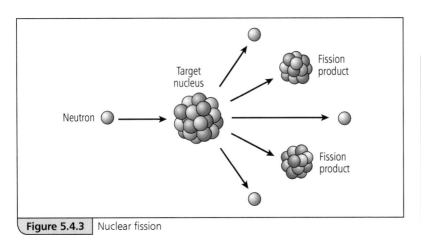

| **Figure 5.4.3** | Nuclear fission |

Write a decay equation for caesium-137 which undergoes beta decay to form an isotope of barium.

$$^{137}_{55}Cs \longrightarrow ^{0}_{-1}\beta + ^{137}_{56}Ba$$

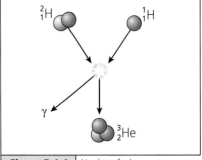

| **Figure 5.4.4** | Nuclear fusion |

Nuclear fusion

Stars produce their energy using the process of nuclear **fusion**. In this process small nuclei are merged together to form larger ones (Figure 5.4.4). The Sun produces all of its energy by nuclear fusion processes, mostly fusing isotopes of hydrogen to form helium isotopes. An example of a fusion reaction is shown below.

$$^{2}_{1}H + ^{1}_{1}H \longrightarrow ^{3}_{2}He + \gamma$$

ACTIVITY

Most nuclear fission takes place in nuclear reactors but there have been some naturally formed reactors. Find out about these and how they worked.

SUMMARY QUESTIONS

1 Write complete decay equations for the following.
   a The alpha decay of americium-241 $\left(^{241}_{95}Am\right)$ into an isotope of neptunium (Np).
   b The beta decay of caesium-137 $\left(^{137}_{55}Cs\right)$ into an isotope of barium.

2 Copy and complete these nuclear fission and fusion equations by adding the missing values for proton number and nucleon number:
   a $^{235}_{92}U + ^{1}_{0}n \longrightarrow ^{?}_{54}Xe + ^{90}_{?}Sr + 2^{1}_{0}n$
   b $^{2}_{1}H + ^{?}_{1}H \longrightarrow ^{4}_{?}He + ^{?}_{?}n$

KEY POINTS

1 Alpha decay involves the release of an alpha particle (helium nucleus) from a parent nucleus.

2 Beta decay involves the release of a beta particle (electron) when a neutron converts to a proton in a nucleus.

3 Gamma decay involves energy changes in the nucleus.

A model of radioactive decay

Radioactive decay

Radioactive decay is a random process but, because a very large number of identical nuclei are involved, the decay process can be modelled fairly simply.

For an effective model of the decay process all of the particles involved need to be identical so that they each have exactly the same chance of decaying. In the model all of the particles (dice) are identical (Figure 5.5.1). They all have the same chance of decay as each other when they are rolled.

Follow the procedure described in the Activity to gather data about decay and the patterns produced.

Figure 5.5.1 A large number of dice can be used to simulate radioactive decay.

ACTIVITY

1 Put 60 dice in a tray or box so that you don't lose them.

2 Make sure each dice is marked clearly on one face.

  • If you have simple cubes then colour in a spot on one face.

  • If you are using normal numbered dice then the number six counts as the spot.

3 Roll all the dice, a handful at a time.

4 Remove any dice that end up spot upwards (or showing a six). These dice have 'decayed'. Put the decayed dice to the side but do not lose them.

5 Record the number of dice left (not the number of dice that decayed) in a results table, like Table 5.5.1.

6 Roll all of the remaining dice.

7 Repeat rolling and recording the number of dice left until you have no dice left or you have rolled 20 times.

8 Repeat the whole process from stage 3 two times to fill in the results table.

  • The more sets of rolls you complete the better the final graph will be. If you do not have time for three sets then you may share results or just use one or two sets.

9 Work out the total number of dice left for each roll number by adding the three sets of results across the table.

Table 5.5.1 Results table

Roll number	Dice left Try 1	Dice left Try 2	Dice left Try 3	Dice left Total
0	60	60	60	180
1				
2				
3				
...				
19				
20				

Analysing the data

You should see that the three sets of data are not identical although the pattern of decay is similar. This shows that, when using large enough numbers, the decay process follows predictable patterns.

Producing a graph

Plot a scatter graph with the roll number on the *x*-axis and total number of dice remaining on the *y*-axis. Add a line of best fit to the graph. This should be a smooth curve following the pattern of the points. A curve like this is called an exponential decay curve. You can use a spreadsheet to plot the graph but you must make sure that you label the axes clearly.

Analysing the graph

The graph can be used to determine what fraction of the original dice remain after a certain number of rolls. Use the graph to answer these questions. You may use fractions of a roll.

- How many rolls did it take to get down to $\frac{1}{2}$ the original number of dice?
- How many more rolls to get down to $\frac{1}{4}$ of the original?
- How many more rolls to get down to $\frac{1}{8}$ of the original?

You should see a pattern. The number of rolls required for the remaining dice to halve is always 3.8.

Limitations of the model

Because a limited number of dice were used you may find that your results do not follow this pattern exactly. The decay curve may not be entirely smooth and you may find that it did not take exactly 3.8 rolls for the dice to halve each time.

If you use thousands or millions of dice the curve would be much smoother and the relationship would be more precise. When monitoring the decay of radioactive nuclei there are generally billions of nuclei. Even though the decay of an individual nucleus is unpredictable there is a consistent pattern to the number of nuclei remaining after a certain time.

Example results

Table 5.5.2 shows the example (idealised) results produced by completing the experiment with 6000 dice. You may use this data to plot graphs if you don't have enough dice. The table also shows the results that would be obtained when using eight- and ten-sided dice.

KEY POINTS

1 The random 'decay' of large numbers of dice can be used to model the decay of nuclei.
2 Although the decay of a single dice cannot be predicted the pattern in the decay of large numbers can.

Table 5.5.2 Example results

Roll number	Dice remaining		
	Six-sided dice	Eight-sided dice	Ten-sided dice
0	6000	6000	6000
1	5000	5250	5400
2	4167	4594	4860
3	3472	4020	4374
4	2894	3517	3937
5	2411	3077	3543
6	2009	2693	3189
7	1674	2356	2870
8	1395	2062	2583
9	1163	1804	2325
10	969	1578	2092
11	808	1381	1883
12	673	1209	1695
13	561	1057	1525
14	467	925	1373
15	389	810	1235
16	325	708	1112
17	270	620	1001
18	225	542	901
19	188	475	811
20	157	415	729

SUMMARY QUESTIONS

1 a Plot a graph showing the dice remaining for all three types of dice shown in the table.

   b Do all of the types of dice follow the same pattern of decay?

   c How may rolls does it take for the number of eight-sided dice to halve?

   d How many rolls for the number of ten-sided dice to halve?

2 Why are there more dice left after twenty rolls for the ten-sided dice when compared to the six-sided dice?

Nuclear decay and half-life

Rate of decay

Although the time when a specific nucleus decays is random, a large sample of a nuclide will decay exponentially in the same way as the dice model described in 5.5. This regular decay pattern can be used to predict the behaviour of a sample of radioactive material. The rate of decay is not affected by external conditions such as temperature or pressure.

Decay constant

The **decay constant** of a nuclide is the likelihood a nucleus will decay in one second. This is similar to the chance of a dice 'decaying' in the model. Some nuclei are very unstable and have a high likelihood of decaying and so have a large decay constant while other nuclei have a very small chance. All nuclei of the same nuclide have exactly the same decay constant. For example, all carbon-14 nuclei have exactly the same chance of decaying each second.

Activity

The **activity** of a radioactive sample is the rate of decay of the nuclei. This is the number of nuclei that decay each second. As the number of nuclei decaying is proportional to the number of nuclei that are left, the activity of a sample falls over a period of time.

Decay curves

A graph showing the number of radioactive nuclei remaining in a sample over a period of time is called a *decay curve*. The number of nuclei remaining approaches zero but the rate of decay slows as the number of nuclei remaining decreases. This leads to a curve which approaches but never reaches zero.

A graph showing the activity of the sample will have exactly the same shape because the activity is proportional to the number of nuclei remaining (Figure 5.6.1).

Half-life

The **half-life** of a nuclide is the time it takes for one half of the active nuclei to decay. The half-life of a particular nuclide is a constant. As the activity is proportional to the number of nuclei remaining, the half-life can also be defined as the length of time taken for the activity of a sample to fall to half of its original value.

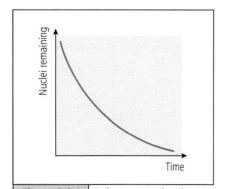

Figure 5.6.1 A decay curve showing the number of nuclei remaining over a perod of time.

Table 5.6.1

Number of half-lives	Fraction of sample remaining
0	1
1	$\frac{1}{2}$
2	$\frac{1}{4}$
3	$\frac{1}{8}$

Figure 5.6.2 shows the decay curve for a sample with a half-life of 45 minutes. It is important to note that the half-life can be found by measuring the time for half of the remaining sample to decay. This means that the time taken for the activity fall from 600 to 300 is the same as the time taken for it to fall from 300 to 150.

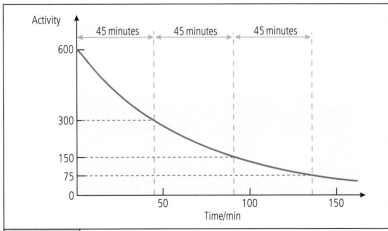

Figure 5.6.2 | The decrease in activity for a radioactive sample with a half-life of 45 minutes. The activity (and number of nuclei remaining) halves every 45 minutes.

Some nuclides have very short half-lives, fractions of a second. This indicates that the nuclei are very unstable and decay very quickly. For example, dubnium-261 has a half-life of 27 seconds

Some nuclides have very long half-lives, millions or billions of years. For example, uranium-238 has a half-life of 4.5 billion years.

KEY POINTS

1   The half-life of a sample of a radioisotope is the time taken for the activity of that sample to fall to half of the original activity.

2   Half-lives can vary from milliseconds to billions of years.

3   The longer the half-life the lower the activity (rate of decay) of the radioisotope.

4   The decay process is independent of external conditions.

SUMMARY QUESTIONS

1   The isotope fermium-253 has a half-life of three days. What fraction of the original sample will remain after fifteen days?

2   If the activity of an isotope falls from 2000 counts per second to 500 counts per second in one day what is the half-life of the sample?

5.7 Applications of radioisotopes

LEARNING OUTCOMES

At the end of this topic you should be able to:

- explain how radioactive materials can be used in medicine and industry
- describe how the age of organic materials can be found using carbon dating.

Although radioactive materials are potentially very dangerous they are also very useful in fields from medicine to archaeology.

Medical uses of radioisotopes

Medical tracers

Compounds containing radioisotopes can be used as tracers inside patients. They are injected into the body and move through the bloodstream, gathering in target organs. The tracers emit gamma radiation which is detected outside the body with a gamma camera. A computer produces images from the information and problems such as blockages in blood vessels can be identified. Figure 5.7.1 shows a gamma trace being used to detect a blocked kidney (Chart B).

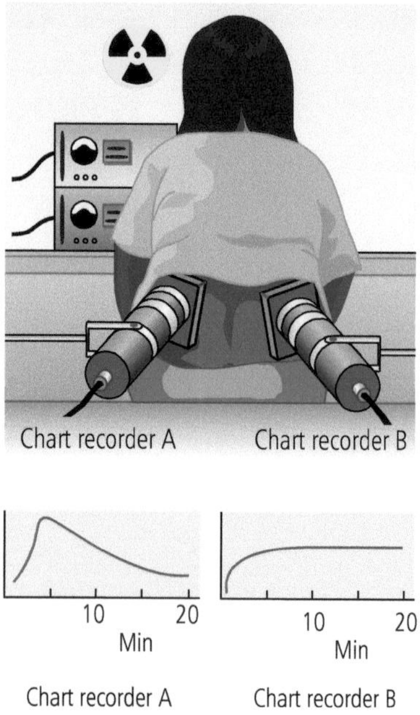

Chart recorder A
Chart recorder B
10
20
Min
10
20
Min
Chart recorder A
Chart recorder B

Figure 5.7.1 A gamma trace can be detected from outside the body during medical diagnosis.

Technecium-99m (Tc-99m) is the most common tracer used in diagnostic medicine. This isotope decays by releasing gamma radiation which is easily detectable by gamma cameras. Tc-99m also has a short half-life and therefore does not stay in the patient for a long time.

Radiotherapy

Radioactive emissions can be highly ionising and can cause cancers. However, cancer cells are more susceptible to damage from gamma rays than normal cells and so can be destroyed by the gamma radiation. During radiotherapy a high intensity beam of gamma radiation is directed at a tumour. The cancer cells receive a high dose of the radiation and, hopefully, die off. The gamma rays may be produced by cobalt-60.

Industrial and civilian applications

When gas leaks from a pipeline it can be difficult to find out the exact location of the leak. A radioactive tracer can be added to the gas and a Geiger counter can be used to detect the radiation leak even if the pipe is underground.

The thickness of aluminium foil can be measured with a beam of beta radiation. If the foil is too thick then the count rate drops. If the foil is too thin the count rate increases (Figure 5.7.2).

Smoke detectors rely on the ionising effect of radiation. An alpha source produces radiation which passes through a small air gap, ionises the air in the gap and the resulting current is detected. Smoke from a fire absorbs the ions created by the alpha particles and the fall in current is detected. This sets off an alarm.

Radiocarbon dating

Any organism contains carbon atoms absorbed from the atmosphere during its lifetime. Most of the carbon is carbon-12, a stable isotope, but a small proportion is carbon-14, a beta emitter. When carbon-14 decays it forms a stable isotope, nitrogen-14.

$$^{14}_{6}C \longrightarrow \ ^{14}_{7}N + \ ^{0}_{-1}\beta$$

The proportions of carbon-12 and carbon-14 in the atmosphere are constant, as new carbon-14 is produced by interaction with cosmic rays at the same rate that carbon-14 decays. This means that all living organisms maintain a constant ratio of carbon-14 to carbon-12. Once the organism dies it no longer takes in new carbon. The carbon-12 nuclei are stable but the carbon-14 nuclei continue to decay and so the ratio of carbon-14 to carbon-12 decreases over time.

Scientists can measure the ratio of the two isotopes by measuring the activity of a sample of carbon taken from biological remains. This ratio can then be used to find out how long ago the organism died.

Carbon-14 has a half-life of 5700 years and so the remains of an organism which died 5700 years ago would have half as much carbon-14 as an organism that died today. For example, the Turin Shroud is an important religious artefact originally thought to be 2000 years old. However, radiocarbon dating on the Shroud showed that the plants used to make it died only 700–800 years ago. Similar techniques can be used with uranium to find the ages of rocks formed billions of years ago.

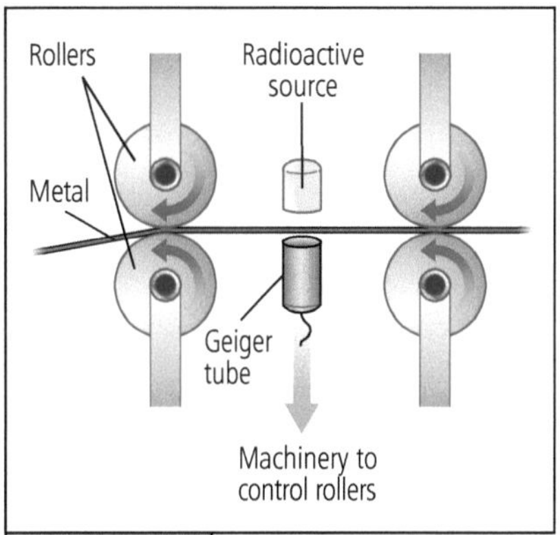

Figure 5.7.2 A beta source can be used to control the thickness of paper or aluminium foil.

ACTIVITY

Find out some of the diagnostic procedures that are carried out using Tc-99m. What safety precautions need to be in place?

WORKED EXAMPLE

An ancient piece of cotton cloth is found to have an activity, due to carbon-14 decay, ¼ of that of a modern cotton sample.

Estimate the age of the ancient piece of cloth.

The cloth has decayed over 2 half-lives and so is 2×5700 = 11 400 years old.

SUMMARY QUESTIONS

1 Why would an alpha particle emitter not be suitable for use as a medical tracer?

2 A sample of wood taken from an arrow is found by radiocarbon dating to have an activity $\frac{1}{8}$ of that for a modern piece of the same type of wood. Estimate the age of the arrow.

KEY POINTS

1 In medicine radioactive materials are used as tracers and to treat cancers (radiotherapy).

2 Radioactive materials can be used to measure the thickness of a material or detect flaws in it.

3 Radioactive dating techniques can be used to find the age of organic materials.

The release of nuclear energy

The law of conservation of energy states that energy cannot be created or destroyed. Energy must be conserved. Albert Einstein realised that mass was equivalent to energy and this relationship was given by:

$$\text{energy} = \text{mass} \times \text{speed of light}^2$$
$$\text{or} \quad E = mc^2$$

Converting mass to energy

Whenever there is a change in energy there is an associated change in mass. This also means that mass can be transformed into energy. In nuclear fission (splitting) a large nucleus is split into two small nuclei. The mass of these smaller nuclei is less than the original nucleus and this mass change leads to a large release of energy.

WORKED EXAMPLE 1

How much energy is released during the nuclear fission shown in this equation?

$$^{235}_{92}U + {}^{1}_{0}n \longrightarrow {}^{144}_{56}Ba + {}^{90}_{36}Kr + 2{}^{1}_{0}n$$

- mass of uranium-235 = 3.902996×10^{-25} kg
- mass of barium-144 = 2.389897×10^{-25} kg
- mass of krypton-90 = 1.493157×10^{-25} kg
- mass of a neutron = 1.674927×10^{-27} kg

Calculate the difference between the starting mass and the end mass.

Δm = mass before fission − mass after fission

$\Delta m = (3.902996 \times 10^{-25} + 1.674927 \times 10^{-27})$ kg
$\quad - (2.389897 \times 10^{-25} + 1.493157 \times 10^{-25}$
$\quad + 2 \times 1.674927 \times 10^{-27})$ kg

$\Delta m = 3.1927 \times 10^{-28}$ kg

Now convert this loss of mass to energy.

$E = mc^2 = 3.1927 \times 10^{-28}$ kg $\times (3.00 \times 10^8\,\mathrm{m\,s^{-1}})^2$
$\quad\quad = 2.8734 \times 10^{-11}$ J

Figure 5.8.1 | A nuclear explosion

Although the energy released by one nuclear decay is very small, there are a vast number of nuclei in every gram of matter and so a very large amount of energy could potentially be released.

Once this was understood scientists began to develop ideas about how to convert mass into energy. The first application of the idea was the nuclear bomb. The conversion of a small amount of matter would release enough energy to provide an explosion thousands of times greater than any seen before.

Nuclear fission power stations

Nuclear fission power stations use the thermal energy released to heat water into steam which drives turbines. These are then used to drive generators which produce electricity.

Induced fission is caused by a neutron colliding with a large nucleus. During this process several other neutrons are released and these can be used to split other nuclei, releasing more energy and yet more neutrons. This process is called a chain reaction (Figure 5.8.2).

Key components of a fission reactor

- *Fuel*: Uranium or plutonium is used inside canisters called *fuel rods*.
- *Moderators*: These slow down the neutrons so that they can be absorbed by the fuel and cause fission.
- *Coolant*: This removes the thermal energy from the reactor core and carries it to a heat exchanger.

There are arguments for and against the use of nuclear power, which national governments must consider (Table 5.8.1).

Table 5.8.1   Arguments for and against the use of nuclear power

For	Against
• Running costs are low. • Only a small amount of waste produced. • Large supplies of nuclear fuel available. • No carbon dioxide is produced so no contribution to global warming.	• Commissioning (building) and decommissioning (dismantling) costs are high. • Nuclear waste contains radioactive isotopes. • Waste products can be used in nuclear weapons. • Accidents such as occurred in Chernobyl and Fukushima can contaminate large areas.

Nuclear fusion in stars

Nuclear energy is also released when very small nuclei combine to form larger ones. This process occurs in the cores of stars and is only possible at very high temperatures and pressures, which have not yet been reproduced sustainably.

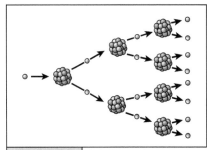

Figure 5.8.2   A chain reaction

1 The activity of a sample of radon-220 is measured over a period of time as shown in the table.

a   Plot a graph of activity against time for the sample.

b   Identify the anomalous result.

c   Use the graph to find the half-life of radon-220.

d   Predict the time it would take for the activity to fall to 10 counts per second.

Time/s	Activity/s^{-1}
0	500
20	389
40	302
60	235
80	182
100	150
120	110
140	86
160	67
180	52
200	40

2 Copy and complete this table showing the components of the different nuclides.

	Nuclide	Number of protons, Z	Nucleon number, A	Number of neutrons, N	Number of electrons	Electron configuration
a	hydrogen-2 (deuterium)	1				
b	hydrogen-3 (tritium)		3			
c	nitrogen-14				7	
d	chlorine-35					2,8,7

3 During the Geiger–Marsden experiment to explore the structure of the atom, the following results were noted:

• Most of the alpha particles passed directly through the gold foil.

• A small percentage of the alpha particles were deflected by angles between 0 and 90 degrees.

• A few alpha particles were deflected by angles greater than 90 degrees.

a   For each describe the conclusions about the structure of the atom that can be made based on this evidence.

b   Why was gold used as the material for the foil?

c   Why was the experiment carried out in an evacuated chamber?

4 Electrons in atoms are found in energy levels or shells.

a   What is the electron configuration of the atoms of the following elements?

   i   Magnesium

   ii   Sodium

   iii Calcium

   iv   Neon

b   Which two of the elements will have the most similar chemical properties?

5 Which of the isotopes listed in the table:

   a are isotopes of the same element?

   b contain the same number of nucleons?

   c contain the same number of neutrons?

   d contain the same number of protons?

$^{35}_{17}Cl$	$^{40}_{18}Ar$	$^{36}_{18}Ar$
$^{38}_{18}Ar$	$^{36}_{16}S$	$^{37}_{17}Cl$
$^{35}_{16}S$	$^{36}_{17}Cl$	$^{40}_{18}Ar$

6 The nuclide thorium-223 $\left(^{223}_{90}Th\right)$ undergoes nuclear decay by alpha emission to form an isotope of radium (Ra).

   a Which nucleons are present in an alpha particle?

   b Write a decay equation representing the alpha decay.

7 This graph shows the relationship between the proton number (atomic number) and the neutron number for all of the stable nuclides.

   a Describe the relationship for nuclides of a low proton number (Z < 20).

   b Describe the relationship for nuclides of a higher proton number (Z > 20).

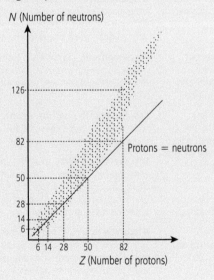

8 This graph shows the activity of a sample of argon-39 and a sample of silver-108.

   a Determine the half-life of argon-39.

   b Determine the half-life of silver-108.

   c Which sample has the higher initial activity?

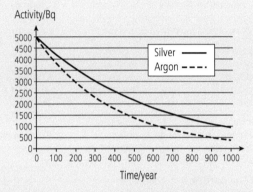

9 Write decay equations for the following:

   a The alpha decay of tellurium-107 $\left(^{107}_{52}Te\right)$ into an isotope of tin (Sn).

   b The beta decay of potassium-40 $\left(^{40}_{19}K\right)$ into an isotope of calcium (Ca).

   c The gamma decay of strontium-90 $\left(^{90}_{38}Sr\right)$.

10 A single nuclear fission reactor could provide all of the electricity requirements for Trinidad.

   a Write a few paragraphs supporting the idea of building a nuclear power station on Trinidad.

   b Write a few paragraphs opposing the idea of building the power station.

11 Nuclear radiation can be used to measure the thickness of materials during their manufacture. Describe how the thickness of a metal foil can be measured using beta radiation so that a constant thickness can be maintained during the manufacturing process.

Glossary

Absolute zero The lowest possible temperature (0 K or $-273\,°C$). At this temperature all of the thermal energy has been removed from a material.

Absorb To take in radiation. This results in an increase in temperature.

Acceleration The rate of change of velocity. The unit of acceleration is metres per second squared ($m\,s^{-2}$). $a = \Delta v/t$

Accuracy An accurate measurement is one which is close to the true value. A set of measurements of a quantity can be accurate if their mean is close to the true value.

Activity The activity of a radioactive sample is the rate of decay of the nuclei (the number of nuclei which decay each second).

Alpha particle A radioactive emission consisting of two protons and two neutrons (a helium nucleus).

Alpha radiation The emission of two protons and two neutrons from a nucleus. The emitted particles form a helium nucleus.

Ammeter A meter used to measure the electric current (in ampere, A) in a circuit.

Amplitude The maximum distance of a particle from its rest position in a vibration.

Angle of incidence The angle between an incident ray and the normal.

Angle of reflection The angle between the reflected ray and the normal.

Average speed The rate of change of distance measured over a period of time. Average speed = distance travelled ÷ time taken.

Background radiation The radioactivity in the surroundings. This includes radiation from rocks, radon gas and cosmic rays.

Beta radiation A radioactive emission consisting of a fast-moving electron ejected from the nucleus.

Boiling A change of state from a liquid into a gas which happens throughout the whole body of a liquid at a specific temperature (the boiling point).

Boyle's law For a fixed mass of gas the pressure is inversely proportional to the volume if the temperature is kept constant.

Celsius scale A centigrade scale for temperature with $0\,°C$ at the freezing point of water and $100\,°C$ at the boiling point of water.

Centre of gravity The point at which all of the weight of an object seems to act.

Chain reaction During nuclear fission neutrons are released. These neutrons can cause further fissions of nuclei and release even more neutrons causing an increasing rate of energy release.

Charles' law For a fixed mass of gas the volume is proportional to the absolute temperature if the pressure is kept constant.

Compression An area of higher air pressure in a sound wave.

Conduction The transfer of thermal energy through a material when atoms pass energy though vibrations. Metals also conduct via free electrons which can transfer energy more quickly.

Conductor A material that allows electricity (or thermal energy) to flow through it.

Constructive interference When two waves meet in phase (e.g. a crest meeting a crest), the waves superimpose and increase the amplitude at that point.

Contact force A force which acts when two objects are in direct contact with each other.

Control variable A variable that must be kept constant during an experiment or investigation in order to allow the relationship between the dependent and independent variable to be determined.

Convection current The movement of particles within a fluid caused by the transfer of thermal energy throughout the fluid. A convection current is caused by the changes in density of a fluid as it heats up or contracts.

Cooling curve The line on a temperature–time graph that shows how a substance cools down.

Critical angle The angle of incidence at which an incident ray will be refracted parallel to the boundary.

Current The rate of flow of charge through an object. The current is measured in amperes where 1 A is the transfer of 1 C of charge per second.

Decay constant The chance of a nucleus decaying per second.

Decoupled Two circuits that do not share a connection through a current but which transfer energy between them.

Density The mass per unit volume of a material. Density = mass ÷ volume.

Dependent variable A variable that changes in response to an independent variable during an experiment or investigation.

Destructive interference When two waves meet out of phase (e.g. a crest meeting a trough), the waves superimpose and partly cancel each other's displacement out at that point.

Diffraction The spreading of a wave when it passes through a gap or past an edge. The amount of diffraction depends on the relationship between the wavelength and the size of the gap; the greatest diffraction occurs when these are the same size.

Diffuse reflection Reflection from a surface which is not smooth. The reflected rays travel in different directions and so no image can be seen.

Diminished An image reduced in size when compared to the original object.

Dispersion The spreading of different frequencies of light caused by the difference in their speeds in a medium. White light can be dispersed by a prism.

Displacement The distance from an origin (starting point) in a particular direction. Displacement is measured in metres.

Displacement–position graph A graph representing the positions of the particles in a wave at a particular instant.

Displacement–time graph A graph showing the changes in displacement of an object over a period of time. The gradient of a section of the graph is the speed of the object at that time.

Dissipate To spread out into the surroundings. Thermal energy dissipates into the surroundings where it cannot be used to do any additional work.

Distance How far an object moves from a point. The SI unit of distance is the metre.

Glossary

Echo The reflection of a sound wave.

Efficiency A measure of how effective a device is at transferring or transforming energy usefully. Efficiency = useful energy out ÷ total energy in. Efficiency can be expressed as a decimal or as a percentage (e.g. 0.4 or 40% efficient).

Elastic limit The point beyond which a spring will no longer return to its original length when the force on the spring is removed.

Electromagnetic Related to electric and magnetic fields.

Electromagnetic relay Switch operated by an electromagnet.

Electromagnetic spectrum A set of waves with similar properties.

Electromotive force (e.m.f.) The amount of energy provided to each coulomb of charge as it passes through a battery. e.m.f. = E/Q

Electron A negatively charged particle. Electrons are found in energy levels or shells around the nucleus of an atom or can be ejected from the nucleus during beta decay.

Electrostatic precipitation Using a charged metal grid to induce charge onto smoke particles so that they can be removed from the air. Used in power station chimneys.

Emit To give out radiation, e.g. infra-red radiation or light.

Energy The capacity to do work.

Evaporation A process where particles escape from the surface of a liquid. The most energetic particles escape first and so reduce the average energy of the particles in the liquid. This reduces the temperature of the liquid.

Extension The increase in length of a spring (or other object) when a force is applied to it. For a spring the extension is proportional to the size of the force unless the spring is extended beyond the limit of proportionality.

Fission The splitting of a nucleus accompanied by a release of energy. Fission can be induced using neutrons.

Fluid A liquid or gas. The particles are able to move past each other allowing the fluid to flow.

Focal length The distance from a lens to where parallel rays parallel to the optical axis will be brought together (converging lens) or seem to come from (diverging lens).

Focal plane The plane, perpendicular to a lens axis, were the principal focus lies.

Free electrons Metals form a structure in which the outer electrons are free to move between atoms. These free electrons are responsible for electrical conduction and most thermal conduction in metals.

Frequency How many complete waves pass a point each second. The unit of frequency is s^{-1} which is also called hertz (Hz).

Friction The contact force acting between two surfaces which opposes movement.

Fusion The joining of small nuclei releasing energy. Fusion is the process which releases energy in the Sun.

Gamma radiation High frequency electromagnetic radiation released from a nucleus.

Gas equation A relationship between the pressure, volume and temperature of a fixed amount of an ideal gas. pV/T = constant.

Gas thermometer A thermometer which uses the pressure of a gas to indicate temperature.

Gravitational potential energy The energy associated with an object when it is inside a gravitational field. The change in gravitational potential energy can be found from the relationship $\Delta E = mg\Delta h$.

Gravity The force of attraction between two objects due to their mass.

Greenhouse effect The capture of thermal energy by the atmosphere due to greenhouse gases reflecting infra-red radiation emitted by the Earth.

Half-life The time taken for the activity of a radioactive sample to fall to half of its initial value.

Hard magnetic A material which retains its magnetic properties well.

Heat capacity The amount of energy which can be stored in a body per degree kelvin (or Celsius).

Impulse The change in momentum caused by a force acting on an object. Impulse = Ft.

Incident ray The ray which strikes a surface such as a mirror.

Independent variable A variable which is changed in an experiment to see how that change affects the dependent variable.

Induce To transfer magnetic or electrical properties without physical contact.

Induction The production of an electromotive force (a voltage) in a wire by a magnetic field moving relative to it.

Inertia The reluctance of an object to change its motion. Large objects, such as planets, have large amounts of inertia and so are difficult to speed up or slow down.

Infra-red thermometer A thermometer that measures the intensity and frequency of the infra-red radiation emitted by an object to determine the temperature.

Instantaneous speed The speed of an object at a particular moment. Measured in metres per second ($m\,s^{-1}$).

Insulator A poor conductor of heat or electricity.

Interference pattern The pattern formed by the constructive and destructive interference of waves. Clear interference patterns are formed in Young's two-slit experiment as the overlapping waves have the same frequency.

Inverted An image is said to be inverted if it is upside down.

Ionisation The removal of an electron from an atom creating an ion.

Isotopes Atoms of the same element (having the same number of protons) that have different numbers of neutrons.

K

Kelvin scale A temperature scale based on the properties of ideal gases and the energy of particles.

Kinetic energy The energy associated with the movement of an object. $E_k = \frac{1}{2}mv^2$.

Kinetic theory The particle model of the behaviour of solids, liquids and gases. The kinetic theory is used to explain the changes of state and pressures within gases and liquids.

Glossary

Laser A device which produces a narrow and intense beam of monochromatic light (light with a single wavelength).

Latent heat The energy required to change the state of an object (from a solid to a liquid or liquid to a solid).

Latent heat of fusion The energy required to melt a substance. The same quantity of energy is released when the substance solidifies.

Latent heat of vaporisation The energy required to vaporise a liquid (change it from a liquid to a gas). The same amount of energy is released when the vapour condenses back into a liquid.

Laterally displaced When a ray passes through a rectangular block of transparent material it is refracted on entry and when it leaves the block. This results in the ray travelling in the original direction but shifted (displaced) sideways from its original path.

Lattice vibration The vibrations of the particles in a solid which cause thermal conduction.

Light dependent resistor (LDR) A resistor which changes resistance depending on the light level it is exposed to. In bright light, LDRs have low resistance but in dark conditions they have very high resistances.

Limit of proportionality The limit to which a spring can be stretched with the extension remaining proportional to the force acting on the spring (still obeying Hooke's law).

Linear magnification A comparison of the size of the image to the size of the object. Linear magnification = height of image ÷ height of object.

Longitudinal A wave motion where the oscillations of the particles are parallel to the direction of wave motion. Sound is a longitudinal wave.

Magnet A magnet exerts a force on nearby magnetic materials by producing a magnetic field.

Moment The turning effect of a force measured in N m. The moment of a force is defined as the force multiplied by the perpendicular distance to the pivot.

Momentum The movement property of an object as defined by the relationship momentum = mass × velocity.

Motor effect A current-carrying wire placed inside a magnetic field will experience a force. This is the motor effect.

Negatively charged Electrons carry negative electric charge. This charge causes an electric field which will affect other charged objects.

Neutron An uncharged particle found in the nucleus of an atom.

Neutron number The number of neutrons within a particular nucleus.

Newton (N) The unit of force. Forces are vector quantities. This means that the direction in which they act is significant.

Non-renewable An energy source which will eventually run out or become very scarce.

Normal A line at right angles to the surface. Angles of incidence, reflection and refraction are all measured relative to this normal.

Nuclear Related to the nucleus of an atom. Nuclear energy is released when nuclei are split (fission) or merged (fusion).

Nucleon A particle found in the nucleus. The two possible nucleons are protons and neutrons.

Nucleon number The total number of protons and neutrons in a nucleus.

Nucleus The central part of an atom. The nucleus occupies only a very small amount of the volume of the atom but contains nearly all of the mass.

Nuclide A particular type of nucleus. For example, carbon-14 is a different nuclide to nitrogen-14.

Optical centre The central point of a lens. A ray which passes through the optical centre does not change path.

Origin The starting point of a movement or the central point in an oscillation.

Oscillation A regular movement around a point. Most oscillations studied are sinusoidal. The object or particle moves in the pattern of a sine wave.

Parallel Circuits that have junctions at which the current can diverge or merge are parallel circuits.

Pascal (Pa) A unit of pressure. The pascal is equivalent to $N\,m^{-2}$.

Penumbra The partial shadow during an eclipse.

Period The time it takes for one complete oscillation of a system. It is measured in seconds.

Photon A packet of energy carried by light. The higher the frequency of light the more energy each photon carries.

Pitch A high frequency sound has high pitch.

Positively charged A proton carries positive charge.

Potential difference (p.d.) The energy transferred by a unit charge, measured in volts. A potential difference of 1 volt will cause 1 coulomb of charge to transfer 1 joule of energy.

Power The rate of transfer of energy measured in watts (W). $P = E/t$.

Precision The degree to which repeated measurements agree. A set of precise measurements will all be very similar.

Pressure law For a fixed mass of gas the pressure is directly proportional to the absolute temperature if the volume is kept constant.

Primary cell A cell which cannot be recharged. Zinc–carbon cells are primary cells.

Principal axis A line which runs through the centre of a lens and perpendicular to the lens.

Principal focus (pl. **foci**) The point at which rays that enter a converging lens parallel to the principal axis are brought together by the lens. For a diverging lens the principal focus is the point from which the original parallel rays seem to pass through.

Principle of moments For an object to be in equilibrium, the clockwise moment is equal to the anticlockwise moment.

Propagation The spreading of energy by a wave. The wave is said to travel in the direction of propagation. For example, the ripples on a pond propagate in a circle and light rays propagate in all directions from a lamp.

Proton A positively charged particle found in the nucleus of an atom.

Proton number The number of protons in the nucleus of an atom.

Rarefaction An area of lower pressure in a sound wave.

Real image An image which can be projected onto a screen. Rays of light pass through a real image.

Rectification The conversion of an alternating current into direct current.

Reflected ray The ray which leaves a mirror or other reflecting surface.

Refractive index The ratio of the speed of light in a vacuum (or air) to the speed of light in a material. The larger the refractive index the slower light travels in the material.

Regular reflection The reflection from a smooth, flat surface such as a mirror which produces a clear image.

Renewable An energy source which has an inexhaustible (or effectively inexhaustible) supply.

Resistance The opposition to an electric current. $R = V/I$.

Resolution The smallest increment a measuring instrument can detect. For example, the resolution of a ruler may be 1 mm. The resolution of a thermometer may be 0.5 °C.

Resultant force The sum of the forces acting on an object. As forces are vectors the direction of the forces must be taken into account (e.g. forces acting in opposite directions must be subtracted from each other).

Scalar A quantity which only has magnitude. For example, scalar quantities include mass and energy.

Secondary cell A cell which can be recharged. A lead–acid cell is a secondary cell.

Semiconductor A material which will conduct in certain conditions.

Series Components placed one after each other in an electrical circuit.

Soft magnetic A material that loses its magnetic properties easily.

Specific heat capacity The amount of energy required to raise the temperature of one kilogram of a specific material by one kelvin.

Specific latent heat The energy required to change the state of 1 kg of a material. The specific latent heat of fusion is the energy required to change the state of 1 kg of the material from a solid into a liquid. The specific latent heat of vaporisation is the energy required to change the state from liquid to a gas. Unit is $J\,Kg^{-1}$ (or $J\,g°C^{-1}$).

Spring constant The force required to extend a spring by 1 metre. Unit is $N\,m^{-1}$.

Stable equilibrium An object is in stable equilibrium if it returns to the original position after being disturbed (pushed).

Standard form A numbering format used for large or small numbers by scientists and engineers. In standard form numbers are represented in the form $a \times 10^b$, where a is a number between 1 and 10 and b is an integer. For example, 3.4×10^4 is used to represent 34 000.

Thermal conductivity The rate at which a material transfers thermal energy by conduction. A material with high thermal conductivity will transfer energy quickly.

Thermal energy (sometimes referred to as heat energy or internal energy) is the energy associated with the movement and arrangement of the particles within an object or material.

Thermistor Temperature-sensitive resistor. The resistance of a thermistor changes with the temperature.

Transformation A change from one form of energy into another. For example, energy can be transformed from electrical energy into light energy by a lamp.

Transformer A device which is used to change the voltage of an alternating supply. A step-up transformer increases the voltage while a step-down transformer reduces the voltage.

Transverse A wave motion where the oscillations are perpendicular to the direction of propagation.

Ultrasound High-frequency sound above the range of human hearing. Ultrasound is used in depth measurement and pre-natal scanning.

Umbra The region in complete darkness during an eclipse.

Unit A system of measurements of quantities. For example, the unit for length is the metre. Scientists use the Système International (SI) of Units.

Unstable equilibrium An object is in unstable equilibrium if, when it is disturbed, it falls over.

Upthrust The force acting on an object submerged or floating on the surface of a liquid. If the upthrust is less than the weight of the object it will sink.

Van de Graaff (VdG) generator A device used to generate charges by friction. A VdG generator can generate potential differences large enough to produce large sparks.

Vector A quantity with magnitude and direction. For example, vectors include force, displacement and velocity.

Velocity–time graph A graph displaying the velocity (on the y-axis) of an object over a period of time (on the x-axis). The graph can be used to find the acceleration (shown by the gradient) or the distance travelled (shown by the area below the line of the graph).

Virtual image The image of an object from which the rays of light appear to come. A virtual image cannot be projected onto a screen as the rays of light never actually pass through the image.

Voltmeter A meter used to measure the potential difference (in volts, V) between two points in a circuit. The voltmeter must be placed in parallel in the circuit and must have very high resistance.

Wave pulse A single oscillation.

Wave train A continuous series of wave pulses.

Wavefront The points on a wave as it propagates. For example, all of the points on the crest of a ripple on a pond.

Wavelength The distance between successive peaks (or troughs) in a wave. Wavelength is measured in metres and has the symbol λ (lambda).

Work The transfer of energy. Work is measured in joules (J).

Index

Key terms are in **bold** and are also listed in the glossary

Index

Index

The author and the publisher would also like to thank the following for permission to reproduce material:

Alamy: A.T. Willett: 4.17.1, Alchemy: 4.19.2, Arcaid Images: 2.1.1, Aurora Photos: 2.3.3, Blend Images: 1.18.2, Chris Rout: 4.2.4, Clive Streeter: 4.8.2, David Lyons: 2.12.2, David J. Green: 4.14.1, John Rendle NZ: 1.21.2, Leslie Garland Picture Library: 4.5.1, Lyroky: 2.12.3, Metta Stock: 4.18.1, Rachko: 1.2.1, sciencephotos: 2.7.1, 3.9.2, 4.12.2, Simone Lunardi: 1.14.2; **Corbis**: Inspirestock: 1.2.2, Ocean: 4.13.3; **Getty Images**: AFP: 5.8.1, Bert Hoferichter: 1.8.2; **Fotolia**: 2.6.4; **iStockphoto**: 1.15.3, 1.20.1, 2.9.4, 3.4.1, 3.13.4, 4.5.2, 4.20.4, 4.24.2, 5.5.1; **Martyn f. Chillmaid**: 2.2.1; **Ministry of Transport, Works & Housing, Jamaica**: 1.1.1; **Reuters**: Darren Staples: 1.8.4; **Rex Features**: 1.12.1; **Science Photo Library**: Adrienne Hart Davis: 2.2.2, ESA-CNES-ARIANESPACE / Optique Vidéo du CSG: 1.12.3, GIPhotoStock/Photo Researchers, Inc: 1.9.1, NASA: 1.5.1; **SuperStock**: Stockbroker: 2.6.3; **Wikimedia Commons**: 2.12.4.

Every effort has been made to trace the copyright holders but if any have been inadvertently overlooked the publisher will be pleased to make the necessary arrangements at the first opportunity.